A Passion for Freedom: Personal Stories on Human Rights

Introduced and Edited by Mary Louise Loe
James Madison University

KENDALL/HUNT PUBLISHING COMPANY
4050 Westmark Drive   Dubuque, Iowa 52002

Contents

Acknowledgments

I would like to express my deepest gratitude to the many people who helped me with this project. My parents, Guido and Frances Cavicchi, and my uncle, Alexander Sterne, inspired my interest in human rights and questions of justice by their teachings and example. My work on this book began with the creation of a new course at James Madison University on the Modern Struggle for Human Rights. After teaching the course for several years, I decided, based on the suggestion of my students, to create an anthology of personal stories. The General Education Program helped by giving me a Summer Grant to begin the project and the College of Arts and Letters awarded me a Summer Teaching Grant to complete it. Michael J. Galgano, Head of the History Department, was very encouraging and supportive of the course and book. I would particularly like to thank Philip F. Riley who shared his vast knowledge and passionate interest in the subject of human rights and was always extremely helpful. Ann Crabb and I had many fruitful discussions regarding the selections.

I would like to dedicate this book to my students in the belief that they will certainly be inspired by the words and lives of the courageous people who tell their stories in this book.

Introduction

This book contains a selection of autobiographical narratives and interviews. Together they tell a story of people who were denied their human rights: freedom of speech, press, assembly, the right to vote. Most of them were imprisoned or exiled because they took a stand against racial discrimination, political oppression, or their nation's subordination to another power. Some were persecuted because of their ethnic identity, race or religion. But they all have in common their decision to oppose the violations of their rights and to maintain their personal dignity, even though their opposition to oppression meant risking their lives. All of the stories are non-fictional, autobiographical narratives except for the interviews with Aung San Suu Kyi and the fifteen Afghan women. The Afghan women were included even though they are not activists but refugees of war, because they tell us what it was like to live under the Taliban. The Taliban not only terrorized the people of Afghanistan, but also helped the al Qaeda leaders who inflicted terror on the United States on September 11, 2001, and continue to threaten the world today.

This book includes the stories of a wide spectrum of people, some of whom became world famous, others known only nationally; the Afghan women remain identified only by their first names. Mahatma Gandhi worked in South Africa and then in his native India for the independence of his people. He was more responsible than anyone for developing the principles and methods of nonviolent resistance to oppression and the eventual independence of India in 1947. Viktor Frankl, a Viennese psychiatrist, spent four years in concentration camps and emerged to develop a life-affirming philosophy and school of psychology, known as logotherapy. The Dalai Lama, the spiritual and secular leader of the Tibetan people, has worked for over forty years to liberate Tibet from the Chinese occupation. Nelson Mandela spent twenty-seven years in prison, and it was to a large degree his perseverance and courage which led to the collapse of the system of apartheid in South Africa and the establishment of a democratic government in that country. Andrei Sakharov, the developer of the hydrogen bomb, became a leader of the human rights movement in the Soviet Union and played a leading role in contributing to the major changes in Soviet society initiated by President Gorbachev. These reforms quickly led to the collapse of the Soviet system and to the end of the Cold War. Aung San Suu Kyi has emerged as the leader of the pro-democracy movement in Burma and has spent many of the past thirteen years under house arrest. She was released in May 2002.

Others included here may not be quite so well known internationally, but played a significant role in the human rights struggle. John Lewis was a leader in the Civil Rights movement in the United States in the late 1950s and 1960s, and is currently a Congressman representing Georgia in the House of Representatives. Liang Heng grew up in China during the 1950s and 1960s, and he presents a vivid portrait of how the Chinese authoritarian system shattered individual lives and families. Violeta Morales organized a group of women who, like herself, had lost their relatives in the first years of General Pinochet's regime in Chile; together they sewed tapestries to create a visual story made from cloth of what had happened to their "disappeared" loved ones. We only know the first names of the women of Afghanistan; when the Revolutionary Association of the Women of Afghanistan (RAWA) interviewed these women in the Spring of 2000, the release of their full names would have placed their lives in danger. As the war continues in Afghanistan today, and a new government comes to power, these women will return to their native land and perhaps one day be free to give a name to their stories. Yet their stories are no less important because we do not know the names of the people behind them.

What emerges from these stories whether told by spiritual and secular leaders or by poor refugees is the universal human experience—the desire to be free, to think one's own thoughts, to speak out as one wishes, and to live in a society where one is not fearful of the government. The people in this book come from all corners of the globe, of varied social and economic backgrounds, of different races, religions, and cultures. They lived under oppressive governments which span the political spectrum from left to right, including the democratic United States. Thousands of other similar stories exist. Yet this particular group includes especially courageous and determined people, whose actions have affected the lives of millions; their message is both inspiring and challenging. They offer us a deep understanding of how people behave under the most extraordinary conditions of oppression and violence. Repeatedly we learn from Gandhi, Frankl, Mandela, Lewis, and Aung San Suu Kyi that even under the most stressful conditions of imprisonment, individuals are free to make choices to preserve their integrity and internal freedom. After reading their stories it is not surprising that these men and women emerged from prison, exile, and house arrest, ready to forgive and to shake hands with their oppressors.

Questions about human rights have been around since the beginning of recorded history. The moral issues of human rights are discussed in all of the great religious texts as well as by early political philosophers. Yet, when one begins to study the history of human rights and its international implications, one becomes aware of its great complexity. In Western Europe it was in the 17th and 18th centuries that the questions of rights were examined with great thoroughness by the Enlightenment thinkers, like John Locke, Voltaire and Rousseau, who wanted to understand human nature and also to create a better society. Their views would have a tremendous impact on the founders of the American government and the leaders in the French Revolution and extend right up until the present; when Chinese students protested in Tiananmen Square in June 1989, calling for human rights, they publicly read aloud the Declaration of Independence.

Yet it was not until the end of World War II, which witnessed the greatest genocide in history, that people came together from nations around the world to form the United Nations and to write a Universal Declaration of Human Rights in 1948. The writing of this document was a difficult process based on cooperation and compromise between the parties involved. What may be seen as a universal human right by some may be viewed as a violation of traditional culture or religion by others. Nonetheless the Declaration was promulgated; since 1948 there have been many other documents and commissions formed in an attempt to uphold a universal moral standard to protect individuals against tyranny and oppression. A major role in this struggle is played in the world today by non-governmental organizations(NGOs). In the year 1900, only a few international human rights organizations existed; today there are over four thousand with thousands of people from all walks of life—students, nurses, doctors, lawyers—dedicating themselves to helping others in a foreign land.

Today governments feel obliged to acknowledge the principles established in the 1948 Universal Declaration in order to gain the respect of others and to be admitted into the community of nations. Unfortunately this does not mean that all members of the United Nations uphold these principles. Conflict certainly did not end with the fall of the Berlin Wall in 1989. Throughout the world there continues to be poverty, injustice, and tyranny, and these problems will certainly not be eliminated in the near future. Many human rights advocates believe that trade should be linked to human rights policies, especially in this age of globalization. As interest in human rights spread during the 1960s, activists called for economic sanctions against the apartheid regime in South Africa. Recently, many Americans objected, unsuccessfully, to the admission of China into the World Trade Organization because of its human rights policies, while others argued that trade would improve the Chinese economy and would do more to create a free society than exclusion. Chinese officials objected to the self-righteousness of these Americans, saying that China had a different culture and tradition, and that Americans had no right to tell them how to run their government. They correctly pointed out that there are more people proportionally in prison in the United States than anywhere else.

Thus human rights is a complex international issue, which is often open to many different interpretations and will continue to be debated and questioned in the future. When civil wars break out, they immediately have an impact on neighboring countries as people flee the conflict and become refugees. Only recently has the desire to seek asylum from political persecution also been recognized by some nations as a human right. Again this right has global consequences; for who is to determine whether someone is seeking asylum from political persecution or simply trying to emigrate to seek economic opportunity? As the world population increases, refugees and their quest for human rights will continue to be a major concern.

Along with the right to seek asylum is the question of military intervention. Today there is a growing consensus that the United Nations and foreign governments have the obligation to intervene, if necessary militarily, in those countries who are violently denying their citizens' human rights. This has occurred recently in Rwanda and the former Yugoslavia. Yet this intervention has also been opposed and portrayed as another form of 19th century Western imperialism and even hypocrisy. While political leaders often approve this type of intervention, controversy has arisen over international laws and courts. The United States, which considers itself one of the most democratic and freest nations in the world, refuses to become a party to the International Criminal Court because it fears that an International Criminal Court may potentially violate America's national sovereignty.

There is no question that the human rights struggle has been helped by technology. Televised scenes of the beatings of civil rights workers and of the horrors of war in Vietnam galvanized into action an entire generation, including my own. When people living in closed societies could view scenes from open societies, and vice-versa, this made the world a smaller place. Today, especially with the internet, information travels instantaneously and transcends national borders. In spite of the many problems, there remains reason for hope, and the hope derives not so much from declarations, treaties and commissions, but from those individuals who dedicate themselves to the cause of justice and insist that governments be forced to abide by universal moral standards in protecting the rights of their citizens. As students of human rights, you will come to understand the complexity of the issue. The people in this book will help you to understand the universality of the human experience beneath the apparent differences of language, culture, religion, skin color, and dress, and to recognize in these individuals the human needs, desires, and concerns which you share with them. I am certain that they will inspire you as they have countless others.

Mohandas Gandhi

Mohandas Gandhi was born on October 2, 1869, in Porbandar, India. His family had long served within the government, and his father was a government minister. He would emerge as the leader of the Indian national independence movement and the most important exponent of nonviolent resistance (*satyagraha*) in the 20th century. He was one of the most important and influential intellectual, spiritual and political figures of the twentieth century and did more than anyone to challenge Western imperialism. He influenced many human rights leaders, including the Dalai Lama, Nelson Mandela, John Lewis and Aung San Suu Kyi.

At the age of eighteen Gandhi went to study law in England for several years. There he became familiar with English society and thought. But despite his attempts to dress and talk like an English man, he was treated as a foreigner and never fully accepted. His sense of being an outsider led to "his experiments with truth"—his quest for self-knowledge as well as knowledge of the world. Upon returning to India Gandhi accepted a position with a law firm in South Africa, which like India, was part of the British Empire at the time. It was in South Africa that he confronted the racial discriminatory policies and laws which started him on his long journey of nonviolent resistance to evil and civil disobedience. For the next twenty-one years Gandhi remained in South Africa, working with Indians and others in South Africa who were second-class citizens like himself.

With the approach of World War I he returned, with his family, to India. Having already achieved fame, he soon emerged as the leader of the Indian National Congress and became dedicated to fighting for independence using the same principles of non-violent resistance he had followed while in South Africa. He would oppose not only English colonial rule, but also some of the Indian traditions, such as the isolation of people called "untouchables." In his protest against English cultural dominance and his desire for Indians to assert their independence, not only politically but also culturally, Gandhi adopted the dress of simple Indian peasants; he wore a *dhoti*, a tunic outfit made of homespun cotton. In one of the selections below he describes his attempt to get the Indian people to begin spinning their own cloth. In 1922, he would become famous throughout the world when he led a march of Indian people to the sea to protest the British salt tax and prohibition against Indians manufacturing their own salt.

Gandhi believed in self-discipline, self-purification through special dietary rules and fasting, and the dignity of manual labor. Influenced by the Russian writer Leo Tolstoy, he often worked and lived on the land, in an attempt to carry out his principles of discipline and manual labor. In the mass protests he organized he refused to compromise his principles and for his total honesty and courage he was soon called the Mahatma—"great soul." He spent years in prison and was often near death due to his hunger strikes to protest various policies and actions. His goals for independence were finally realized in 1947, but his dream of one unified Indian state of Hindus, Muslims and people of all faiths and beliefs was not achieved as two states were created—India and Pakistan. Gandhi was assassinated in 1948 just after India had achieved independence. His moral, philosophical and political influence on the world was unprecedented.

In the selections below from his autobiography, Gandhi describes the organization of a mass strike (*hartal*) to protest the Rowlett Act of March 1919 which established the continuation of wartime rules in India after the first world war had ended. He also discusses his first attempts to get Indians to spin their own cotton cloth, known as *khadi*, as a means of gaining financial independence. In the conclusion, his farewell, Gandhi explains that truth must be based on a complete realization of *ahimsa*. Ahimsa means complete nonviolence, including the refusal to destroy any living organism.

That Memorable Week!—I

After a short tour in South India I reached Bombay, I think on the 4th April, having received a wire from Sjt. Shankarlal Banker asking me to be present there for the 6th of April celebrations.

But in the meanwhile Delhi had already observed the *hartal* on the 30th March. The word of the late Swami Shraddhanandji and Hakim Ajmal Khan Saheb was law there. The wire about the postponement of the *hartal* till the 6th of April had reached there too late. Delhi had never witnessed a *hartal* like that before. Hindus and Musalmans seemed united like one man. Swami Shraddhanandji was invited to deliver a speech in the Jumma Masjid, which he did. All this was more than the authorities could bear. The police checked the *hartal* procession as it was proceeding towards the railway station, and opened fire, causing a number of casualties, and the reign of repression commenced in Delhi. Shraddhanandji urgently summoned me to Delhi. I wired back, saying I would start for Delhi immediately after the 6th of April celebrations were over in Bombay.

The story of happenings in Delhi was repeated with variations in Lahore and Amritsar. From Amritsar Drs. Satyapal and Kitchlu had sent me a pressing invitation to go there. I was altogether unacquainted with them at that time, but I communicated to them my intention to visit Amritsar after Delhi.

On the morning of the 6th the citizens of Bombay flocked in their thousands to the Chowpati for a bath in the sea, after which they moved on in a procession to Thakurdvar. The procession included a fair sprinkling of women and children, while the Musalmans joined it in large numbers. From Thakurdvar some of us who were in the procession were taken by the Musalman friends to a mosque near by, where Mrs. Naidu and myself were persuaded to deliver speeches. Sjt. Vithaldas Jerajani proposed that we should then and there administer the Swadeshi and Hindu-Muslim unity pledges to the people, but I resisted the proposal on the ground that pledges should not be administered or taken in precipitate hurry, and that we should be satisfied with what was already being done by the people. A pledge once taken, I argued, must not be broken afterwards; therefore it was necessary that the implications of the Swadeshi pledge should be clearly understood, and the grave responsibility entailed by the pledge regarding Hindu-Muslim unity fully realized by all concerned. In the end I suggested that those who wanted to take the pledges should again assemble on the following morning for the purpose.

Needless to say the *hartal* in Bombay was a complete success. Full preparation had been made for starting civil disobedience. Two or three things had been discussed in this connection. It was decided that civil disobedience might be offered in respect of such laws only as easily lent themselves to being disobeyed by the masses. The salt tax was extremely unpopular and a powerful movement had been for some time past going on to secure its repeal. I

From *Autobiography: The Story of My Experiments with Truth* by Mohandas K. Gandhi, translated by Mahadev Desai.

therefore suggested that the people might prepare salt from sea-water in their own houses in disregard of the salt laws. My other suggestion was about the sale of proscribed literature. Two of my books, *viz.*, *Hind Swaraj* and *Sarvodaya* (Gujarati adaptation of Ruskin's *Unto This Last*), which had been already proscribed, came handy for this purpose. To print and sell them openly seemed to be the easiest way of offering civil disobedience. A sufficient number of copies of the books was therefore printed, and it was arranged to sell them at the end of the monster meeting that was to be held that evening after the breaking of the fast.

On the evening of the 6th an army of volunteers issued forth accordingly with this prohibited literature to sell it among the people. Both Shrimati Sarojini Devi and I went out in cars. All the copies were soon sold out. The proceeds of the sale were to be utilized for furthering the civil disobedience campaign. Both these books were priced at four annas per copy, but I hardly remember anybody having purchased them from me at their face value merely. Quite a large number of people simply poured out all the cash that was in their pockets to purchase their copy. Five and ten rupee notes just flew out to cover the price of a single copy, while in one case I remember having sold a copy for fifty rupees! It was duly explained to the people that they were liable to be arrested and imprisoned for purchasing the proscribed literature. But for the moment they had shed all fear of jail-going.

It was subsequently learnt that the Government had conveniently taken the view that the books that had been proscribed by it had not in fact been sold, and that what we had sold was not held as coming under the definition of proscribed literature. The reprint was held by the Government to be a new edition of the books that had been proscribed, and to sell them did not constitute an offence under the law. This news caused general disappointment.

The next morning another meeting was held for the administration of the pledges with regard to Swadeshi and Hindu-Muslim unity. Vithaldas Jerajani for the first time realized that all is not gold that glitters. Only a handful of persons came. I distinctly remember some of the sisters who were present on that occasion. The men who attended were also very few. I had already drafted the pledge and brought it with me. I thoroughly explained its meaning to those present before I administered it to them. The paucity of the attendance neither pained nor surprised me, for I have noticed this characteristic difference in the popular attitude—partiality for exciting work, dislike for quiet constructive effort. The difference has persisted to this day.

But I shall have to devote to this subject a chapter by itself. To return to the story. On the night of the 7th I started for Delhi and Amritsar. On reaching Mathura on the 8th I first heard rumours about my probable arrest. At the next stoppage after Mathura, Acharya Gidvani came to meet me, and gave me definite news that I was to be arrested, and offered his services to me if I should need them. I thanked him for the offer, assuring him that I would not fail to avail myself of it, if and when I felt it necessary.

Before the train had reached Palwal railway station, I was served with a written order to the effect that I was prohibited from entering the boundary of the Punjab, as my presence there was likely to result in a disturbance of the peace. I was asked by the police to get down from the train. I refused to do so saying, 'I want to go to the Punjab in response to a pressing invitation, not to foment unrest, but to allay it. I am therefore sorry that it is not possible for me to comply with this order.'

At last the train reached Palwal. Mahadev was with me. I asked him to proceed to Delhi to convey to Swami Shraddhanandji the news about what had happened and to ask the people to remain calm. He was to explain why I had decided to disobey the order served upon me and suffer the penalty for disobeying it, and also why it would spell victory for our side if we could maintain perfect peace in spite of any punishment that might be inflicted upon me.

At Palwal railway station I was taken out of the train and put under police custody. A train from Delhi came in a short time. I was made to enter a third class carriage, the police party accompanying. On reaching Mathura, I was taken to the police barracks, but no police official could tell me as to what they proposed to do with me or where I was to be taken next. Early at 4 o'clock the next morning I was waked up and put in a goods train that was going towards Bombay. At noon I was again made to get down at Sawai Madhopur. Mr. Bowring, Inspector of Police, who arrived by the mail train from Lahore, now took charge of me. I was put in a first class compartment with him. And from an ordinary prisoner I became a 'gentleman' prisoner. The officer commenced a long panegyric of Sir Michael O'Dwyer. Sir Michael had nothing against me personally, he

went on, only he apprehended a disturbance of the peace if I entered the Punjab and so on. In the end he requested me to return to Bombay of my own accord and agree not to cross the frontier of the Punjab. I replied that I could not possibly comply with the order, and that I was not prepared of my own accord to go back. Whereupon the officer, seeing no other course, told me that he would have to enforce the law against me. 'But what do you want to do with me?' I asked him. He replied that he himself did not know, but was awaiting further orders. 'For the present,' he said, 'I am taking you to Bombay.'

We reached Surat. Here I was made over to the charge of another police officer. 'You are now free,' the officer told me when we had reached Bombay. 'It would however be better,' he added, 'if you get down near the Marine Lines where I shall get the train stopped for you. At Colaba there is likely to be a big crowd.' I told him that I would be glad to follow his wish. He was pleased and thanked me for it. Accordingly I alighted at the Marine Lines. The carriage of a friend just happened to be passing by. It took me and left me at Revashankar Jhaveri's place. The friend told me that the news of my arrest had incensed the people and roused them to a pitch of mad frenzy. 'An outbreak is apprehended every minute near Pydhuni, the Magistrate and the police have already arrived there,' he added.

Scarcely had I reached my destination, when Umar Sobani and Anasuyabehn arrived and asked me to motor to Pydhuni at once. 'The people have become impatient, and are very much excited,' they said, 'we cannot pacify them. Your presence alone can do it.'

I got into the car. Near Pydhuni I saw that a huge crowd had gathered. On seeing me the people went mad with joy. A procession was immediately formed, and the sky was rent with the shouts of *Vande mataram* and *Allaho akbar*. At Pydhuni we sighted a body of mounted police. Brickbats were raining down from above. I besought the crowd to be calm, but it seemed as if we should not be able to escape the shower of brickbats. As the procession issued out of Abdur Rahman Street and was about to proceed towards the Crawford Market, it suddenly found itself confronted by a body of the mounted police, who had arrived there to prevent it from proceeding further in the direction of the Fort. The crowd was densely packed. It had almost broken through the police cordon. There was hardly any chance of my voice being heard in that vast concourse. Just then the officer in charge of the mounted police gave the order to disperse the crowd, and at once the mounted party charged upon the crowd brandishing their lances as they went. For a moment, the lances just grazed the car as the lancers swiftly passed by. The ranks of the people were soon broken, and they were thrown into utter confusion, which was soon converted into a rout. Some got trampled under foot, others were badly mauled and crushed. In that seething mass of humanity there was hardly any room for the horses to pass, nor was there any exit by which the people could disperse. So the lancers blindly cut their way through the crowd. I hardly imagine they could see what they were doing. The whole thing presented a most dreadful spectacle. The horsemen and the people were mixed together in mad confusion.

Thus the crowd was dispersed and its progress checked. Our motor was allowed to proceed. I had it stopped before the Commissioner's office, and got down to complain to him about the conduct of the police.

That Memorable Week!—II

So I went to the Commissioner Mr. Griffith's office. All about the staircase leading to the office I saw soldiers armed from top to toe, as though for military action. The verandah was all astir. When I was admitted to the office, I saw Mr. Bowring sitting with Mr. Griffith.

I described to the Commissioner the scenes I had witnessed. He replied briefly: 'I did not want the procession to proceed to the Fort, as a disturbance was inevitable there. And as I saw that the people would not listen to persuasion, I could not help ordering the mounted police to charge through the crowd.'

'But,' said I, 'you knew what the consequences must be. The horses were bound to trample on the people. I think it was quite unnecessary to send that contingent of mounted men.'

'You cannot judge that,' said Mr. Griffith. 'We police officers know better than you the effect of your teaching on the people. If we did not start with drastic measures, the situation would pass out of our hands. I tell you that the people are sure to go out of your control. Disobedience of law will quickly appeal to them; it is beyond them to understand the duty of keeping peaceful. I have no doubt about your intentions, but the people will not understand them. They will follow their natural instinct.'

'It is there that I join issue with you,' I replied. 'The people are not by nature violent but peaceful.'

And thus we argued at length. Ultimately Mr. Griffith said, 'But suppose you were convinced that your teaching had been lost on the people, what would you do?'

'I should suspend civil disobedience if I were so convinced.'

'What do you mean? You told Mr. Bowring that you would proceed to the Punjab the moment you were released.'

'Yes, I wanted to do so by the next available train. But it is out of the question today.'

'If you will be patient, the conviction is sure to grow on you. Do you know what is happening in Ahmedabad? and what has happened in Amritsar? People have everywhere gone nearly mad. I am not yet in possession of all the facts. The telegraph wires have been cut in some places. I put it to you that the responsibility for all these disturbances lies on you.'

'I assure you I should readily take it upon myself wherever I discovered it. But I should be deeply pained and surprised, if I found that there were disturbances in Ahmedabad. I cannot answer for Amritsar. I have never been there, no one knows me there. But even about the Punjab I am certain of this much that, had not the Punjab Government prevented my entry into the Punjab, I should have been considerably helpful in keeping the peace there. By preventing me they gave the people unnecessary provocation.'

And so we argued on and on. It was impossible for us to agree. I told him that I intended to address a meeting on Chowpati and to ask the people to keep the peace, and took leave of him. The meeting was held on the Chowpati sands. I spoke at length on the duty of non-violence and on the limitations of Satyagraha, and said: 'Satyagrahi is essentially a weapon of the truthful. A Satyagrahi is pledged to non-violence, and, unless people observe it in thought, word and deed, I cannot offer mass Satyagraha.'

Anasuyabehn, too, had received news of disturbances in Ahmedabad. Someone had spread a rumour that she also had been arrested. The mill-hands had gone mad over her rumoured arrest, struck work and committed acts of violence, and a sergeant had been done to death.

I proceeded to Ahmedabad. I learnt that an attempt had been made to pull up the rails near the Nadiad railway station, that a Government officer had been murdered in Viramgam, and that Ahmedabad was under martial law. The people were terror-stricken. They had indulged in acts of violence and were being made to pay for them with interest.

A police officer was waiting at the station to escort me to Mr. Pratt, the Commissioner. I found him in a state of rage. I spoke to him gently and expressed my regret for the disturbances. I suggested that martial law was unnecessary, and declared my readiness to cooperate in all efforts to restore peace. I asked for permission to hold a public meeting on the grounds of the Sabarmati Ashram. The proposal appealed to him, and the meeting was held, I think, on Sunday, the 13 of April, and martial law was withdrawn the same day or the day after. Addressing the meeting, I tried to bring home to the people the sense of their wrong, declared a penitential fast of three days for myself, appealed to the people to go on a similar fast for a day, and suggested to those who had been guilty of acts of violence to confess their guilt.

I saw my duty as clear as daylight. It was unbearable for me to—find that the labourers, amongst whom I had spent a good deal of my time, whom I had served, and from whom I had expected better things, had taken part in the riots, and I felt I was a sharer in their guilt.

Just as I suggested to the people to confess their guilt, I suggested to the Government to condone the crimes. Neither accepted my suggestion.

The late Sir Ramanbhai and other citizens of Ahmedabad came to me with an appeal to suspend Satyagraha. The appeal was needless, for I had already made up my mind to suspend Satyagraha so long as people had not learnt the lesson of peace. The friends went away happy.

There were, however, others who were unhappy over the decision. They felt that, if I expected peace everywhere and regarded it as a condition precedent to launching Satyagraha, mass Satyagraha would be an impossibility. I was sorry to disagree with them. If those amongst whom I worked, and whom I expected to be prepared for non-violence and self-suffering, could not be non-violent, Satyagraha was certainly impossible. I was firmly of opinion that those who wanted to lead the people to Satyagraha ought to be able to keep the people within the limited non-violence expected of them. I hold the same opinion even today.

A Himalayan Miscalculation

Almost immediately after the Ahmedabad meeting I went to Nadiad. It was here that I first used the expression 'Himalayan miscalculation' which obtained such a wide currency afterwards. Even at Ahmedabad I had begun to have a dim perception of my mistake. But when I reached Nadiad and saw the actual state of things there and heard reports about a large number of people from Kheda district having been arrested, it suddenly dawned upon me that I had committed a grave error in calling upon the people in the Kheda district and elsewhere to launch upon civil disobedience prematurely, as it now seemed to me. I was addressing a public meeting. My confession brought down upon me no small amount of ridicule. But I have never regretted having made that confession. For I have always held that it is only when one sees one's own mistakes with a convex lens, and does just the reverse in the case of others, that one is able to arrive at a just relative estimate of the two. I further believe that a scrupulous and conscientious observance of this rule is necessary for one who wants to be a Satyagrahi.

Let us now see what that Himalayan miscalculation was. Before one can be fit for the practice of civil disobedience one must have rendered a willing and respectful obedience to the state laws. For the most part we obey such laws out of fear of the penalty for their breach, and this holds good particularly in respect of such laws as do not involve a moral principle. For instance, an honest, respectable man will not suddenly take to stealing, whether there is a law against stealing or not, but this very man will not feel any remorse for failure to observe the rule about carrying head-lights on bicycles after dark. Indeed it is doubtful whether he would even accept advice kindly about being more careful in this respect. But he would observe any obligatory rule of this kind, if only to escape the inconvenience of facing a prosecution for a breach of the rule. Such compliance is not, however, the willing and spontaneous obedience that is required of a Satyagrahi. A Satyagrahi obeys the laws of society intelligently and of his own free will, because he considers it to be his sacred duty to do so. It is only when a person has thus obeyed the laws of society scrupulously that he is in a position to judge as to which particular rules are good and just and which unjust and iniquitous. Only then does the right accrue to him of the civil disobedience of certain laws in well-defined circumstances. My error lay in my failure to observe this necessary limitation. I had called on the people to launch upon civil disobedience before they had thus qualified themselves for it, and this mistake seemed to me of Himalayan magnitude. As soon as I entered the Kheda district, all the old recollections of the Kheda Satyagraha struggle came back to me, and I wondered how I could have failed to perceive what was so obvious. I realized that before a people could be fit for offering civil disobedience, they should thoroughly understand its deeper implications. That being so, before re-starting civil disobedience on a mass scale, it would be necessary to create a band of well-tried, pure-hearted volunteers who thoroughly understood the strict conditions of Satyagraha. They could explain these to the people, and by sleepless vigilance keep them on the right path.

With these thoughts filling my mind I reached Bombay, raised a a corps of Satyagrahi volunteers through the Satyagraha Sabha there, and with their help commenced the work of educating the people with regard to the meaning and inner significance of Satyagraha. This was principally done by issuing leaflets of an educative character bearing on the subject.

But whilst this work was going on, I could see that it was a difficult task to interest the people in the peaceful side of Satyagraha. The volunteers too failed to enlist themselves in large numbers. Nor did all those who actually enlisted take anything like a regular systematic training, and as the days passed by, the number of fresh recruits began gradually to dwindle instead of to grow. I realized that the progress of the training in civil disobedience was not going to be as rapid as I had at first expected.

The Birth of Khadi

I do not remember to have seen a handloom or a spinning wheel when in 1908 I described it in *Hind Swaraj* as the panacea for the growing pauperism of India. In that book I took it as understood that anything that helped India to get rid of the grinding poverty of her masses would in the same process also establish Swaraj. Even in 1915, when I returned to India from South Africa, I had not actually seen a spinning wheel. When the Satyagraha Ashram was founded at Sabarmati, we introduced a few handlooms there. But no sooner had we done this than we found ourselves up against a difficulty. All of us belonged either to the liberal professions or to business; not one of us was an artisan. We needed a weaving expert to teach us to weave before we could work the looms. One was at last procured from Palanpur, but he did not communicate to us the whole of his art. But Maganlal Gandhi was not to be easily baffled. Possessed of a natural talent for mechanics, he was able fully to master the art before long, and one after another several new weavers were trained up in the Ashram.

The object that we set before ourselves was to be able to clothe ourselves entirely in cloth manufactured by our own hands. We therefore forthwith discarded the use of mill-woven cloth, and all the members of the Ashram resolved to wear hand-woven cloth made from Indian yarn only. The adoption of this practice brought us a world of experience. It enabled us to know, from direct contact, the conditions of life among the weavers, the extent of their production, the handicaps in the way of their obtaining their yarn supply, the way in which they were being made victims of fraud, and, lastly, their ever growing indebtedness. We were not in a position immediately to manufacture all the cloth for our needs. The alternative therefore was to get our cloth supply from handloom weavers. But ready-made cloth from Indian mill-yarn was not easily obtainable either from the cloth-dealers or from the weavers themselves. All the fine cloth woven by the weavers was from foreign yarn, since Indian mills did not spin fine counts. Even today the outturn of higher counts by Indian mills is very limited, whilst highest counts they cannot spin at all. It was after the greatest effort that we were at last able to find some weavers who condescended to weave Swadeshi yarn for us, and only on condition that the Ashram would take up all the cloth that they might produce. By thus adopting cloth woven from mill-yarn as our wear, and propagating it among our

friends, we made ourselves voluntary agents of the Indian spinning mills. This in its turn brought us into contact with the mills, and enabled us to know something about their management and their handicaps. We saw that the aim of the mills was more and more to weave the yarn spun by them; their co-operation with the handloom weaver was not willing, but unavoidable and temporary. We became impatient to be able to spin our own yarn. It was clear that, until we could do this ourselves, dependence on the mills would remain. We did not feel that we could render any service to the country by continuing as agents of Indian spinning mills.

No end of difficulties again faced us. We could get neither a spinning wheel nor a spinner to teach us how to spin. We were employing some wheels for filling pearls and bobbins for weaving in the Ashram. But we had no idea that these could be used as spinning wheels. Once Kalidas Jhaveri discovered a woman who, he said, would demonstrate to us how spinning was done. We sent to her a member of the Ashram who was known for his great versatility in learning new things. But even he returned without wrestling the secret of the art.

So the time passed on, and my impatience grew with the time. I plied every chance visitor to the Ashram who was likely to possess some information about handspinning with questions about the art. But the art being confined to women and having been all but exterminated, if there was some stray spinner still surviving in some obscure corner, only a member of that sex was likely to find out her whereabouts.

In the year 1917 I was taken by my Gujarati friends to preside at the Broach

Educational Conference. It was here that I discovered that remarkable lady Gangabehn Majmundar. She was a widow, but her enterprising spirit knew no bounds. Her education, in the accepted sense of the term, was not much. But in courage and commonsense she easily surpassed the general run of our educated women. She had already got rid of the curse of untouchability, and fearlessly moved among and served the suppressed classes. She had means of her own, and her needs were few. She had a well seasoned constitution, and went about everywhere without an escort. She felt quite at home on horseback. I came to know her more intimately at the Godhra Conference. To her I poured out my grief about the charkha, and she lightened my burden by a promise to prosecute an earnest and incessant search for the spinning wheel.

Found at Last!

At last, after no end of wandering in Gujarat, Gangabehn found the spinning wheel in Vijapur in the Baroda State. Quite a number of people there had spinning wheels in their homes, but had long since consigned them to the lofts as useless lumber. They expressed to Gangabehn their readiness to resume spinning, if someone promised to provide them with a regular supply of slivers, and to buy the yarn spun by them. Gangabehn communicated the joyful news to me. The providing of slivers was found to be a difficult task. On my mentioning the thing to the late Umar Sobani, he solved the difficulty by immediately undertaking to send a sufficient supply of slivers from his mill.

I sent to Gangabehn the slivers received from Umar Sobani, and soon yarn began to pour in at such a rate that it became quite a problem how to cope with it.

Mr. Umar Sobani's generosity was great, but still one could not go on taking advantage of it for ever. I felt ill at ease, continuously receiving slivers from him. Moreover, it seemed to me to be fundamentally wrong to use mill-slivers. If one could use mill-slivers, why not use mill-yarn as well? Surely no mills supplied slivers to the ancients? How did they make their slivers then? With these thoughts in my mind I suggested to Gangabehn to find carders who could supply slivers. She confidently undertook the task. She engaged a carder who was prepared to card cotton. He demanded thirty-five rupees, if not much more, per month. I considered no price too high at the time. She trained a few youngsters to make slivers out of the carded cotton. I begged for cotton in Bombay. Sjt. Yashvantprasad Desai at once responded. Gangabehn's enterprise thus prospered beyond expectation. She found out weavers to weave the yarn that was spun in Vijapur, and soon Vijapur Khadi gained a name for itself.

While these developments were taking place in Vijapur, the spinning wheel gained a rapid footing in the Ashram. Maganlal Gandhi, by bringing to bear all his splendid mechanical talent on the wheel, made many improvements in it, and wheels and their accessories began to be manufactured at the Ashram. The first piece of khadi manufactured in the Ashram cost 17 annas per yard. I did not hesitate to commend this very coarse khadi at that rate to friends, who willingly paid the price.

I was laid up in bed at Bombay. But I was fit enough to make searches for the wheel there. At last I chanced upon two spinners. They charged one rupee for a seer of yarn, *i.e.,* *28 tolas* or nearly three quarters of a pound. I was then ignorant of the economics of khadi. I considered no price too high for securing handspun yarn. On comparing the rates paid by me with those paid in Vijapur I found that I was being cheated. The spinners refused to agree to any reduction in their rates. So I had to dispense with their services. But they served their purpose. They taught spinning to Shrimatis Avantikabai, Ramibai Kamdar, the widowed mother of Sjt. Shankarlal Banker and Shrimati Vasumatibehn. The wheel began merrily to hum in my room, and I may say without exaggeration that its hum had no small share in restoring me to health. I am prepared to admit that its effect was more psychological than physical. But then it only shows how powerfully the physical in man reacts to the psychological. I too set my hand to the wheel, but did not do much with it at the time.

In Bombay, again, the same old problem of obtaining a supply of hand-made slivers presented itself. A carder twanging his bow used to pass daily by Sjt. Revashankar's residence. I sent for him and learnt that he carded cotton for stuffing mattresses. He agreed to card cotton for slivers, but demanded a stiff price for it, which, however, I paid. The yarn thus prepared I disposed of to some Vaishnava friends for making from it the garlands for the *pavitra ekadashi.* Sjt. Shivji started a spinning class in Bombay. All these experiments involved considerable expenditure. But it was willingly defrayed by patriotic friends, lovers of the motherland, who had faith in Khadi. The money thus spent, in my humble opinion, was not wasted. It brought us a rich store of experience, and revealed to us the possibilities of the spinning wheel.

I now grew impatient for the exclusive adoption of khadi for my dress. My *dhoti* was still of Indian mill cloth. The coarse khadi manufactured in the Ashram and at Vijapur was only 30 inches in width. I gave notice to Gangabehn that, unless she provided me with a khadi *dhoti* of 45 inches width within a month, I would do with coarse, short khadi *dhoti.* The ultimatum came upon her as a shock. But she proved equal to the demand made upon her. Well within the month she sent me a pair of khadi *dhotis* of 45 inches width, and thus relieved me from what would then have been a difficult situation for me.

At about the same time Sjt. Lakshmidas brought Sjt. Ramji, the weaver, with his wife Gangabehn from Lathi to the Ashram and got khadi *dhotis* woven at the Ashram. The part played by this couple in the spread of khadi was by no means insignificant. They initiated a host of persons in Gujarat and also outside into the art of weaving handspun yarn. To see Gangabehn at her loom is a stirring sight. When this unlettered but self-possessed sister plies at her loom she becomes so lost in it that it is difficult to distract her attention, and much more difficult to draw her eyes off her beloved loom.

An Instructive Dialogue

From its very inception the khadi movement, Swadeshi movement as it was then called, evoked much criticism from the mill-owners. The late Umar Sobani, a capable mill-owner himself, not only gave me the benefit of his own knowledge and experience, but kept me in touch with the opinion of the other mill-owners as well. The argument advanced by one of these deeply impressed him. He pressed me to meet him. I agreed. Mr. Sobani arranged the interview. The mill-owner opened the conversation.

'You know that there has been Swadeshi agitation before now?'

'Yes, I do,' I replied.

'You are also aware that in the days of the Partition we, the mill-owners, fully exploited the Swadeshi movement. When it was at its height, we raised the prices of cloth, and did even worse things.'

'Yes, I have heard something about it, and it has grieved me.'

'I can understand your grief, but I can see no ground for it. We are not conducting our business out of philanthropy. We do it for profit, we have got to satisfy the shareholders. The price of an article is governed by the demand for it. Who can check the law of demand and supply? The Bengalis should have known that their agitation was bound to send up the price of Swadeshi cloth by stimulating the demand for it.'

I interrupted: 'The Bengalis like me were trustful in their nature. They believed, in the fullness of their faith, that the mill-owners would not be so utterly selfish and unpatriotic as to betray their country in the hour of its need, and even to go the length, as they did, of fraudulently passing off foreign cloth as Swadeshi.'

'I knew your believing nature,' he rejoined; 'that is why I put you to the trouble of coming to me, so that I might warn you against falling into the same error as these simple-hearted Bengalis.'

With these words the mill-owner beckoned to his clerk who was standing by to produce samples of the stuff that was being manufactured in his mill. Pointing to it he said: 'Look at this stuff. This is the latest variety turned out by our mill. It is meeting with a widespread demand. We manufacture it from the waste. Naturally, therefore, it is cheap. We send it as far North as the valleys of the Himalayas. We have agencies all over the country, even in places where your voice or your agents can never reach. You can thus see that we do not stand in need of more agents. Besides, you ought to know that India's production of cloth falls far short of its requirements. The question of Swadeshi, therefore, largely resolves itself into one of production. The moment we can increase our production sufficiently, and improve its quality to the necessary extent, the import of foreign cloth will automatically cease. My advice to you, therefore, is not to carry on your agitation on its present lines, but to turn your attention to the erection of fresh mills. What we need is not propaganda to inflate demand for our goods, but greater production.'

'Then, surely, you will bless my effort, if I am already engaged in that very thing,' I asked.

'How can that be?' he exclaimed, a bit puzzled, 'but maybe, you are thinking of promoting the establishment of new mills, in which case you certainly deserve to be congratulated.'

'I am not doing exactly that,' I explained, 'but I am engaged in the revival of the spinning wheel.'

'What is that?' he asked, feeling still more at sea. I told him all about the spinning wheel, and the story of my long quest after it, and I added, 'I am entirely of your opinion; it is no use my becoming virtually an agent for the mills. That would do more harm than good to the country. Our mills will not be in want of custom for a long time to come. My work should be, and therefore is, to organize the production of handspun cloth, and to find means for the disposal of the khadi thus produced. I am, therefore, concentrating my attention on the production of khadi. I swear by this form of Swadeshi, because through it I can provide work to the semi-starved, semi-employed women of India. My idea is to get these women to spin yarn, and to clothe the people of India with khadi woven out of it. I do not know how far this movement is going to succeed, at present it is only in the incipient stage. But I have full faith in it. At any rate it can do no harm. On the contrary to the extent that it can add to the cloth production of the country, be it ever so small, it will represent so much solid gain. You will thus perceive that my movement is free from the evils mentioned by you.'

He replied, 'If you have additional production in view in organizing your movement, I have nothing to say against it. Whether the spinning wheel can make headway in this age of power machinery is another question. But I for one wish you every success.'

Farewell

The time has now come to bring these chapters to a close.

My life from this point onward has been so public that there is hardly anything about it that people do not know. Moreover, since 1921 I have worked in such close association with the Congress leaders that I can hardly describe any episode in my life since then without referring to my relations with them. For though Shraddhanandji, the Deshabandhu, Hakim Saheb and Lalaji are no more with us today, we have the good luck to have a host of other veteran Congress leaders still living and working in our midst. The history of the Congress, since the great changes in it that I have described above, is still in the making. And my principal experiments during the past seven years have all been made through the Congress. A reference to my relations with the leaders would therefore be unavoidable, if I set about describing my experiments further. And this I may not do, at any rate for the present, if only from a sense of propriety. Lastly, my conclusions from my current experiments can hardly as yet be regarded as decisive. It therefore seems to me to be my plain duty to close this narrative here. In fact my pen instinctively refuses to proceed further.

It is not without a wrench that I have to take leave of the reader. I set a high value on my experiments. I do not know whether I have been able to do justice to them. I can only say that I have spared no pains to give a faithful narrative. To describe truth, as it has appeared to me, and in the exact manner in which I have arrived at it, has been my ceaseless effort. The exercise has given me ineffable mental peace, because, it has been my fond hope that it might bring faith in Truth and Ahimsa to waverers.

My uniform experience has convinced me that there is no other God than Truth. And if every page of these chapters does not proclaim to the reader that the only means for the realization of Truth is Ahimsa, I shall deem all my labour in writing these chapters to have been in vain. And, even though my efforts in this behalf may prove fruitless, let the readers know that the vehicle, not the great principle, is at fault. After all, however sincere my strivings after Ahimsa may have been, they have still been imperfect and inadequate. The little fleeting glimpses, therefore, that I have been able to have of Truth can hardly convey an idea of the indescribable lustre of Truth, a million times more intense than that of the sun we daily see with our eyes. In fact what I have caught is only the faintest glimmer of that mighty effulgence. But this much I can say with assurance, as a result of all my experiments, that a perfect vision of Truth can only follow a complete realization of Ahimsa.

To see the universal and all-pervading Spirit of Truth face to face one must be able to love the meanest of creation as oneself. And a man who aspires after that cannot afford to keep out of any field of life. That is why my devotion to Truth has drawn me into the field of politics; and I can say without the slightest hesitation, and yet in all humility, that those who say that religion has nothing to do with politics do not know what religion means.

Identification with everything that lives is impossible without self-purification; without self-purification the observance of the law of Ahimsa must remain an empty dream; God can never be realized by one who is not pure of heart. Self-purification therefore must mean purification in all the walks of life. And purification being highly infectious, purification of oneself necessarily leads to the purification of one's surroundings.

But the path of self-purification is hard and steep. To attain to perfect purity one has to become absolutely passion-free in thought, speech and action; to rise above the opposing currents of love and hatred, attachment and repulsion. I know that I have not in me as yet that triple purity, in spite of constant ceaseless striving for it. That is why the world's praise fails to move me, indeed it very often stings me. To conquer the subtle passions seems to me to be harder far than the physical conquest of the world by the force of arms. Ever since my return to India I have had experiences of the dormant passions lying hidden within me. The knowledge of them has made me feel humiliated though not defeated. The experiences and experiments have sustained me and given me great joy. But I know that I have still before me a difficult path to traverse. I must reduce myself to zero. So long as a man does not of his own free will put himself last among his fellow creatures, there is no salvation for him. Ahimsa is the farthest limit of humility.

In bidding farewell to the reader, for the time being at any rate, I ask him to join with me in prayer to the God of Truth that He may grant me the boon of Ahimsa in mind, word and deed.

Questions

1. What were Gandhi's goals in the civil disobedience campaign?

2. Why did he call the strike a "Himalayan miscalculation?"

3. What were Gandhi's goals in the *Khadi* movement and what difficulties did he encounter?

Recommended Reading

Fischer, Louis. *Gandhi: His Life and Message for the World*. New York: New American Library, 1991.

Gandhi on Non-Violence: Selected texts from Gandhi's Non-Violence in Peace and War, ed. Thomas Merton. New York: New Directions, 1968.

Film

Gandhi

CHAPTER 2

Viktor Frankl

Viktor Emil Frankl was born in Vienna in March 1905. He would live until 1997 and in those remarkable ninety-two years, he became a psychiatrist, wrote thirty-two books and received honorary degrees from universities around the world. He was not strictly a human rights activist, but he developed a philosophy and school of existential psychoanalysis, called logotherapy, which offers deep insight into human survival in the face of oppression and suffering, most decidedly the core of human rights. In 1942 he, along with his parents and young wife, were sent by the Nazis to the Theresienstadt concentration camp. He would never see any of them again; he and one sister were the only survivors in his immediate family. For the next three years he would live in four different concentration camps. From this experience of observing human beings, and their behavior and reactions to the worst possible conditions of oppression, Frankl developed his philosophy and ideas on psychotherapy.

Frankl could have left Austria before his arrest, but decided against it because he could not take his parents with him. When he entered the camp he tried to persuade the guard to allow him to keep his scientific manuscript which contained his life work to that point. His pleas were ignored, and from that moment forward he knew his life was going to take a new path. Upon his release, he wrote the book, *Man's Search for Meaning: An Introduction to Logotherapy,* from which the passages below have been selected.

In 1945 Frankl returned to Vienna and his psychiatric work. He became the head physician of the Neurology Department of the Vienna Polyclinic Hospital. During the next fifty-two years he would practice psychiatry, write books, lecture and teach abroad, and climb mountains, so many in fact, that there is a mountain in Austria named after him. He also married again and had a daughter who followed in his footsteps to become a psychiatrist.

In the two selections below, Frank discusses how his love for his wife helped give meaning to his life while he was in Auschwitz. He would later argue that man's search and need for meaning, whether it be a belief in God, the love of an individual, or one's work, was what was needed above all to sustain people. This faith and optimism, referred to by some as the foundation of existential philosophy, would become the basis of his school of psychoanalysis. Frankl disagreed with his teacher Sigmund Freud that people are primarily driven by instinct and desire. To Frankl, an individual's spiritual side, one's personality or what could be called soul, is more important than one's physical side. He observed that, even in the worst conditions of a concentration camp, people still could assert their will and choose to preserve their internal freedom. Although Frankl was influenced by the writings of many people, including Dostoevsky, Nietzsche, and Freud, it was his own personal experience in the concentration camps which led to his fully mature philosophy and understanding. Like Gandhi, Mandela, the Dalai Lama, and Aung San Suu Kyi, Frankl refused to view himself as a victim, in spite of what had happened to him and his family. He believed that people could endure and survive the most adverse circumstances once they recognized their potential and strength. In his psychiatric work, he brought these convictions to his patients to help them find meaning in their lives.

Experiences in a Concentration Camp

In spite of all the enforced physical and mental primitiveness of the life in a concentration camp, it was possible for spiritual life to deepen. Sensitive people who were used to a rich intellectual life may have suffered much pain (they were often of a delicate constitution), but the damage to their inner selves was less. They were able to retreat from their terrible surroundings to a life of inner riches and spiritual freedom. Only in this way can one explain the apparent paradox that some prisoners of a less hardy make-up often seemed to survive camp life better than did those of a robust nature. In order to make myself clear, I am forced to fall back on personal experience. Let me tell what happened on those early mornings when we had to march to our work site.

There were shouted commands: "Detachment, forward march! Left-2-3-4! Left-2-3-4! Left-2-3-4! Left-2-3-4! First man about, left and left and left and left! Caps off!" These words sound in my ears even now. At the order "Caps off!" we passed the gate of the camp, and searchlights were trained upon us. Whoever did not march smartly got a kick. And worse off was the man who, because of the cold, had pulled his cap back over his ears before permission was given.

We stumbled on in the darkness, over big stones and through large puddles, along the one road leading from the camp. The accompanying guards kept shouting at us and driving us with the butts of their rifles. Anyone with very sore feet supported himself on his neighbor's arm. Hardly a word was spoken; the icy wind did not encourage talk. Hiding his mouth behind his upturned collar, the man marching next to me whispered suddenly: "If our wives could see us now! I do hope they are better off in their camps and don't know what is happening to us."

That brought thoughts of my own wife to mind. And as we stumbled on for miles, slipping on icy spots, supporting each other time and again, dragging one another up and onward, nothing was said, but we both knew: each of us was thinking of his wife. Occasionally I looked at the sky, where the stars were fading and the pink light of the morning was beginning to spread behind a dark bank of clouds. But my mind clung to my wife's image, imagining it with an uncanny acuteness. I heard her answering me, saw her smile, her frank and encouraging look. Real or not, her look was then more luminous than the sun which was beginning to rise.

A thought transfixed me: for the first time in my life I saw the truth as it is set into song by so many poets, proclaimed as the final wisdom by so many thinkers. The truth—that love is the ultimate and the highest goal to which man can aspire. Then I grasped the meaning of the greatest secret that human poetry and human thought and belief have to impart: *The salvation of man is through love and in love.* I understood how a man who has nothing left in this world still may know bliss,

From *Man's Search for Meaning* by Viktor Frankl, trans. by Ilse Lasch. © 1959, 1962, 1984, 1992 by Viktor Frankl. Reprinted by permission of Beacon Press, Boston.

be it only for a brief moment, in the contemplation of his beloved. In a position of utter desolation, when man cannot express himself in positive action, when his only achievement may consist in enduring his sufferings in the right way—an honorable way—in such a position man can, through loving contemplation of the image he carries of his beloved, achieve fulfillment. For the first time in my life I was able to understand the meaning of the words, "The angels are lost in perpetual contemplation of an infinite glory."

In front of me a man stumbled and those following him fell on top of him. The guard rushed over and used his whip on them all. Thus my thoughts were interrupted for a few minutes. But soon my soul found its way back from the prisoner's existence to another world, and I resumed talk with my loved one: I asked her questions, and she answered; she questioned me in return, and I answered.

"Stop!" We had arrived at our work site. Everybody rushed into the dark hut in the hope of getting a fairly decent tool. Each prisoner got a spade or a pickaxe.

"Can't you hurry up, you pigs?" Soon we had resumed the previous day's positions in the ditch. The frozen ground cracked under the point of the pickaxes, and sparks flew. The men were silent, their brains numb.

My mind still clung to the image of my wife. A thought crossed my mind: I didn't even know if she were still alive. I knew only one thing—which I have learned well by now: Love goes very far beyond the physical person of the beloved. It finds its deepest meaning in his spiritual being, his inner self. Whether or not he is actually present, whether or not he is

still alive at all, ceases somehow to be of importance.

I did not know whether my wife was alive, and I had no means of finding out (during all my prison life there was no outgoing or incoming mail); but at that moment it ceased to matter. There was no need for me to know; nothing could touch the strength of my love, my thoughts, the image of my beloved. Had I known then that my wife was dead, I think that I would still have given myself, undisturbed by that knowledge, to the contemplation of her image, and that my mental conversation with her would have been just as vivid and just as satisfying. "Set me like a seal upon thy heart, love is as strong as death."

This intensification of inner life helped the prisoner find a refuge from the emptiness, desolation and spiritual poverty of his existence, by letting him escape into the past. When given free rein, his imagination played with past events, often not important ones, but minor happenings and trifling things. His nostalgic memory glorified them and they assumed a strange character. Their world and their existence seemed very distant and the spirit reached out for them longingly: In my mind I took bus rides, unlocked the front door of my apartment, answered my telephone, switched on the electric lights. Our thoughts often centered on such details, and these memories could move one to tears.

As the inner life of the prisoner tended to become more intense, he also experienced the beauty of art and nature as never before. Under their influence he sometimes even forgot his own frightful circumstances. If someone had seen our faces on the journey from Auschwitz to a Bavarian camp as we beheld the mountains of Salzburg with their summits glowing in the sunset, through the little barred windows of the prison carriage, he would never have believed that those were the faces of men who had given up all hope of life and liberty. Despite that factor—or maybe because of it— we were carried away by nature's beauty, which we had missed for so long.

In camp, too, a man might draw the attention of a comrade working next to him to a nice view of the setting sun shining through the tall trees of the Bavarian woods (as in the famous water color by Dürer), the same woods in which we had built an enormous, hidden munitions plant. One evening, when we were already resting on the floor of our hut, dead tired, soup bowls in hand, a fellow prisoner rushed in and asked us to run out to the assembly grounds and see the wonderful sunset. Standing outside we saw sinister clouds glowing in the west and the whole sky alive with clouds of ever-changing shapes and colors, from steel blue to blood red. The desolate grey mud huts provided a sharp contrast, while the puddles on the muddy ground reflected the glowing sky. Then, after minutes of moving silence, one prisoner said to another, "How beautiful the world *could* be!"

Another time we were at work in a trench. The dawn was grey around us; grey was the sky above; grey the snow in the pale light of dawn; grey the rags in which my fellow prisoners were clad, and grey their faces. I was again conversing silently with my wife, or perhaps I was struggling to find the *reason* for my sufferings, my slow dying. In a last violent protest against

the hopelessness of imminent death, I sensed my spirit piercing through the enveloping gloom. I felt it transcend that hopeless, meaningless world, and from somewhere I heard a victorious "Yes" in answer to my question of the existence of an ultimate purpose. At that moment a light was lit in a distant farmhouse, which stood on the horizon as if painted there, in the midst of the miserable grey of a dawning morning in Bavaria. *"Et lux in tenebris lucet"*—and the light shineth in the darkness. For hours I stood hacking at the icy ground. The guard passed by, insulting me, and once again I communed with my beloved. More and more I felt that she was present, that she was with me; I had the feeling that I was able to touch her, able to stretch out my hand and grasp hers. The feeling was very strong: she was there. Then, at that very moment, a bird flew down silently and perched just in front of me, on the heap of soil which I had dug up from the ditch, and looked steadily at me.

Earlier, I mentioned art. Is there such a thing in a concentration camp? It rather depends on what one chooses to call art. A kind of cabaret was improvised from time to time. A hut was cleared temporarily, a few wooden benches were pushed or nailed together and a program was drawn up. In the evening those who had fairly good positions in camp—the Capos and the workers who did not have to leave camp on distant marches—assembled there. They came to have a few laughs or perhaps to cry a little; anyway, to forget. There were songs, poems, jokes, some with underlying satire regarding the camp. All were meant to help us forget, and they did help. The gatherings were so effective that a few ordinary prisoners went to see the cabaret in spite of their fatigue even though they missed their daily portion of food by going.

▼   ▼   ▼   ▼   ▼

In attempting this psychological presentation and a psychopathological explanation of the typical characteristics of a concentration camp inmate, I may give the impression that the human being is completely and unavoidably influenced by his surroundings. (In this case the surroundings being the unique structure of camp life, which forced the prisoner to conform his conduct to a certain set pattern.) But what about human liberty? Is there no spiritual freedom in regard to behavior and reaction to any given surroundings? Is that theory true which would have us believe that man is no more than a product of many conditional and environmental factors—be they of a biological, psychological or sociological nature? Is man but an accidental product of these? Most important, do the prisoners' reactions to the singular world of the concentration camp prove that man cannot escape the influences of his surroundings? Does man have no choice of action in the face of such circumstances?

We can answer these questions from experience as well as on principle. The experiences of camp life show that man does have a choice of action. There were enough examples, often of a heroic nature, which proved that apathy could be overcome, irritability suppressed. Man *can* preserve a vestige of spiritual freedom, of independence of mind, even in such terrible conditions of psychic and physical stress.

We who lived in concentration camps can remember the men who walked through the huts comforting others, giving away their last piece of bread. They may have been few in number, but they offer sufficient proof that everything can be taken from a man but one thing: the last of the human freedoms—to choose one's attitude in any given set of circumstances, to choose one's own way.

And there were always choices to make. Every day, every hour, offered the opportunity to make a decision, a decision which determined whether you would or would not submit to those powers which threatened to rob you of your very self, your inner freedom; which determined whether or not you would become the plaything of circumstance, renouncing freedom and dignity to become molded into the form of the typical inmate.

Seen from this point of view, the mental reactions of the inmates of a concentration camp must seem more to us than the mere expression of certain physical and sociological conditions. Even though conditions such as lack of sleep, insufficient food and various mental stresses may suggest that the inmates were bound to react in certain ways, in the final analysis it becomes clear that the sort of person the prisoner became was the result of an inner decision, and not the result of camp influences alone. Fundamentally, therefore, any man can, even under such circumstances, decide what shall become of him—mentally and spiritually. He may retain his human dignity even in a concentration camp. Dostoevski said once, "There is only one thing that I dread: not to be worthy of my sufferings." These words frequently came to my mind after I became acquainted with those martyrs whose behavior in camp, whose suffering and death, bore witness to the fact that the last inner freedom cannot be lost. It can be said that they were worthy of their sufferings; the way they bore their suffering was a genuine inner achievement. It is this spiritual freedom—which cannot be taken away—that makes life meaningful and purposeful.

An active life serves the purpose of giving man the opportunity to realize values in creative work, while a passive life of enjoyment affords him the opportunity to obtain fulfillment in experiencing beauty, art, or nature. But there is also purpose in that life which is almost barren of both creation and enjoyment and which admits of but one possibility of high moral behavior: namely, in man's attitude to his existence, an existence restricted by external forces. A creative life and a life of enjoyment are banned to him. But not only creativeness and enjoyment are meaningful. If there is a meaning in life at all, then there must be a meaning in suffering. Suffering is an ineradicable part of life, even as fate and death. Without suffering and death human life cannot be complete.

The way in which a man accepts his fate and all the suffering it entails, the way in which he takes up his cross, gives him ample opportunity—even under the most difficult circumstances to add a deeper meaning to his life. It may remain brave, dignified and unselfish. Or in the bitter fight for self-preservation he may forget his human dignity and become no more than an animal. Here lies the chance for a man either to make use of or to forgo the opportunities of attaining the moral values that a difficult situation may afford him. And this decides whether he is worthy of his sufferings or not.

Do not think that these considerations are unworldly and too far removed from real life. It is true that only a few people are capable of reaching such high moral standards. Of the prisoners only a few kept their full inner liberty and obtained those values which their suffering afforded, but even one such example is sufficient proof that man's inner strength may raise him above his outward fate. Such men are not only in concentration camps. Everywhere man is confronted with fate, with the chance of achieving something through his own suffering.

Take the fate of the sick—especially those who are incurable. I once read a letter written by a young invalid, in which he told a friend that he had just found out he would not live for long, that even an operation would be of no help. He wrote further that he remembered a film he had seen in which a man was portrayed who waited for death in a courageous and dignified way. The boy had thought it a great accomplishment to meet death so well. Now—he wrote—fate was offering him a similar chance.

Those of us who saw the film called *Resurrection*—taken from a book by Tolstoy—years ago, may have had similar thoughts. Here were great destinies and great men. For us, at that time, there was no great fate; there was no chance to achieve such greatness. After the picture we went to the nearest cafe, and over a cup of coffee and a sandwich we forgot the strange metaphysical thoughts which for one moment had crossed our minds. But when we ourselves were confronted with a great destiny and faced with the decision of meeting it with equal spiritual greatness, by then we had forgotten our youthful resolutions of long ago, and we failed.

Perhaps there came a day for some of us when we saw the same film again, or a similar one. But by then other pictures may have simultaneously unrolled before one's inner eye; pictures of people who attained much more in their lives than a sentimental film could show. Some details of a particular man's inner greatness may have come to one's mind, like the story of the young woman whose death I witnessed in a concentration camp. It is a simple story. There is little to tell and it may sound as if I had invented it; but to me it seems like a poem.

This young woman knew that she would die in the next few days. But when I talked to her she was cheerful in spite of this knowledge. "I am grateful that fate has hit me so hard" she told me. "In my former life I was spoiled and did not take spiritual accomplishments seriously." Pointing through the window of the hut, she said, "This tree here is the only friend I have in my loneliness." Through that window she could see just one branch of a chestnut tree, and on the branch were two blossoms. "I often talk to this tree," she said to me. I was startled and didn't quite know how to take her words. Was she delirious? Did she have occasional hallucinations? Anxiously I asked her if the tree replied. "Yes." What did it say to her? She answered, "It said to me, 'I am here—-I am here—I am life, eternal life.' "

We have stated that that which was ultimately responsible for the state of the prisoner's inner self was not so much the enumerated psychophysical causes as it was the result of a free decision. Psychological observations of the prisoners have shown that only the men who allowed their inner hold on their moral and spiritual selves to subside eventually fell victim to the camp's degenerating influences. The question now arises, what could, or should, have constituted this "inner hold"?

Former prisoners, when writing or relating their experiences, agree that the most depressing influence of all was that a prisoner could not know how long his term of imprisonment would be. He had been given no date for his release. (In our camp it was pointless even to talk about it.) Actually a prison term was not only uncertain but unlimited. A well-known research psychologist has pointed out that life in a concentration camp could be called a "provisional existence." We can add to this by defining it as a "provisional existence of unknown limit."

New arrivals usually knew nothing about the conditions at a camp. Those who had come back from other camps were obliged to keep silent, and from some camps no one had returned. On entering camp a change took place in the minds of the men. With the end of uncertainty there came the uncertainty of the end. It was impossible to foresee whether or when, if at all, this form of existence would end.

The latin word *finis* has two meanings: the end or the finish, and a goal to reach. A man who could not see the end of his "provisional existence" was not able to aim at an ultimate goal in life. He ceased living for the future, in contrast to a man in normal life. Therefore the whole structure of his inner life changed; signs of decay set in which we know from other areas of life. The unemployed worker, for example, is in a similar position. His existence has become provisional and in a certain sense he cannot live for the future or aim at a goal. Research work done on unemployed miners has shown that they suffer from a peculiar sort of deformed time—inner time—which is a result of their unemployed state. Prisoners, too, suffered from this strange "time-experience." In camp, a small time unit, a day, for example, filled with hourly tortures and fatigue, appeared endless. A larger time unit, perhaps a week, seemed to pass very quickly. My comrades agreed when I said that in camp a day lasted longer than a week. How paradoxical was our time-experience! In this connection we are reminded of Thomas Mann's *The Magic Mountain*, which contains some very pointed psychological remarks. Mann studies the spiritual development of people who are in an analogous psychological position, i.e., tuberculosis patients in a sanatorium who also know no date for their release. They experience a similar existence—without a future and without a goal.

One of the prisoners, who on his arrival marched with a long column of new inmates from the station to the camp, told me later that he had felt as though he were marching at his own funeral. His life had seemed to him absolutely without future. He regarded it as over and done, as if he had already died. This feeling of lifelessness was intensified by other causes: in time, it was the limitlessness of the term of imprisonment which was most acutely felt; in space, the narrow limits of the prison. Anything outside the barbed wire became remote—out of reach and, in a way, unreal. The events and the people outside, all the normal life there, had a ghostly aspect for the prisoner. The outside life, that is, as much as he could see of it, appeared to him almost as it might have to a dead man who looked at it from another world.

A man who let himself decline because he could not see any future goal found himself occupied with retrospective thoughts. In a different connection, we have already spoken of the tendency there was to look into the past, to help make the present, with all its horrors, less real. But in robbing the present of its reality there lay a certain danger. It became easy to overlook the opportunities to make something positive of camp life, opportunities which really did exist. Regarding our "provisional existence" as unreal was in itself an important factor in causing the prisoners to lose their hold on life; everything in a way became pointless. Such people forgot that often it is just such an exceptionally difficult external situation which gives man the opportunity to grow spiritually beyond himself. Instead of taking the camp's difficulties as a test of their inner strength, they did not take their life seriously and despised it as something of no consequence. They preferred to close their eyes and to live in the past. Life for such people became meaningless.

Naturally only a few people were capable of reaching great spiritual heights. But a few were given the chance to attain human greatness even through their apparent worldly failure and death, an accomplishment which in ordinary circumstances they would never have achieved. To the others of us, the mediocre and the half-hearted, the words of Bismarck could be applied: "Life is like being at the dentist. You always think that the worst is still to come, and yet it is over already." Varying this, we could say that most men in a concentration camp believed that the real opportunities of life had passed. Yet, in reality, there was an opportunity and a challenge. One could make a victory of those experiences, turning life into an inner triumph, or one could ignore the challenge and simply vegetate, as did a majority of the prisoners.

Any attempt at fighting the camp's psychopathological influence on the prisoner by psychotherapeutic or psychohygienic methods had to aim at giving him inner strength by pointing out to him a future goal to which he could look forward. Instinctively some of the prisoners attempted to find one on their own. It is a peculiarity of man that he can only live by looking to the future—*sub specie aeternitatis.* And this is his salvation in the most difficult moments of his existence, although he sometimes has to force his mind to the task.

I remember a personal experience. Almost in tears from pain (I had terrible sores on my feet from wearing torn shoes), I limped a few kilometers with our long column of men from the camp to our work site. Very cold, bitter winds struck us. I kept thinking of the endless little problems of our miserable life. What would there be to eat tonight? If a piece of sausage came as extra ration, should I exchange it for a piece of bread? Should I trade my last cigarette, which was left from a bonus I received a fortnight ago, for a bowl of soup? How could I get a piece of wire to replace the fragment which served as one of my shoelaces? Would I get to our work site in time to join my usual working party or would I have to join another, which might have a brutal foreman? What could I do to get on good terms with the Capo, who could help me to obtain work in

camp instead of undertaking this horribly long daily march?

I became disgusted with the state of affairs which compelled me, daily and hourly, to think of only such trivial things. I forced my thoughts to turn to another subject. Suddenly I saw myself standing on the platform of a well-lit, warm and pleasant lecture room. In front of me sat an attentive audience on comfortable upholstered seats. I was giving a lecture on the psychology of the concentration camp! All that oppressed me at that moment became objective, seen and described from the remote viewpoint of science. By this method I succeeded somehow in rising above the situation, above the sufferings of the moment, and I observed them as if they were already of the past. Both I and my troubles became the object of an interesting psychoscientific study undertaken by myself. What does Spinoza say in his *Ethics?*— *Affectus, qui passio est, desinit esse passio simulatque eius claram et distinctam formamus ideam."* Emotion, which is suffering, ceases to be suffering as soon as we form a clear and precise picture of it.

The prisoner who had lost faith in the future— his future—was doomed. With his loss of belief in the future, he also lost his spiritual hold; he let himself decline and became subject to mental and physical decay. Usually this happened quite suddenly, in the form of a crisis, the symptoms of which were familiar to the experienced camp inmate. We all feared this moment—not for ourselves, which would have been pointless, but for our friends. Usually it began with the prisoner refusing one morning to get dressed and wash or to go out on the parade grounds. No entreaties, no blows, no threats had any effect. He just lay there, hardly moving. If this crisis was brought about by an illness, he refused to be taken to the sick-bay or to do anything to help himself. He simply gave up. There he remained, lying in his own excreta, and nothing bothered him any more.

I once had a dramatic demonstration of the close link between the loss of faith in the future and this dangerous giving up. F——, my senior block warden, a fairly well-known composer and librettist, confided in me one day: "I would like to tell you something, Doctor. I have had a strange dream. A voice told me that I could wish for something, that I should only say what I wanted to know, and all my questions would be answered. What do you think I asked? That I would like to know when the war would be over for me. You know what I mean, Doctor—for me! I wanted to know when we, when our camp, would be liberated and our sufferings come to an end."

"And when did you have this dream?" I asked. "In February, 1945," he answered. It was then the beginning of March.

"What did your dream voice answer?" Furtively he whispered to me, "March thirtieth."

When F—— told me about his dream, he was still full of hope and convinced that the voice of his dream would be right. But as the promised day drew nearer, the war news which reached our camp made it appear very unlikely that we would be free on the promised date. On March twenty-ninth, F—— suddenly became ill and ran a high temperature. On March thirtieth, the day his prophecy had told him that the war and suffering would be over for him, he became delirious and lost consciousness. On March thirty-first, he was dead. To all outward appearances, he had died of typhus.

▼   ▼   ▼   ▼   ▼

Those who know how close the connection is between the state of mind of a man—his courage and hope, or lack of them—and the state of immunity of his body will understand that the sudden loss of hope and courage can have a deadly effect. The ultimate cause of my friend's death was that the expected liberation did not come and he was severely disappointed. This suddenly lowered his body's resistance against the latent typhus infection. His faith in the future and his will to live had become paralyzed and his body fell victim to illness—and thus the voice of his dream was right after all.

The observations of this one case and the conclusion drawn from them are in accordance with something that was drawn to my attention by the chief doctor of our concentration camp. The death rate in the week between Christmas, 1944, and New Year's, 1945, increased in camp beyond all previous experience. In his opinion, the explanation for this increase did not lie in the harder working conditions or the deterioration of our food supplies or a change of weather or new epidemics. It was simply that the majority of the prisoners had lived in the naive hope that they would be home again by Christmas. As the time drew near and there was no encouraging news, the prisoners lost courage and disappointment overcame them. This had a dangerous influence on their powers of resistance and a great number of them died.

As we said before, any attempt to restore a man's inner strength in the camp had first to succeed in showing him some future goal. Nietzsche's words, "He who has a *why* to live for can bear with almost any *how*," could be the guiding motto for all psychotherapeutic and psychohygienic efforts regarding prisoners. Whenever there was an opportunity for it, one had to give them a why—an aim—for their lives, in order to strengthen them to bear the terrible *how* of their existence. Woe to him who saw no more sense in his life, no aim, no purpose, and therefore no point in carrying on. He was soon lost. The typical reply with which such a man rejected all encouraging arguments was, "I have nothing to expect from life any more." What sort of answer can one give to that?

What was really needed was a fundamental change in our attitude toward life. We had to learn ourselves and, furthermore, we had to teach the despairing men, that *it did not really matter what we expected from life, but rather what life expected from us*. We needed to stop asking about the meaning of life, and instead to think of ourselves as those who were being questioned by life—daily and hourly. Our answer must consist, not in talk and meditation, but in right action and in right conduct. Life ultimately means taking the responsibility to find the right answer to its problems and to fulfill the tasks which it constantly sets for each individual.

These tasks, and therefore the meaning of life, differ from man to man, and from moment to moment. Thus it is impossible to define the meaning of life in a general way. Questions about the meaning of life can never be answered by sweeping statements. "Life" does not mean something vague, but something very real and concrete, just as life's tasks are also very real and concrete. They form man's destiny, which is different and unique for each individual. No man and no destiny can be compared with any other man or any other destiny. No situation repeats itself, and each situation calls for a different response. Sometimes the situation in which a man finds himself may require him to shape his own fate by action. At other times it is more advantageous for him to make use of an opportunity for contemplation and to realize assets in this way. Sometimes man may be required simply to accept fate, to bear his cross. Every situation is distinguished by its uniqueness, and there is always only one right answer to the problem posed by the situation at hand.

When a man finds that it is his destiny to suffer, he will have to accept his suffering as his task; his single and unique task. He will have to acknowledge the fact that even in suffering he is unique and alone in the universe. No one can relieve him of his suffering or suffer in his place. His unique opportunity lies in the way in which he bears his burden.

For us, as prisoners, these thoughts were not speculations far removed from reality. They were the only thoughts that could be of help to us. They kept us from despair, even when there seemed to be no chance of coming out of it alive. Long ago we had passed the stage of asking what was the meaning of life, a naïve query which understands life as the attaining of some aim through the active creation of something of value. For us, the meaning of life embraced the wider cycles of life and death, of suffering and of dying.

Once the meaning of suffering had been revealed to us we refused to minimize or alleviate the camp's tortures by ignoring them or harboring false illusions and entertaining artificial optimism. Suffering had become a task on which we did not want to turn out backs. We had realized its hidden opportunities for achievement, the opportunities which caused the poet Rilke to write, *"Wie viel ist aufzuleiden!"* (How much suffering there is to get through!) Rilke spoke of "getting through suffering" as others would talk of "getting through work." There was plenty of suffering for us to get through. Therefore, it was necessary to face up to the full amount of suffering, trying to keep moments of weakness and furtive tears to a minimum. But there was no need to be ashamed of tears, for tears bore witness that a man had the greatest of courage, the courage to suffer. Only very few realized that. Shamefacedly some confessed occasionally that they had wept, like the comrade who answered my question of how he had gotten over his edema, by confessing, "I have wept it out of my system."

The tender beginnings of a psychotherapy or psychohygiene were, when they were possible at all in the camp, either individual or collective in nature. The individual psychotherapeutic attempts were often a kind of "life-saving procedure." These efforts were usually concerned with the prevention of suicides. A very strict camp ruling forbade any efforts to save a man who attempted suicide. It was forbidden, for example, to cut down a man who was trying to hang himself. Therefore, it was all important to prevent these attempts from occurring.

I remember two cases of would-be suicide, which bore a striking similarity to each other. Both men had talked of their intentions to commit suicide. Both used the typical argument—they had nothing more to expect from life. In both cases it was a question of getting them to realize that life was still expecting something from them; something in the future was expected of them. We found, in fact, that for the one it was his child whom he adored and who was waiting for him in a foreign country. For the other it was a thing, not a person. This man was a scientist and had written a series of books which still needed to be finished. His work could not be done by anyone else, any more than another person could ever take the place of the father in his child's affections.

This uniqueness and singleness which distinguishes each individual and gives a meaning to his existence has a bearing on creative work as much as it does on human love. When the impossibility of replacing a person is realized, it allows the responsibility which a man has for his existence and its continuance to appear in all its magnitude. A man who becomes conscious of the responsibility he bears toward a human being who affectionately waits for him, or to an unfinished work, will never be able to throw away his life. He knows the "why" for his existence, and will be able to bear almost any "how."

The opportunities for collective psychotherapy were naturally limited in camp. The right example was more effective than words could ever be. A senior block warden who did not side with the authorities had, by his just and encouraging behavior, a thousand opportunities to exert a far-reaching moral influence on those under his jurisdiction. The immediate influence of behavior is always more effective than that of words. But at times a word was effective too, when mental receptiveness had been intensified by some outer circumstances. I remember an incident when there was occasion for psychotherapeutic work on the inmates of a whole hut, due to an intensification of their receptiveness because of a certain external situation.

It had been a bad day. On parade, an announcement had been made about the many actions that would, from then on, be regarded as sabotage and therefore punishable by immediate death by hanging. Among these were crimes such as cutting small strips from our old blankets (in order to improvise ankle supports) and very minor "thefts." A few days previously a semi-starved prisoner had broken into the potato store to steal a few pounds of potatoes. The theft had been discovered and some prisoners had recognized the "burglar." When the camp authorities heard about it they ordered that the guilty man be given up to them or the whole camp would starve for a day. Naturally the 2,500 men preferred to fast.

On the evening of this day of fasting we lay in our earthen huts—in a very low mood. Very little was said and every word sounded irritable. Then, to make matters even worse, the light went out. Tempers reached their ebb. But our senior block warden was a wise man. He improvised a little talk about all that was on our minds at that moment. He talked about the many comrades who had died in the last few days, either of sickness or of suicide. But he also mentioned what may have been the real reason for their deaths: giving up hope. He maintained that there should be some way of preventing possible future victims from reaching this extreme state. And it was to me that the warden pointed to give this advice.

God knows, I was not in the mood to give psychological explanations or to preach any sermons—to offer my comrades a kind of medical care of their souls. I was cold and hungry, irritable and tired, but I had to make the effort and use this unique opportunity. Encouragement was now more necessary than ever.

So I began by mentioning the most trivial of comforts first. I said that even in this Europe in the sixth winter of the Second World War, our situation was not the most terrible we could think of. I said that each of us had to ask himself what irreplaceable losses he had suffered up to then. I speculated that for most of them these losses had really been few. Whoever was still alive had reason for hope. Health, family, happiness, professional abilities, fortune, position in society—all these were things that could be achieved again or restored. After all, we still had all our bones intact. Whatever we had gone through could still be an asset to us in the future. And I quoted from Nietzsche: *"Was mich nicht umbringt, macht mich stärker."* (That which does not kill me, makes me stronger.)

Then I spoke about the future. I said that to the impartial the future must seem hopeless. I agreed that each of us could guess for himself how small were his chances of survival. I told them that although there was still no typhus epidemic in the camp, I estimated my own chances at about one in twenty. But I also told them that, in spite of this, I had no intention of losing hope and giving up. For no man knew what the future would bring, much less the next hour. Even if we could not expect any sensational military events in the next few days, who knew better than we, with our experience of camps, how great chances sometimes opened up, quite suddenly, at least for the individual. For instance, one might be attached unexpectedly to a special group with exceptionally good working conditions—for this was the kind of thing which constituted the "luck" of the prisoner.

But I did not only talk of the future and the veil which was drawn over it. I also mentioned the past; all its joys, and how its light shone even in the present darkness. Again I quoted a poet—to avoid sounding like a preacher myself—who had written, *"Was Du erlebst, kann keine Macht der Welt Dir rauben."* (What you have experienced, no power on earth can take from you.) Not only our experiences, but all we have done, whatever great thoughts we may have had, and all we have suffered, all this is not lost, though it is past; we have brought it into being. Having been is also a kind of being, and perhaps the surest kind.

Then I spoke of the many opportunities of giving life a meaning. I told my comrades (who lay motionless, although occasionally a sigh could be heard) that human life, under any circumstances, never ceases to have a meaning, and that this infinite meaning of life includes suffering and dying, privation and death. I asked the poor creatures who listened to me attentively in the darkness of the hut to face up to the seriousness of our position. They must not lose hope but should keep their courage in the certainty that the hope-

lessness of our struggle did not detract from its dignity and its meaning. I said that someone looks down on each of us in difficult hours—a friend, a wife, somebody alive or dead, or a God—and he would not expect us to disappoint him. He would hope to find us suffering proudly—not miserably—knowing how to die.

And finally I spoke of our sacrifice, which had meaning in every case. It was in the nature of this sacrifice that it should appear to be pointless in the normal world, the world of material success. But in reality our sacrifice did have a meaning. Those of us who had any religious faith I said frankly, could understand without difficulty. I told them of a comrade who on his arrival in camp had tried to make a pact with Heaven that his suffering and death should save the human being he loved from a painful end. For this man, suffering and death were meaningful; his was a sacrifice of the deepest significance. He did not want to die for nothing. None of us wanted that.

The purpose of my words was to find a full meaning in our life, then and there, in that hut and in that practically hopeless situation. I saw that my efforts had been successful. When the electric bulb flared up again, I saw the miserable figures of my friends limping toward me to thank me with tears in their eyes. But I have to confess here that only too rarely had I the inner strength to make contact with my companions in suffering and that I must have missed many opportunities for doing so.

We now come to the third stage of a prisoner's mental reactions: the psychology of the prisoner after his liberation. But prior to that we shall consider a question which the psychologist is asked frequently, especially when he has personal knowledge of these matters: What can you tell us about the psychological make-up of the camp guards? How is it possible that men of flesh and blood could treat others as so many prisoners say they have been treated? Having once heard these accounts and having come to believe that these things did happen, one is bound to ask how, psychologically, they could happen. To answer this question without going into great detail, a few things must be pointed out:

First, among the guards there were some sadists, sadists in the purest clinical sense.

Second, these sadists were always selected when a really severe detachment of guards was needed.

There was great joy at our work site when we had permission to warm ourselves for a few minutes (after two hours of work in the bitter frost) in front of a little stove which was fed with twigs and scraps of wood. But there were always some foremen who found a great pleasure in taking this comfort from us. How clearly their faces reflected this pleasure when they not only forbade us to stand there but turned over the stove and dumped its lovely fire into the snow! When the SS took a dislike to a person, there was always some special man in their ranks known to have a passion for, and to be highly specialized in, sadistic torture, to whom the unfortunate prisoner was sent.

Third, the feelings of the majority of the guards had been dulled by the number of years in which, in ever-increasing doses, they had witnessed the brutal methods of the camp. These morally and mentally hardened men at least refused to take active part in sadistic measures. But they did not prevent others from carrying them out.

Fourth, it must be stated that even among the guards there were some who took pity on us. I shall only mention the commander of the camp from which I was liberated. It was found after the liberation—only the camp doctor, a prisoner himself, had known of it previously—that this man had paid no small sum of money from his own pocket in order to purchase medicines for his prisoners from the nearest market town.[1] But the senior camp warden, a prisoner himself, was harder than any of the guards. He beat the other prisoners at every slightest opportunity, while the camp commander, to

---

[1]An interesting incident with reference to this SS commander is in regard to the attitude toward him of some of his Jewish prisoners. At the end of the war when the American troops liberated the prisoners from our camp, three young Hungarian Jews hid this commander in the Bavarian woods. Then they went to the commandant of the American Forces who was very eager to capture this SS commander and they said they would tell him where he was but only under certain conditions: the American commander must promise that absolutely no harm would come to this man. After a while, the American officer finally promised these young Jews that the SS commander when taken into captivity would be kept safe from harm. Not only did the American officer keep his promise but, as a matter of fact, the former SS commander of this concentration camp was in a sense restored to his command, for he supervised the collection of clothing among the nearby Bavarian villages, and its distribution to all of us who at that time still wore the clothes we had inherited from other inmates of Camp Auschwitz who were not as fortunate as we, having been sent to the gas chamber immediately upon their arrival at the railway station.

my knowledge, never once lifted his hand against any of us.

It is apparent that the mere knowledge that a man was either a camp guard or a prisoner tells us almost nothing. Human kindness can be found in all groups, even those which as a whole it would be easy to condemn. The boundaries between groups overlapped and we must not try to simplify matters by saying that these men were angels and those were devils. Certainly, it was a considerable achievement for a guard or foreman to be kind to the prisoners in spite of all the camp's influences, and, on the other hand, the baseness of a prisoner who treated his own companions badly was exceptionally contemptible. Obviously the prisoners found the lack of character in such men especially upsetting, while they were profoundly moved by the smallest kindness received from any of the guards. I remember how one day a foreman secretly gave me a piece of bread which I knew he must have saved from his breakfast ration. It was far more than the small piece of bread which moved me to tears at that time. It was the human "something" which this man also gave to me—the word and look which accompanied the gift.

From all this we may learn that there are two races of men in this world, but only these two—the "race" of the decent man and the "race" of the indecent man. Both are found everywhere; they penetrate into all groups of society. No group consists entirely of decent or indecent people. In this sense, no group is a "pure race"—and therefore one occasionally found a decent fellow among the camp guards.

Life in a concentration camp tore open the human soul and exposed its depths. Is it surprising that in those depths we again found only human qualities which in their very nature were a mixture of good and evil? The rift dividing good from evil, which goes through all human beings, reaches into the lowest depths and becomes apparent even on the bottom of the abyss which is laid open by the concentration camp.

And now to the last chapter in the psychology of a concentration camp—the psychology of the prisoner who has been released. In describing the experiences of liberation, which naturally must be personal, we shall pick up the threads of that part of our narrative which told of the morning when the white flag was hoisted above the camp gates after days of high tension. This state of inner suspense was followed by total relaxation. But it would be quite wrong to think that we went mad with joy. What, then, did happen?

With tired steps we prisoners dragged ourselves to the camp gates. Timidly we looked around and glanced at each other questioningly. Then we ventured a few steps out of camp. This time no orders were shouted at us, nor was there any need to duck quickly to avoid a blow or kick. Oh no! This time the guards offered us cigarettes! We hardly recognized them at first; they had hurriedly changed into civilian clothes. We walked slowly along the road leading from the camp. Soon our legs hurt and threatened to buckle. But we limped on; we wanted to see the camp's surroundings for the first time with the eyes of free men. "Freedom"—we repeated to ourselves, and yet we could not grasp it. We had said this word so often during all the years we dreamed about it, that it had lost its meaning. Its reality did not penetrate into our consciousness; we could not grasp the fact that freedom was ours.

We came to meadows full of flowers. We saw and realized that they were there, but we had no feelings about them. The first spark of joy came when we saw a rooster with a tail of multicolored feathers. But it remained only a spark; we did not yet belong to this world.

In the evening when we all met again in our hut, one said secretly to the other, "Tell me, were you pleased today?"

And the other replied, feeling ashamed as he did not know that we all felt similarly, "Truthfully, no!" We had literally lost the ability to feel pleased and had to relearn it slowly.

Psychologically, what was happening to the liberated prisoners could be called "depersonalization." Everything appeared unreal, unlikely, as in a dream. We could not believe it was true. How often in the past years had we been deceived by dreams! We dreamt that the day of liberation had come, that we had been set free, had returned home, greeted our friends, embraced our wives, sat down at the table and started to tell of all the things we had gone through—even of how we had often seen the day of liberation in our dreams. And then—a whistle shrilled in our ears, the signal to get up, and our dreams of freedom came to an end. And now the dream had come true. But could we truly believe in it?

The body has fewer inhibitions than the mind. It made good use of the new freedom from the first moment on. It began to eat ravenously, for hours and days, even half the night. It is amazing what quantities one can eat. And when one of the prisoners was invited out by a friendly farmer in the neighborhood, he ate and ate and then drank coffee, which loosened his tongue, and he then began to talk, often for hours. The pressure which had been on his mind for years was released at last. Hearing him talk, one got the impression that he *had* to talk, that his desire to speak was irresistible. I have known people who have been under heavy pressure only for a short time (for example, through a cross-examination by the Gestapo) to have similar reactions. Many days passed, until not only the tongue was loosened, but something within oneself was well; then feeling suddenly broke through the strange fetters which had restrained it.

One day, a few days after the liberation, I walked through the country past flowering meadows, for miles and miles, toward the market town near the camp. Larks rose to the sky and I could hear their joyous song. There was no one to be seen for miles around; there was nothing but the wide earth and sky and the larks' jubilation and the freedom of space. I stopped, looked around, and up to the sky— and then I went down on my knees. At that moment there was very little I knew of myself or of the world—I had but one sentence in mind—always the same: "I called to the Lord from my narrow prison and He answered me in the freedom of space."

How long I knelt there and repeated this sentence memory can no longer recall. But I know that on that day, in that hour, my new life started. Step for step I progressed, until I again became a human being.

The way that led from the acute mental tension of the last days in camp (from that war of nerves to mental peace) was certainly not free from obstacles. It would be an error to think that a liberated prisoner was not in need of spiritual care any more. We have to consider that a man who has been under such enormous mental pressure for such a long time is naturally in some danger after his liberation, especially since the pressure was released quite suddenly. This danger (in the sense of psychological hygiene) is the psychological counterpart of the bends. Just as the physical health of the caisson worker would be endangered if he left his diver's chamber suddenly (where he is under enormous atmospheric pressure), so the man who has suddenly been liberated from mental pressure can suffer damage to his moral and spiritual health.

During this psychological phase one observed that people with natures of a more primitive kind could not escape the influences of the brutality which had surrounded them in camp life. Now, being free, they thought they could use their freedom licentiously and ruthlessly. The only thing that had changed for them was that they were now the oppressors instead of the oppressed. They became instigators, not objects, of willful force and injustice. They justified their behavior by their own terrible experiences. This was often revealed in apparently insignificant events. A friend was walking across a field with me toward the camp when suddenly we came to a field of green crops. Automatically, I avoided it, but he drew his arm through mine and dragged me through it. I stammered something about not treading down the young crops. He became annoyed, gave me an angry look and shouted, "You don't say! And hasn't enough been taken from us? My wife and child have been gassed—not to mention everything else— and you would forbid me to tread on a few stalks of oats!"

Only slowly could these men be guided back to the commonplace truth that no one has the right to do wrong, not even if wrong has been done to them. We had to strive to lead them back to this truth, or the consequences would have been much worse than the loss of a few thousand stalks of oats. I can still see the prisoner who rolled up his shirt sleeves, thrust his right hand under my nose and shouted, May this hand be cut off if I don't stain it with blood on the day when I get home!" I want to emphasize that the man who said these words was not a bad fellow. He had been the best of comrades in camp and afterwards.

Apart from the moral deformity resulting from the sudden release of mental pressure, there were two other fundamental experiences which threatened to damage the character of the liberated prisoner: bitterness and disillusionment when he returned to his former life.

Bitterness was caused by a number of things he came up against in his former home town. When, on his return, a man found that in many places he was met only with a shrug of the shoulders and with hackneyed phrases, he tended to become bitter and to ask himself why he had gone through all that he had. When he heard the same phrases nearly everywhere—"We did not know about it," and "We, too, have suffered," then he asked himself, have they really nothing better to say to me?

The experience of disillusionment is different. Here it was not one's fellow man (whose superficiality and lack of feeling was so disgusting that one finally felt like creeping into a hole and neither hearing nor seeing human beings any more) but fate itself which seemed so cruel. A man who for years had thought he had reached the absolute limit of all possible suffering now found that suffering has no limits, and that he could suffer still more, and still more intensely.

When we spoke about attempts to give a man in camp mental courage, we said that he had to be shown something to look forward to in the future. He had to be reminded that life still waited for him, that a human being waited for his return. But after liberation? There were some men who found that no one awaited them. Woe to him who found that the person whose memory alone had given him courage in camp did not exist any more! Woe to him who, when the day of his dreams finally came, found it so different from all he had longed for! Perhaps he boarded a trolley, traveled out to the home which he had seen for years in his mind, and only in his mind, and pressed the bell, just as he has longed to do in thousands of dreams, only to find that the person who should open the door was not there, and would never be there again.

We all said to each other in camp that there could be no earthly happiness which could compensate for all we had suffered. We were not hoping for happiness—it was not that which gave us courage and gave meaning to our suffering, our sacrifices and our dying. And yet we were not prepared for unhappiness. This disillusionment, which awaited not a small number of prisoners, was an experience which these men have found very hard to get over and which, for a psychiatrist, is also very difficult to help them overcome. But this must not be a discouragement to him; on the contrary, it should provide an added stimulus.

But for every one of the liberated prisoners, the day comes when, looking back on his camp experiences, he can no longer understand how he endured it all. As the day of his liberation eventually came, when everything seemed to him like a beautiful dream, so also the day comes when all his camp experiences seem to him nothing but a nightmare.

The crowning experience of all, for the homecoming man, is the wonderful feeling that, after all he has suffered, there is nothing he need fear any more—except his God.

Questions

1. How did the prison guards differ from one another?

2. In what different ways did the prisoners react to their imprisonment?

3. How did the prisoners react to their release from the camp?

4. Is Frankl's philosophy of value to people who are not in prison? Why? Why not?

Recommended Reading

Levi, Primo. *Survival in Auschwitz: The Nazi Assault on Humanity,* trans. Stuart Woolf. New York: Collier, 1961.

Wiesel, Eli, *The Trilogy: Night, Dawn, The Accident.* New York: Farrar, Strauss & Giroux, 1994.

Films

Night and Fog
Mein Kampf

CHAPTER 3

The Dalai Lama

The fourteenth Dalai Lama Tenzin Gyatso is both the spiritual leader of the Tibetan people and the head of the Tibetan government-in-exile, located in Dharamsala, India. He was born on July 6, 1935, in northeastern Tibet. At the age of two he was selected as the reincarnation of the 13th Dalai Lama. He was then raised and educated in Lhasa, the capital of Tibet, completing the Doctorate of Buddhist Philosophy in 1958 shortly before he escaped into exile.

In 1950 Tibet was invaded by the Chinese People's Liberation Army (PLA). The Dalai Lama attempted to negotiate with the Chinese to leave, visiting China and Mao Zedong in 1954, but the occupation of Tibet and the violence against the Tibetan people continued. In March 1959 thousands of Tibetan demonstrators were killed by the PLA, and with his own life in danger, the Dalai Lama decided to leave Tibet, hoping that he could accomplish more from abroad. Approximately 80,000 Tibetans followed him into exile. Since that time the Dalai Lama has emerged as a world leader in the struggle for human rights. He remains particularly concerned that the Tibetan culture and way of life are being destroyed by the Chinese occupiers, who have moved into Tibet by the millions. When the Dalai Lama received a Noble Peace Prize in 1989, he presented to the world his Five Point Peace Plan to transform the Tibetan Plateau into a zone of Ahimsa, a sanctuary of peace. The entire Tibetan plateau would be demilitarized and become a protected natural environment, where all living beings including wildlife would be preserved. While it has universal appeal, the Plan has not been accepted by the occupying Chinese government. Nonetheless the words of the Dalai Lama, who always calls himself a simple monk, will certainly outlive the current occupation of the Tibetan lands. The Dalai Lama's philosophy derives from Buddhism and a deep understanding of other religious traditions, philosophy and politics. He believes in the fundamental unity of all things and the commonality of all people. His optimism that people can work together to solve the many problems of poverty, injustice, and oppression remains an inspiration to all.

Escape into Exile

Once over the Tibetan border, I drove back to Lhasa via Dromo, Gyantse and Shigatse. At each place I addressed large public gatherings, to which I invited both Tibetan and Chinese officials. As usual, I gave a short, spiritual teaching combined with what I had to say about temporal matters. In doing so, I laid great emphasis on the obligation of all Tibetans to deal honestly and justly with the Chinese authorities. I insisted that it was the duty of everyone to right wrongs whenever they saw them, no matter who had committed them. I also urged my people to adhere strictly to the principles of the Seventeen-Point 'Agreement'. I told them of my talks with Nehru and Chou En-lai and of how, during the first week of February that year, Chairman Mao himself had publicly acknowledged that Tibet was not yet ready for reform. Finally, I reminded them of the Chinese claim that they were in Tibet to help Tibetans. If any of the authorities failed to be co-operative, they were acting against Communist Party policy. I added that others could be left to sing praises, but we, according to Chairman Mao's own directive, should be self-critical. At this, the Chinese present became clearly uncomfortable.

In this way I tried to assure my people that I was doing all I could for them and to send warning to our new, foreign masters that, from now on, there would be no hesitation in pointing out malpractices whenever necessary.

However, at every stage along the journey, my forced optimism was dealt fresh blows by the news and reports of widespread fighting in the east. Then one day, General Tan Kuan-sen, the Political Commissar, came to meet me and asked that I send a representative to ask the freedom fighters to lay down their arms. Since this was my own wish, I agreed to do so and sent a lama to talk with them. But they did not, and by the time I reached Lhasa on 1 April 1957, I knew that the situation throughout Tibet was rapidly slipping not only from Chinese control, but also from my own.

In midsummer there was open warfare throughout Kham and Amdo. The freedom fighters, under the command of a man named Gompo Tashi, were increasing their numbers on a daily basis and becoming ever more audacious in their raids. The Chinese, for their part, showed no restraint. As well as using aircraft to bomb towns and villages, whole areas were laid waste by artillery barrage. The result was that thousands of people from Kham and Amdo had fled to Lhasa and were now camped on the plains outside the city. Some of the stories they brought with them were so horrifying that I did not really believe them for many years. The methods that the Chinese used to intimidate the population were so abhorrent that they were almost beyond the capacity of my imagination. It was not until I read the report published in 1959 by the International Commission of Jurists, that I fully accepted

Pages 123–143 from *Freedom in Exile: The Autobiography of the Dalai Lama* by Tenzin Gyatso. Copyright © 1990 by Tenzin Gyatso, His Holiness, The Fourteenth Dalai Lama of Tibet. Reprinted by permission of HarperCollins Publisher Inc.

what I had heard: crucifixion, vivisection, disemboweling and dismemberment of victims was commonplace. So too were beheading, burning, beating to death and burying alive, not to mention dragging people behind galloping horses until they died or hanging them upside down or throwing them bound hand and foot into icy water. And, in order to prevent them shouting out 'Long live the Dalai Lama,' on the way to execution, they tore out their tongues with meat hooks.

Realising that disaster was in the offing, I announced that I would present myself for my final monastic examinations during the *Monlam* festival of 1959, eighteen months from now. I felt that I must graduate as soon as possible, lest time run out. At the same time, I began very much to look forward to the arrival in Lhasa of Pandit Nehru, who had accepted my invitation (warmly approved by the Chinese Ambassador) to visit Tibet the following year. I hoped that his presence would compel the Chinese authorities to start behaving in a civilised way.

Meanwhile, life in the capital continued much as it always had since the Chinese first arrived six years before, although they themselves became significantly more aggressive. From now on, whenever the Generals came to see me, they were armed. They did not wear their guns openly, however, but concealed them under their clothes. This forced them to adopt very awkward positions when they sat down, and even then the barrels were clearly visible. When they spoke, they continued to offer me the usual assurances, but their faces betrayed their real feelings by turning the colour of radishes.

Also, the Preparatory Committee continued to meet on a regular basis to discuss meaningless policy amendments. It was extraordinary to what lengths the Chinese authorities went to provide a façade behind which they could carry out their abominations elsewhere in the country. I felt powerless. Yet I was certain that if I resigned (which I did consider doing) or opposed the Chinese directly, the consequences would be devastating. And I could not allow Lhasa and those areas of Tibet that were not so far engulfed in bloodshed to succumb as well. Already there were at least eight divisions of the PLA operating in the east: over 150,000 trained men with sophisticated battlefield technology confronting an irregular band of horsemen and mountain warriors. The more I thought about the future, the less hope I felt. It seemed that no matter what I or any of my people did, sooner or later all of Tibet would be turned into a mere vassal state in the new Chinese Empire, without religious or cultural freedoms, let alone those of free speech.

Life at the Norbulingka, where I stayed permanently now, also continued much as ever. The thousands of gilded Buddhas that stood flickering in the gentle light of countless butter lamps were a pointed reminder that we live in a world of Impermanence and Illusion. My routine was much the same as it always had been, although now I got up earlier, usually before five o'clock, to pray and study texts alone for the first part of the morning. Later on, one of my tutors would come to discuss the text I was reading. Then we would be joined by my *tsenshap*, of whom there were now four, and I spent much of the rest of the day debating—for this was how I would be examined. And, as usual, I would, on certain days of the calendar, preside over a *puja* in one of the many palace shrine-rooms.

Lhasa itself had changed considerably since the Chinese invasion, however. A whole new district had sprung up to accommodate the Communist officials and their dependents. Already there was evidence of a modern Chinese city which would one day swamp the ancient capital. They had built a hospital and a new school—although I regret to say that these were of little benefit to the Tibetan population—and several new barracks. Also, in view of the deteriorating situation, the military had begun to dig trenches around their quarters and fortify them with sandbags. And now when they went out, whereas before they had felt secure enough to go in pairs (though never alone), they did so only in convoys. But my contact with this world was slight and most of my information about it came from the dismal reports brought to me by my sweepers and various officials.

In the spring of 1958, I moved into a new palace at the Norbulingka, it being the tradition for each successive Dalai Lama to found his own building within the Jewel Park. Like the others, mine was quite small and designed to be used as no more than my own personal living quarters. What made it special, however, were the modern fittings and appliances with which it was furnished. I had a modern, iron bed in place of my old wooden box; and there was a bathroom complete with running water. There was plumbing for heating it too, but unfortunately my tenure at the Norbulingka was interrupted before it could be got to work properly. Electric lighting was also fitted

throughout, on both floors. In my audience-room I had chairs and tables rather than the traditional Tibetan cushions (for the benefit of foreign visitors), as well as a large radio, a gift from the Indian Government, if I remember correctly. It was the perfect home. Outside, there was a small pond and a beautiful rockery and a garden whose planting I personally supervised. Everything grows well in Lhasa and it was soon electric with colour. Altogether, I was extremely happy there, but not for long.

The fighting throughout Kham and Amdo and now central Tibet continued to gain momentum. By early summer several tens of thousands of freedom fighters had joined forces and were pressing their raids closer and closer to Lhasa, despite being poorly supplied with small arms and ammunition. Some of what they had was captured from the Chinese, some of it had come from a raid on a Tibetan Government ammunition dump near Tashilhunpo, and a small amount of it had duly materialised courtesy of the CIA, but they were still hopelessly ill-equipped.

When I went into exile, I heard stories of how weapons and money were dropped into Tibet by aircraft. However, these missions caused almost more harm to the Tibetans than to the Chinese forces. Because the Americans did not want their assistance to be attributable, they took care not to supply US-manufactured equipment. Instead, they dropped only a few badly made bazookas and some ancient British rifles which had once been in general service throughout India and Pakistan and thus could not be traced to their source in the event of capture. But the mishandling they received whilst being air-dropped rendered them almost useless.

Naturally, I never saw any of the fighting but, during the 1970s, an old lama who had recently escaped from Tibet told me of how he had observed a skirmish from his hermitage cell high up in the mountains in a remote part of Amdo. A small posse of six horsemen had attacked a PLA encampment several hundred strong, just near the bend of a river. The result was chaos. The Chinese panicked and started shooting wildly in all directions, killing large numbers of their own troops. Meanwhile the horsemen, having escaped across the river, turned back and, approaching from a different direction, attacked again from the flank before disappearing into the hills. I was very moved to hear of such bravery.

The inevitable crisis point was finally reached during the second half of 1958, when members of *Chushi Gangdruk*, the freedom-fighters' alliance, besieged a major PLA garrison at Tsethang, hardly more than two days' travel from the gates of Lhasa itself. At this point, I began to see more and more of General Tan Kuan-sen. He looked like a peasant and had yellow teeth and close-cropped hair, and he now came on an almost weekly basis, accompanied by very arrogant interpreters, to urge, cajole and abuse me. Previously his visits had rarely been more than once a month. As a result, I grew to loathe my new audience-room at the Norbulingka. Its very atmosphere was tainted by the tension of our interviews and I began to dread going in there.

At first the General demanded that I mobilise the Tibetan army against the 'rebels'. It was my duty to do so, he said. He was furious when I pointed out that if I did, he could

be sure that the soldiers would take it as an opportunity to go over to the side of the freedom fighters. After this he confined himself to railing against the ungratefulness of Tibetans and saying that it would all end badly for us. Finally, he identified Taktser Rinpoché and Gyalo Thondup and several of my ex-officials (each of whom was out of the country) as culprits and ordered me to revoke their Tibetan citizenship. This I did, thinking that firstly they were abroad and therefore safe, and secondly that for the time being it was better to acquiesce than provoke the Chinese into open military confrontation within Lhasa itself. I wanted to avoid this by almost any means. I felt that if the people of Lhasa became involved in fighting, there could be no hope of restoring peace.

Meanwhile, the freedom fighters were in no mood to compromise. They even tried to secure my approval for what they were doing. Alas I could not give it, even though as a young man and a patriot I had some thought now to do so. I was still pinning hope on Nehru's impending visit, but at the last moment the Chinese authorities cancelled it. General Tan Kuan-sen announced that he could not guarantee the Indian Prime Minister's safety and the invitation would have to be withdrawn. This was a disaster, I felt.

At the end of summer 1958, I went to Drepung, followed by Sera monastery, for the initial part of my final monastic examination. This involved several days of debates with the most outstanding scholars of these two centers of learning. The first day at Drepung began with the wonderfully harmonious chanting of several thousand monks in the public assembly hall. Their praise of the Buddha, his saints and successors (many of them Indian sages and teachers), moved me to tears.

Before leaving Drepung, I went, as per tradition, to the top of the tallest mountain behind the monastery, from which it was possible to obtain a panoramic view over literally hundreds of miles. It was so high that even for Tibetans there was a danger of altitude sickness—but not too high for the beautiful birds that nested far above the plateau, nor the profusion of wild flowers known in Tibetan as *upel*. These spectacular plants were light blue in colour, tall and thorny, and shaped like a delphinium.

Unfortunately, these pleasant observations were marred by the fact that it was necessary to deploy Tibetan soldiers in the mountains to protect me. For just in front of Drepung, there was a Chinese military garrison, set about with barbed wire and bunkers, within whose perimeter could be heard troops practising with small arms and artillery every day.

When I returned to Lhasa after my examinations were over, I learned that, so far, I had passed very well. One of the abbots, a most learned monk named Pema Gyaltsen, told me that if I had had the same opportunities for study as an ordinary monk, my performance would have been unsurpassed. So I felt very happy that this lazy student did not in the end disgrace himself.

Back in the capital, after this short interlude of sanity, I found the situation considerably worse than when I left. Thousands more refugees from Chinese atrocity outside Lhasa had arrived and were bivouacked on its outskirts. By now, the Tibetan population of the city must have been about double the usual

number. Yet still there was an uneasy truce and no fighting actually took place. All the same, when, during the autumn, I went to Ganden to continue my debates, I was encouraged by some of my advisors to take the opportunity to head south, where much of the country was in the hands of the 'defenders of the Buddha *Dharma*'. The tentative plan was that I should then repudiate the Seventeen-Point 'Agreement' and reinstate my own Government as the rightful administration of Tibet. I gave serious thought to their proposition, but I was again forced to conclude that to do so would achieve nothing positive. Such a declaration would only provoke the Chinese into launching a full-scale attack.

So I returned to Lhasa to continue my studies throughout the long, cold, winter months. I had one final examination to take during *Monlam* at the beginning of the following year. It was hard to concentrate on my work. Almost every day I heard new reports of Chinese outrages against the non-combatant population. Sometimes the news was favourable to Tibet—but this gave me no comfort. Only the thought of my responsibility to the six million Tibetans kept me going. That and my faith. Early every morning, as I sat in prayer in my room before the ancient altar with its clutter of statuettes standing in silent benediction, I concentrated hard on developing compassion for all sentient beings. I reminded myself constantly of the Buddha's teaching that our enemy is in a sense our greatest teacher. And if this was sometimes hard to do, I never really doubted that it was so.

At last the New Year came upon us and I left the Norbulingka to take up residence at the

Jokhang for the *Monlam* festival, after which came my final examination. Just before I did so, I received General Chiang Chin-wu, who came, as was his custom, with a New Year message. He also announced the arrival in Lhasa of a new dance troupe from China. Might I be interested to see them? I replied that I would be. He then said that they could perform anywhere, but since there was a proper stage with footlights at the Chinese military headquarters, it might be better if I could go there. This made sense as there were no such facilities at the Norbulingka, so I indicated that I would be happy to do so.

When I arrived at the Jokhang, I found, as I had expected, more people thronging the temple than ever before. In addition to the laity drawn from the furthest reaches of Tibet, there must have been 25–30,000 monks mingled with the huge crowd.

Each day, the *Barkhor* and *Lingkhor* were packed with devotees earnestly circumambulating. Some went, prayer-wheel in hand, chanting the sacred words '*Om Mani Padme Hum*', almost our national *mantra*. Others silently clasped their hands to forehead, to throat and to heart before prostrating themselves full-length on the ground. The marketplace in front of the temple was also bursting with people: women, in floor-length dresses decorated with colourful aprons; jaunty Khampas, their long hair tied with bright red braid and rifles slung across their shoulders; wizened nomads from the hills; and everywhere gleeful children.

Never had I seen such bustle as I squinted through the curtains of my apartment windows. Only this year there was an air of expectancy that even I, secluded as I was, could not fail to notice. It was as if everyone knew that something momentous was about to happen.

Shortly after the main *Monlam* ceremony was over (the one involving a long recital), two junior Chinese officials came unannounced to renew General Chiang Chin-wu's invitation to sec the dance troupe. They also asked for a date when I could attend. I replied that I would be pleased to go after the festival was over. But for the moment I had rather more important things to think about, namely my final examination, which was soon to take place.

The night beforehand I prayed earnestly and, as I did so, felt more deeply than ever before the awesome, unending responsibility that my office entails. Then, next morning, I presented myself for the debates which were to be held before an audience of many thousands of people. Before noon the subject was logic and epistemology, and my opponents were undergraduates like myself. In the middle of the day, the topics were *Madhyamika* and *Prajnaparamita*, again debated with undergraduates. Then in the evening, all five major subjects were hurled at me, this time by graduates, all of them considerably older and more experienced than myself. At last, at around seven o'clock in the evening, it was all over. I felt exhausted—but relieved and delighted that the panel of judges had unanimously agreed that I was worthy to receive my degree and with it the title of *geshe,* or Doctor of Buddhist Studies. On 5 March, I left the Jokhang to return to the Norbulingka, as usual in a splendid procession. For the last time, the full pageantry of more than a thousand years of uninterrupted civilisation was on display. My bodyguard, dressed in their brightly coloured ceremonial uniforms, surrounded the palanquin in which I rode. Beyond them were the members of the *Kashag* and nobles of Lhasa sumptuously clad in silk and flowing robes, their horses stepping high as, if they knew that the bits in their mouths were made of gold. Behind them came the most eminent abbots and lamas in the land, some lean and ascetic, others looking more like prosperous merchants than the highly evolved spiritual masters they were.

Finally, thousands upon thousands of citizens lined the route, and the road was packed with eager spectators along the full four-mile distance between the two buildings. The only people missing were the Chinese who, for the first time since their arrival, had neglected to send a contingent. This did nothing to reassure either my bodyguard or the army. The latter had posted men up in the hills nearby, ostensibly to 'protect' me from the freedom fighters. But in reality they had a very different enemy in mind. My bodyguards had a similar fear. Several of them openly established a position and kept their Bren gun pointing at the Chinese military headquarters.

It was not until two days later that I again had indirect communication with the Chinese authorities. They wanted to know for definite when I would be free to attend the theatrical show. I replied that the 10th of March would be convenient. Two days later, the day before the performance, some Chinese called on the *Kusun Depon*, commander of my bodyguard, at home, saying that they had been told to take

him to the headquarters of Brigadier Fu, the military advisor. He wanted to brief him about arrangements for my visit the following evening.

The Brigadier began by telling him that the Chinese authorities wanted us to dispense with the usual formality and ceremony of my visits. Pointedly, he insisted that no Tibetan soldiers accompany me, only two or three unarmed bodyguards if absolutely necessary, adding that they wanted the whole affair to be conducted in absolute secrecy. These all seemed strange requests and there was much discussion about them amongst my advisors afterwards. Nevertheless, all agreed that I could not refuse without causing a severe breach of diplomacy which might have very negative consequences. So I agreed to go with a minimum of fuss and to take along only a handful of staff.

Tenzin Choegyal, my younger brother, was also invited. He was by this time studying at Drepung monastery, so he was to travel independently. In the meantime, word went out that on the following day there were to be traffic restrictions in the vicinity of the stone bridge that led over the river adjacent to the Chinese headquarters.

Of course, it was completely impossible for my movements to be kept secret and the very fact that the Chinese wanted to do so shocked my people, who were already greatly concerned about my safety. The news spread like flames on dry grass.

The result was catastrophic. Next morning, after my prayers and then breakfast, I went outside in the quiet early morning light for a walk in the garden. Suddenly, I was startled by shouting in the distance. I hurried back inside and instructed some attendants to find out what the noise was all about. When they came back, they explained that people were pouring out of Lhasa and heading in our direction. They had decided to come and protect me from the Chinese. All morning their numbers grew. Some remained in groups at each entrance to the Jewel Park, others began to circumambulate it. By noon an estimated thirty thousand people had gathered. And during the morning, three members of the *Kashag* had difficulty getting past the crowds at the front entrance. The people were showing hostility to anyone they thought guilty of collaboration with the Chinese. One senior official, who was accompanied in his car by a bodyguard, was stoned and badly injured because people thought he was a traitor. They were mistaken. (During the 1980s, his son, who was a member of the delegation forced to sign the Seventeen-Point 'Agreement', came to India, where he wrote a detailed account of what really happened.) But later, someone was actually killed.

I was appalled at this news. Something had to be done to defuse the situation. It sounded to me as though, in a fit of anger, the crowd might even be tempted to attack the Chinese garrison. A number of popular leaders had been spontaneously elected and were calling for the Chinese to leave Tibet to the Tibetans. I prayed for calm. At the same time I realised that whatever my own personal feelings might be, there was no question of my going over to the Chinese headquarters that evening. Accordingly, my Lord Chamberlain telephoned to pass on my regrets, adding, on my instructions, that I hoped normality would be restored very soon and that the crowds could be persuaded to disperse.

However, the crowd at the gates of the Norbulingka was determined not to move. As far as the people and their leaders were concerned, the life of the Dalai Lama was in danger from the Chinese and they would not leave until I gave a personal assurance that I would not go to the Chinese military headquarters that night. This I did, via one of my officials. But it was not enough. They then demanded that I should never go to the camp. Again they were given my assurance, at which point most of the leaders left and went into the city, where further demonstrations were held; but many of the people outside the Norbulingka remained. Unfortunately, they did not realise that their continued presence constituted a far greater threat than if they had gone away.

That same day, I sent three of my most senior ministers to meet with General Tan Kuan-sen. When eventually they reached his headquarters, they found that Ngabo Ngawang Jigme was already there. At first the Chinese were polite. But when the General arrived he was in an ill-concealed rage. He and two other senior officers harangued the Tibetans for several hours about the treachery of the 'imperialist rebels', adding the accusation that the Tibetan Government had been secretly organising agitation against the Chinese authorities. Furthermore, it had defied the orders of the Chinese and refused to disarm the 'rebels' in Lhasa. They could now expect drastic measures to be taken to crush this opposition.

When they reported back to me that evening in my audience-room at the Norbulingka, I realised that the Chinese were issuing an ultimatum. Meanwhile, at about six o'clock, around seventy junior government officials, together with the remaining popular leaders and members of my personal bodyguard, held a meeting outside the Jewel Park and endorsed a declaration denouncing the Seventeen-Point 'Agreement', adding that Tibet no longer recognised Chinese authority. When I heard of this, I sent a message saying that it was the duty of the leaders to reduce the existing tension and not to aggravate it. But my advice seemed to fall on ears that could not hear.

Later that same evening a letter arrived from General Tan Kuan-sen suggesting, in suspiciously moderate tones, that I move to his headquarters for my own safety. I was amazed at his effrontery. There was no question of doing any such thing. However, in order to try to buy time, I wrote him a conciliatory reply.

The next day, 11 March, the crowd leaders announced to the Government that they would post guards outside the Cabinet office, which was situated within the outer wall of the Norbulingka. This was to prevent any ministers from leaving the palace grounds. They feared that if they did not take the law into their own hands the Government might be forced into a compromise by the Chinese authorities. The *Kashag* in turn held a meeting with these leaders and requested them to call off the demonstration as it was in danger of precipitating an open confrontation.

A day later, the women of Lhasa staged a mass demonstration. Meanwhile, the crowd leaders showed some willingness to listen to my

ministers, but then two more letters arrived from General Tan Kuan-sen. One of these was addressed to me, the other to the *Kashag*. To the former, which was similar to the first, I again replied politely, agreeing that there were dangerous elements within the crowd which sought to undermine relations between Tibet and China. I also agreed that it might be a good idea if, for my safety, I went to his headquarters.

In his other letter, the General ordered the ministers to instruct the crowd to take down the barricades that had been erected on the road outside Lhasa that led to China. Unfortunately, this had a calamitous effect. It seemed to the crowd leaders that, by saying they wanted these removed, the Chinese were making a clear indication that they planned to bring in reinforcements which would be used to attack the Dalai Lama. They refused.

On hearing this, I decided that I must speak to these men myself. I did so, explaining that there was a serious danger that Chinese troops would use force to dispel the crowd if people did not leave very soon. Evidently my entreaty was partially successful, as afterwards they announced that they would move to Shöl, the village at the foot of the Potala, where many angry demonstrations were subsequently held. But, the majority of the people outside the Norbulingka remained.

It was at around this point that I consulted the Nechung oracle which was hurriedly summoned. Should I stay or should I try to escape? What was I to do? The oracle made it clear that I should stay and keep open the dialogue with the Chinese. For once, I was unsure of whether this really was the best course of action. I was reminded of Lukhangwa's remark about the gods lying when they too became desperate. So I spent the afternoon performing *Mo,* another form of divination. The result was identical.

The next days passed in a dizzying, frightening blur. I began to receive reports of a Chinese military build-up and the mood of the crowd grew almost hysterical. I consulted the oracle a second time but his advice was the same as before. Then, on the 16th, I received a third and final letter from the General, together with an enclosure from Ngabo. General Tan's letter was much along the lines of his last two. Ngabo's, on the other hand, made clear what I and everyone else had dimly concluded, namely that the Chinese were planning to attack the crowd and shell the Norbulingka. He wanted me to indicate on a map where I would be—so that the artillerymen could be briefed to aim off whichever building I marked. It was a horrifying moment as the truth sank in. Not only was my own life in danger but the lives of thousands upon thousands of my people now seemed certain to be lost. If only they could be persuaded to go away to return to their homes. Surely they could see that they had demonstrated to the Chinese the strength of their feelings? But it was no use They were in such a pitch of fury against these unwelcome foreigners with their brutal methods that nothing could move them. They would stay till the end and die keeping guard over their Precious Protector.

Reluctantly, I set about replying to Ngabo and General Tan, saying something along the lines that I was dismayed by the disgraceful behaviour of reactionary elements amongst the population of Lhasa. I assured them that I still thought it a good idea that I should move to the sanctuary of the Chinese headquarters, but that it was very difficult just at the moment; and that I hoped they too have the patience to sit out the disturbances. Anything to buy time! After all, the crowd could not stay put indefinitely. I took care not to say where I was in the hope that this lack of knowledge would cause uncertainty and delay.

Having dispatched my replies, I was at a loss as to what to do next. The following day, I again sought the counsel of the oracle. To my astonishment, he shouted, 'Go! Go! Tonight!' The medium, still in his trance, then staggered forward and, snatching up some paper and a pen, wrote down, quite clearly and explicitly, the route that I should take out of the Norbulingka, down to the last Tibetan town on the Indian border. His directions were not what might have been expected. That done, the medium, a young monk named Lobsang Jigme, collapsed in a faint, signifying that Dorje Drakden had left his body. Just then, as if to reinforce the oracle's instructions, two mortar shells exploded in the marsh outside the northern gate of the Jewel Park.

Looking back on this event at a distance of more than thirty-one years, I am certain that Dorje Drakden had known all along that I must leave Lhasa on the 17th, but he did not say so for fear of word getting out. If no plans were made, nobody could find out about them.

I did not begin preparations for my escape immediately, however. First I wanted to confirm the oracle's decision, which I did by performing *Mo* once more. The answer agreed with the oracle, even though the odds against making a successful break seemed terrifyingly high. Not only was the crowd refusing to let anyone into or out of the palace grounds without first searching and interrogating them, but also Ngabo's letter made it clear that the Chinese had already considered the possibility that I might try to escape. They must have taken precautions. Yet the supernatural counsels fitted in with my own reasoning: I was convinced that leaving was the only thing I could do to make the crowd disperse. If I was no longer inside, there could be no reason for people to remain. I therefore decided to accept the advice.

Because the situation was so desperate, I realised that I should tell as few people as possible of my decision and at first informed only my Lord Chamberlain and the *Chikyab Kenpo*. They then had the task of making preparations for a party to leave the palace that night, but without anyone knowing who would be amongst it. At the same time as we discussed how they were to go about this, we decided on the composition of the escape party. I would take with me only my closest advisors, including my two tutors, and those members of my immediate family who were present.

Later that afternoon, my tutors and the four members of the *Kashag* left the palace hidden under a tarpaulin in the back of a lorry; in the evening, my mother, Tenzin Choegyal and Tsering Dolma went out, disguised, on the pretext of going to a nunnery on the south side of the Kyichu river. I then summoned the popular leaders and told them of my plan, stressing the need not only for maximum co-operation (which I knew was assured), but also

for absolute secrecy. I was certain that the Chinese would have spies amongst the crowd. When these men had gone, I wrote them a letter explaining my reasons for leaving and begging them not to open fire except in self-defence, trusting that they would relay this message to the people. It was to be delivered next day.

At nightfall, I went for the last time to the shrine dedicated to Mahakala, my personal protector divinity. As I entered the room through its heavy, creaking door, I paused for a moment to take in what I saw before me. A number of monks sat chanting prayers at the base of a large statue of the Protector. There was no electric light in the room, only the glow of dozens of votive butter lamps set in rows of golden and silver dishes. Numerous frescoes covered the walls. A small offering of *tsampa* sat on a plate on the altar. A server, his face half in shadow, was bending over a large urn from which he was ladling out butter for the lamps. No one looked up, although I knew that my presence must have been noticed. To my right, one of the monks took up his cymbals, whilst another put a horn to his lips and blew a long, mournful note. The cymbals clashed together and were held, vibrating. Its sound was comforting.

I went forward and presented a *kata*, a length of white silk, to the divinity. This is the traditional Tibetan gesture on departure and signifies not only propitiation, but also implies the intention of return. For a moment I lingered in silent prayer. The monks would now suspect that I was going, but I was assured of their silence. Before leaving the room, I sat down for a few minutes and read from the Buddha's *sutras,* stopping at the one which talks of the need to 'develop confidence and courage'.

On leaving, I instructed someone to dim the lights throughout the remainder of the building before going downstairs, where I found one of my dogs. I patted it and was glad that it had never been very friendly with me. Our parting was not too difficult. I was much more sad to be leaving behind my bodyguards and sweepers. I then went outside into the chill March air. At the main entrance to the building was a landing with steps running off either side down to the ground. I walked round it, pausing on the far side to visualise reaching India safely. On coming back to the door, I visualised returning to Tibet.

At a few minutes before ten o'clock, now wearing unfamiliar trousers and a long, black coat, I threw a rifle over my right shoulder and, rolled up, an old *thangka* that had belonged to the Second Dalai Lama over my left. Then, slipping my glasses into my pocket, stepped outside. I was very frightened. I was joined by two soldiers, who silently escorted me to the gate in the inner wall, where I was met by the *Kusun Depon*. With them, I groped my way across the park, hardly able to see a thing. On reaching the outer wall, we joined up with *Chikyab Kenpo*, who, I could just make out, was armed with a sword. He spoke to me in a low, reassuring voice. I was to keep by him at all costs. Going through the gate, he announced boldly to the people gathered there that he was undertaking a routine tour of inspection. With that, we were allowed to pass through. No further words were spoken.

I could sense the presence of a great mass of humanity as I stumbled on, but they did not take any notice of us and, after a few minutes' walk, we were once more alone. We had successfully negotiated our way through the crowd, but now there were the Chinese to deal with. The thought of being captured terrified me. For the first time in my life I was truly afraid—not so much for myself but for the millions of people who put their faith in me. If I was caught, all would be lost. There was also some danger that we could be mistaken for Chinese soldiers by freedom fighters unaware of what was happening.

Our first obstacle was the tributary of the Kyichu river that I used to visit as a small child, until forbidden to do so by Tathag Rinpoché. To cross it, we had to use stepping-stones, which I found extremely difficult to negotiate without my glasses. More than once I almost lost my balance. We then made our way to the banks of the Kyichu itself. Just before reaching it, we came across a large group of people. The Lord Chamberlain spoke briefly with their leaders and then we passed on to the river-bank. Several coracles were waiting for us, together with a small party of ferrymen.

The crossing went smoothly, although I was certain that every splash of oars would draw down machine-gun fire on to us. There were many tens of thousands of PLA stationed in and around Lhasa at that time and it was inconceivable that they would not have patrols out. On the·other side, we met up with a party of freedom fighters who were waiting with some ponies. Here we were also joined by my mother, my brother and sister and my tutors. We then paused to wait for my senior officials, who were following, to join us. Whilst we did so, we took the opportunity to exchange, in highly charged whispers, remarks about the iniquitous behaviour of the Chinese which had driven us to this pass. I also put my glasses back on—I could bear sightlessness no longer—but then almost wished I hadn't as I could now make out the torchlight of PLA sentries guarding the garrison that lay only a few hundred yards from where we stood. Fortunately, the moon was obscured by low cloud and visibility was poor.

As soon as the others arrived, we set off towards the hill and the mountain pass, called Che-La, that separates the Lhasa valley from the Tsangpo valley. At around three o'clock in the morning, we stopped at a simple farm house, the first of many to provide us with shelter over the next few weeks. But we did not remain long and after only a little while left to continue the trek up to the pass, which we reached at around eight o'clock. Not long before we reached it, the first light of day dawned and we saw to our amusement the result of our haste. There had been a mix-up with the ponies, their harnesses and their riders. Because the monastery that had provided the animals had had almost no warning, and because of the dark, the best of them had been fitted with the worst saddles and given to the wrong people, whereas some of the oldest and shaggiest mules wore the finest harnesses and were being ridden by the most senior officials!

At the top of the 16,000-foot pass, the groom who was leading my pony stopped and turned it round, telling me that this was the last opportunity on the journey for a look at Lhasa. The ancient city looked serene as ever as it lay spread out far below. I prayed for a few

minutes before dismounting and running on foot down the sandy slopes that gave the place its name—Che-La means Sandy Pass. We then rested again for a short while before pushing on towards the banks of the Tsangpo, which we reached finally not long before noon. There was only one place to cross it, by ferry, and we had to hope that the PLA had not reached it first. They had not.

On the far side, we stopped in a small village whose inhabitants turned out to greet me, many weeping. We were now on the fringes of some of Tibet's most difficult country: an area with only a few remote settlements. It was a region that the freedom fighters had made their own. From here on, I knew we were invisibly surrounded by hundreds of guerrilla warriors who had been warned of our impending arrival and whose job it was to protect us as we travelled.

It would have been difficult for the Chinese to follow us, but if they had information on our whereabouts it was possible that they might calculate our intended route and mobilise forces ahead to try to intercept us. So for our immediate protection an escort of about three hundred and fifty Tibetan soldiers had been assembled, along with a further fifty or so irregulars. The escape party itself had by now grown to approaching one hundred people.

Almost everyone but myself was heavily armed, including even the man appointed as my personal cook, who carried an enormous bazooka and wore a belt hung with its deadly shells. He was one of the young men trained by the CIA. So eager was he to use his magnificent and terrible-looking weapon that, at one point, he lay down and fired off several shots at what he claimed looked like an enemy position. But it took such a long time to reload that I felt sure he would have been made short work of by a real enemy. Altogether, it was not an impressive performance.

There was another of these CIA operatives amongst the party, a radio operator who was apparently in touch with his headquarters throughout the journey. Exactly whom he was in contact with, I do not know to this day. I only know that he was equipped with a Morse-key transmitter.

That night we stopped at a monastery called Ra-Me, where I wrote a hurried letter to the Panchen Lama telling him of my escape and advising him to join me in India if he could. I had not heard from him since the middle of winter, when he had written to offer his good wishes for the year ahead. In a separate, secret note he had also said he thought that, with the situation deteriorating throughout the country, we needed to formulate a strategy for the future. This was the first indication he had given of being no longer in the thrall of our Chinese masters. Unfortunately, my message never reached him and he remained in Tibet.

The next pass was called Sabo-La, which we reached two or three days later. At the top, it was very cold and snowing a blizzard. I began to be deeply worried about some of my companions. Although I was young and fit, some of the older ones amongst my entourage found the going very difficult. But we dared not slacken the pace as we were still in grave danger of being intercepted by Chinese forces. Particularly we were in danger of being caught in a pincer movement by troops stationed at Gyantse and in the Kongpo region.

At first, it was my intention to halt at Lhuntse Dzong, not far from the Indian border, where I would repudiate the Seventeen-Point 'Agreement', re-establish my Government as the rightful administration of all Tibet, and try to open negotiations with the Chinese. However, on about the fifth day, we were over-taken by a posse of horsemen who brought terrible news. Just over forty-eight hours after my departure, the Chinese had begun to shell the Norbulingka and to machine-gun the defence-less crowd, which was still in place. My worst fears had come true. I realised that it would be impossible to negotiate with people who behaved in this cruel and criminal fashion. There was nothing for it now but for us to get as far away as possible, though India still lay many days' journey distant, with several more high mountain passes in between.

When eventually we reached Lhuntse Dzong, after more than a week's travel, we paused for only two nights, just long enough for me formally to repudiate the Seventeen-Point 'Agreement' and to announce the for-mation of my own Government, the only legally constituted authority in the land. Over a thousand people attended the ceremony of consecration. I wanted very much to stay longer, but reports informed us that there were Chinese troop movements not far away. So reluctantly we prepared to move on to the Indian border, which now lay just sixty miles away in a straight line, though actually about double that on the ground. There was still another range of mountains to cross and it would take several more days to cover the dis-tance, especially as our ponies were already worn out and there was very little fodder to give them. They would need frequent halts to conserve their energy. Before we left, I sent on a small party of the fittest men, who were to reach India as quickly as possible, find the nearest officials and warn them that I was planning to seek asylum there.

From Lhuntse Dzong we passed to the small village of Jhora and from there to the Karpo pass, the last before the border. Just as we were nearing the highest point of the track we received a bad shock. Out of nowhere, an aeroplane appeared and flew directly over-head. It passed quickly—too quickly for any-one to be able to see what markings it had—but not so fast that the people on board could have missed spotting us. This was not a good sign. If it was Chinese, as it probably was, there was a good chance that they now knew where we were. With this information they could return to attack us from the air, against which we had no protection. Whatever the identity of the aircraft, it was a forceful reminder that I was not safe anywhere in Tibet. Any misgivings I had about going into exile vanished with this realisation: India was our only hope.

A little later, the men I had sent on from Lhuntse Dzong returned with the news that the Indian Government had signalled its willingness to receive me. I was very relieved to hear this, as I had not wanted to set foot in India without permission.

I spent my last night in Tibet at a tiny village called Mangmang. No sooner had we reached this final outpost of the Land of Snows than it began to rain. This was on top of a week of appalling weather, which threw blizzards and snow glare at us by turns as we straggled along.

We were all exhausted and it was the last thing that we needed, but it continued torrentially throughout the night. To make matters worse, my tent leaked and no matter where I dragged my bedding I could not escape the water which ran in rivulets down the inside. The result was that the fever I had been fighting off for the past few days developed overnight into a case of full-blown dysentery.

The following morning, I was too ill to continue, so we remained where we were. My companions moved me to a small house nearby, but it provided little more protection than my tent. Moreover I was oppressed by the stench of cows that rose from the ground floor to where I lay above. That day, I heard on the small portable radio we had with us a report on All-India Radio saying that I was en route to India, but that I had fallen off my horse and was badly injured. This cheered me up rather, as it was one misfortune that I had managed to avoid, though I knew my friends would be concerned.

Next day, I decided to move on. I now had the difficult task of saying goodbye to the soldiers and freedom fighters who had escorted me all the way from Lhasa, and who were now about to turn and face the Chinese. There was one official too who decided to remain. He said that he did not think that he could be of much use in India, therefore it would be better to stay and fight. I really admired his determination and courage.

After bidding these people a tearful farewell, I was helped on to the broad back of a *dzomo,* for I was still too ill to ride a horse. And it was on this humble form of transport that I left my native land.

Questions

1. What are some of the changes which occurred in Tibet as a result of the Chinese occupation?

2. In what ways does the Dalai Lama's actions reflect his role as spiritual and secular leader?

3. Why did the Dalai Lama finally decide to go into exile? What do you think would have happened had he remained in Tibet?

Recommended Reading

Dalai Lama, *The Art of Happiness*. New York: Penguin, 1998.

Harrer, Heinrich. *Seven Years in Tibet*. New York: Putnam, 1997.

Ani Pachen and Donnelly, Adelaide. *Sorrow Mountain: The Journey of A Tibetan Warrior Nun*. New York: Kodansha, 2000.

Films

Kundun
Seven Years in Tibet

CHAPTER 4

Nelson Rolihlahla Mandela

Nelson Mandela was born in Mvezo, a tiny village in the Transkei in South Africa in July 1918, a member of the Thembu tribe which belongs to the Xhosa nation. His father had been a chief and an advisor to kings, and after he died when Mandela was nine, the acting Regent of the Thembu people, Chief Jongentaba Dalindyebo, became his guardian and benefactor. Mandela attended the Healdtown Boarding School and the University College at Fort Hare. When he was expelled for participating in a student strike, he left for Johannesburg. He would complete his B.A. degree by correspondence, and later become a lawyer, founding the first all-black firm in South Africa.

In Johannesburg, he became involved in politics as he observed firsthand the effects of the system of apartheid, a system of laws and regulations established in South Africa to separate the races. In 1942 Mandela joined the African National Congress (ANC). He soon joined and became a leader in the African National Congress Youth League (ANCYL), which opposed the system of apartheid, calling for self-determination, free elections, education, and redistribution of land. By 1952 the ANC launched a mass nonviolent civil disobedience campaign against apartheid for the Defiance of Unjust Laws, based on the tactics used earlier in South Africa and India by Gandhi. The campaign rapidly spread throughout South Africa.

By 1961 Mandela decided that nonviolence would not work as a political strategy because the government was responding to peaceful demonstrators with violence. Mandela formed a new military wing, *Umkhonto we Sizwe* (The Spear of the Nation), which carried out violent acts of sabotage against the government. In 1961 he attended the Conference of the Pan-Africa Freedom Movement in Ethiopia. Remaining abroad, he received military training in guerrilla warfare so that he could return to South Africa and train others.

Soon after his return to South Africa, he was arrested for illegally leaving the country and for inciting people to strike. It is this trial in 1962 which he describes in the first selection below. At the end of this trial Mandela was sentenced to five years imprisonment. Two years later, he was brought to trial again, this time with six other defendants, on charges of high treason. All of the men, active figures in the African National Congress, were sentenced to life imprisonment, and exiled to prison on Robben Island. In the second selection, Mandela describes his initial arrival at Robben Island where he remained until he was transferred in 1984. During the twenty-seven years that he spent in prison, Mandela followed a very disciplined life and developed his ideas and personal philosophy, including a rejection of violent methods of revolt. By the 1970s, as worldwide opposition to the South African government's system of apartheid led to protests and economic sanctions, Mandela became a symbol of the struggle against apartheid, achieving the global fame and admiration attained only by Mahatma Gandhi. The new President of South Africa, F.W. de Klerk, finally freed Mandela in February 1990. Mandela immediately began working with President de Klerk to end apartheid and to hold democratic elections open to all citizens, regardless of race. In 1993 he was awarded the Noble Peace Prize along with President de Klerk. In 1994, in the first multiracial democratic elections ever held in South Africa, Mandela was elected President. He served one five-year term and retired in 1999, but even now, as he approaches his 84th birthday, he continues to play an active role in the cause of global peace and human rights.

The initial hearing was set for Monday, October 15, 1962. The organization had set up a Free Mandela Committee and launched a lively campaign with the slogan "Free Mandela." Protests were held throughout the country and the slogan began to appear scrawled on the sides of buildings. The government retaliated by banning all gatherings relating to my imprisonment, but this restriction was ignored by the liberation movement.

In preparation for Monday's hearing, the Free Mandela Committee had organized a mass demonstration at the courthouse. The plan was to have people line both sides of the road along the route my van would take. From press reports, conversations with visitors, and even the remarks of prison guards, I learned that a large and vociferous turnout was expected.

On Saturday, while I was preparing myself for the Monday hearing, I was ordered to pack my things immediately: the hearing had been shifted to Pretoria. The authorities had made no announcement, and had I not managed to get word out through a sympathetic jailer, no one would have known that I had left Johannesburg.

But the movement reacted quickly, and by the time my case began on Monday morning, the Old Synagogue was packed with supporters. The synagogue was like a second home to me after four years of the Treason Trial. My legal adviser, Joe Slovo, could not be present as he was confined to Johannesburg by bans and I was ably assisted instead by Bob Hepple.

I entered the court that Monday morning wearing a traditional Xhosa leopard-skin kaross instead of a suit and tie. The crowd of supporters rose as one and with raised, clenched fists shouted *"Amandla!"* and *"Ngawethu!"* The kaross electrified the spectators, many of whom were friends and family, some of whom had come all the way from the Transkei. Winnie also wore a traditional beaded headdress and an ankle-length Xhosa skirt.

I had chosen traditional dress to emphasize the symbolism that I was a black African walking into a white man's court. I was literally carrying on my back the history, culture, and heritage of my people. That day, I felt myself to be the embodiment of African nationalism, the inheritor of Africa's difficult but noble past and her uncertain future. The kaross was also a sign of contempt for the niceties of white justice. I well knew the authorities would feel threatened by my kaross as so many whites feel threatened by the true culture of Africa.

When the crowd had quieted down and the case was called, 1 formally greeted the prosecutor, Mr. Bosch, whom I had known from my attorney days, and the magistrate, Mr. Van Heerden, who was also familiar to me. I then immediately applied for a two-week remand on the grounds that I had been transferred to Pretoria without being given the opportunity of notifying my attorneys. I was granted a week's postponement.

When I was on my way back to my cell, a very nervous white warder said that the commanding officer, Colonel Jacobs, had ordered me to hand over the kaross. I said, "You can tell him that he is not going to have it." This warder was a weak fellow, and he started trembling. He practically begged me for it and said he would be fired if he did not bring it back. I felt sorry for him and I said, "Look, here, just tell your commanding officer that it is Mandela speaking, not you." A short while later Colonel Jacobs himself appeared and ordered me to turn over what he referred to as my "blanket." I told him that he had no jurisdiction over the attire I chose to wear in court and if he tried to confiscate my kaross I would take the matter all the way to the Supreme Court. The colonel never again tried to take my "blanket," but the authorities would permit me to wear it only in court, not on my way to or from court for fear it would "incite" other prisoners.

When the case resumed a week later I was given permission to address the court before I was asked to plead. "I hope to be able to indicate," I explained, "that this case is a trial of the aspirations of the African people, and because of that I thought it proper to conduct my own defense." I wanted to make it clear to the bench, the gallery, and the press that I intended to put the state on trial. I then made application for the recusal of the magistrate on the grounds that I did not consider myself morally bound to obey laws made by a Parliament in which I had no representation. Nor was it possible to receive a fair trial from a white judge:

> Why is it that in this courtroom I am facing a white magistrate, confronted by a white prosecutor, escorted by white orderlies? Can anybody honestly and seriously suggest that in this type of atmosphere the scales of justice are evenly balanced? Why is it that no African in the history of this country has ever had the honor of being tried by his own kith and kin, by his own flesh and blood? I will tell Your Worship why: the real purpose of this rigid color bar is to ensure that the justice dispensed by the courts should conform to the policy of the country, however much that policy might be in conflict with the norms of justice accepted in judiciaries throughout the civilized world. . . . Your Worship, I hate racial discrimination most intensely and in all its manifestations. I have fought it all my life. I fight it now, and I will do so until the end of my days. I detest most intensely the set-up that surrounds me here. It makes me feel that I am a black man in a white man's court. This should not be.

During the trial the prosecutor called more than one hundred witnesses from all over the country, including the Transkei and South West Africa. They were policemen, journalists, township superintendents, printers. Most of them gave technical evidence to show that I left the country illegally and that I had incited African workers to strike during the three-day stay-at-home in May 1961. It was indisputable—and in fact I did not dispute—that I was technically guilty of both charges.

The prosecutor had called Mr. Barnard, the private secretary to the prime minister, to testify to the letter I had sent the prime minister demanding that he call a national convention and informing him that if he did not, we would organize a three-day strike. In my cross-examination of Mr. Barnard I first read the court the letter I sent requesting that the prime minister call a national convention for all South Africans to write a new nonracial constitution.

NM: Did you place this letter before your prime minister?

WITNESS: Yes.

NM: Now was any reply given to this letter by the prime minister?

WITNESS: He did not reply to the writer.

NM: He did not reply to the letter. Now, will you agree that this letter raises matters of vital concern to the vast majority of the citizens of this country?

WITNESS: I do not agree.

NM: You don't agree? You don't agree that the question of human rights, of civil liberties, is a matter of vital importance to the African people?

WITNESS: Yes, that is so, indeed.

NM: Are these things mentioned here?

WITNESS: Yes, I think so.

NM: . . . You have already agreed that this letter raises questions like the rights of freedom, civil liberties, and so on?

WITNESS: Yes, the letter raises it.

NM: Now, you know of course that Africans don't enjoy the rights demanded in this letter? They arc denied these rights of government.

WITNESS: Some rights.

NM: No African is a member of Parliament?

WITNESS: That is right.

NM: No African can be a member of the provincial council, of the municipal councils.

WITNESS: Yes.

NM: Africans have no vote in this country?

WITNESS: They have got no vote as far as Parliament is concerned.

NM: Yes, that is what I am talking about, I am talking about Parliament and other government bodies of the country, the provincial councils, the municipal councils. They have no vote?

WITNESS: That is right.

NM: Would you agree with me that in any civilized country in the world it would be scandalous for a prime minister to fail to reply to a letter raising vital issues affecting the majority of the citizens of that country. Would you agree with that?

WITNESS: I don't agree with that.

NM: You don't agree that it would be irregular for a prime minister to ignore a letter raising vital issues affecting the vast majority of the citizens of that country?

WITNESS: This letter has not been ignored by the prime minister.

NM: Just answer the question. Do you regard it proper for a prime minister not to respond to pleas made in regard to vital issues by the vast majority of the citizens of the country? You say that is wrong?

WITNESS: The prime minister did respond to the letter.

NM: Mr. Barnard, I don't want to be rude to you. Will you confine yourself to answering my questions. The question I am putting to you is, do you agree that it is most improper on the part of a prime minister not to reply to a communication raising vital issues affecting the vast majority of the country?

Mr. Barnard and I never did agree. In the end, he simply said that the tone of the letter was aggressive and discourteous and for that reason the prime minister did not answer it.

▼   ▼   ▼   ▼   ▼

Throughout the proceedings the prosecutor and the magistrate repeatedly inquired about the number of witnesses I intended to call. I would always reply, "I plan to call as many witnesses as the state, if not more." When the state finally concluded its case, there was a stillness in the courtroom in anticipation of the beginning of my defense. I rose and instead of calling my first witness, I declared quite matter-of-factly that I was not calling any witnesses at all, at which point I abruptly closed my case. There was a murmur in the courtroom and the prosecutor could not help exclaiming "Lord!"

I had misled the court from the beginning because I knew the charge was accurate and the state's case was solid, and I saw no point in attempting to call witnesses and defend myself. Through my cross-examination and attempts to force the judge to recuse himself, I had made the statements I wanted about the unfairness of the court. I saw no advantage in calling witnesses to try to disprove something that was incontrovertible.

The magistrate was taken by surprise by my action and asked me with some incredulity, "Have you anything more to say?"

"Your Worship, I submit that I am guilty of no crime."

"Is that all you have to say?"

"Your Worship, with respect, if I had something more to say I would have said it."

The prosecutor then shuffled through his papers attempting to get ready for an address he did not expect to have to make. He briefly addressed the court and asked the magistrate to find me guilty on both counts. The court was then adjourned until the following day, when I would have a chance to address the court in what is known as the plea in mitigation before the magistrate gave his sentence.

The following morning, before court was called into session, I was in an office off the courtroom talking with Bob Hepple, who had been advising me on the case, and we were praising the fact that the day before, the General Assembly of the U.N. had voted in favor of sanctions against South Africa for the first time. Bob also told me that acts of sabotage in Port Elizabeth and Durban had occurred both celebrating the U.N. vote and protesting my trial. We were in the midst of this discussion when the prosecutor, Mr. Bosch, entered the room and then asked Bob to excuse himself.

"Mandela," he said, after Bob had left, "I did not want to come to court today. For the first time in my career, I despise what I am doing. It hurts me that I should be asking the court to send you to prison." He then reached out and shook my hand, and expressed the hope that everything would turn out well for me. I thanked him for his sentiments, and assured him that I would never forget what he had said.

The authorities were on alert that day. The crowd inside the courtroom seemed even larger than on the first day of the case. All one hundred fifty "non-European" seats were filled. Winnie was present, in Xhosa dress, as well as a number of my relatives from the Transkei. Hundreds of demonstrators stood a block from the courthouse, and there seemed to be as many policemen as spectators.

When I walked in the courtroom, I raised my right fist and called out *"Amandla!"* which was met by a mighty *"Ngawethu!"* The magistrate pounded his gavel and cried for order. When the court was quiet, he summed up the charges, after which I had my opportunity to speak. My plea in mitigation lasted over an hour. It was not a judicial appeal at all but a political testament. I wanted to explain to the court how and why I had become the man I was, why I had done what I had done, and why, if given the chance, I would do it again.

Many years ago, when I was a boy brought up in my village in the Transkei, I listened to the elders of the tribe telling stories about the good old days before the arrival of the white man. Then our people lived peacefully, under the democratic rule of their kings and their *amapakati* [literally "insiders," but meaning those closest in rank to the king], and moved freely and confidently up and down the country without let or hindrance. The country was our own, in name and right. We occupied the land, the forests, the rivers; we extracted the mineral wealth beneath the soil and all the riches of this beautiful country. We set up and operated our own government, we controlled our own arms and we organized our trade and commerce. The elders would tell tales of the wars fought by our ancestors in defense of the Fatherland, as well as the acts of valor by generals and soldiers during these epic days. . . .

The structure and organization of early African societies in this country fascinated me very much and greatly influenced the evolution of my political outlook. The land, then the main means of production, belonged to the whole tribe and there was no individual ownership whatsoever. There were no classes, no rich or poor and no exploitation of man by man. All men were free and equal and this was the foundation of government. Recognition of this general principle found expression in the constitution of the council, variously called "Imbizo" or "Pitso" or "Kgotla," which governs the affairs of the tribe. The council was so completely democratic that all members of the tribe could participate in its deliberations. Chief and subject, warrior and medicine man, all took part and endeavored to influence its decisions. It was so weighty and influential a body that no step of any importance could ever be taken by the tribe without reference to it.

There was much in such a society that was primitive and insecure and it certainly could never measure up to the demands of the present epoch. But in such a society are contained the seeds of revolutionary democracy in which none will be held in slavery or servitude, and in which poverty, want and insecurity shall be no more. This is the history which, even today, inspires me and my colleagues in our political struggle.

I told the court how I had joined the African National Congress and how its policy of democracy and nonracialism reflected my own deepest convictions. I explained how as a lawyer I was often forced to choose between compliance with the law and accommodating my conscience.

I would say that the whole life of any thinking African in this country drives him continuously to a conflict between his conscience on the one hand and the law on the other. This is not a conflict peculiar to this country. The conflict arises for men of conscience, for men who think and who feel deeply in every country. Recently in Britain, a peer of the realm. Earl [Bertrand] Russell, probably the most respected philosopher of the Western world, was sentenced and convicted for precisely the type of activities for which I stand before you today—for following his conscience in defiance of the law, as a protest against the nuclear weapons policy being pursued by his own government. He could do no other than to oppose the law and to suffer the consequences for it. Nor can I. Nor can many Africans in this country. The law as it is applied, the law as it has been developed over a long period of history, and especially the law as it is written and designed by the Nationalist government is a law which, in our views, is immoral, unjust, and intolerable. Our consciences dictate that we must protest against it, that we must oppose it and that we must attempt to alter it. . . . Men, I think, are not capable of doing nothing, of saying nothing, of not reacting to injustice, of not protesting against oppression, of not striving for the good society and the good life in the ways they see it.

I recounted in detail the numerous times the government had used the law to hamper my life, career, and political work, through bannings, restrictions, and trials.

> I was made, by the law, a criminal, not because of what I had done, but because of what I stood for, because of what I thought, because of my conscience. Can it be any wonder to anybody that such conditions make a man an outlaw of society? Can it be wondered that such a man, having been outlawed by the government, should be prepared to lead the life of an outlaw, as I have led for some months, according to the evidence before this court?
>
> It has not been easy for me during the past period to separate myself from my wife and children, to say good-bye to the good old days when, at the end of a strenuous day at an office I could look forward to joining my family at the dinnertable, and instead to take up the life of a man hunted continuously by the police, living separated from those who are closest to me, in my own country, facing continually the hazards of detection and of arrest. This has been a life infinitely more difficult than serving a prison sentence. No man in his right senses would voluntarily choose such a life in preference to the one of normal, family, social life which exists in every civilized community.
>
> But there comes a time, as it came in my life, when a man is denied the right to live a normal life, when he can only live the life of an outlaw because the government has so decreed to use the law to impose a state of outlawry upon him. I was driven to this situation, and I do not regret having taken the decisions that I

did take. Other people will be driven in the same way in this country, by this very same force of police persecution and of administrative action by the government, to follow my course, of that I am certain.

I enumerated the many times that we had brought our grievances before the government and the equal number of times that we were ignored or shunted aside. I described our stay-away of 1961 as a last resort after the government showed no signs of taking any steps to either talk with us or meet our demands. It was the government that provoked violence by employing violence to meet our nonviolent demands. I explained that because of the government's actions we had taken a more militant stance. I said that I had been privileged throughout my political life to fight alongside colleagues whose abilities and contributions were far greater than my own. Many others had paid the price of their beliefs before me, and many more would do so after me.

Before sentencing, I informed the court that whatever sentence the state imposed, it would do nothing to change my devotion to the struggle.

> I do not believe, Your Worship, that this court, in inflicting penalties on me for the crimes for which I am convicted should be moved by the belief that penalties will deter men from the course that they believe is right. History shows that penalties do not deter men when their conscience is aroused, nor will they deter my people or the colleagues with whom I have worked before.
>
> I am prepared to pay the penalty even though I know how bitter and desperate is the situation of an African in the prisons of this country. I have been in these prisons and I know how gross is the discrimination, even

behind the prison wall, against Africans. . . . Nevertheless these considerations do not sway me from the path that I have taken nor will they sway others like me. For to men, freedom in their own land is the pinnacle of their ambitions, from which nothing can turn men of conviction aside. More powerful than my fear of the dreadful conditions to which I might be subjected in prison is my hatred for the dreadful conditions to which my people are subjected outside prison throughout this country. . . .

Whatever sentence Your Worship sees fit to impose upon me for the crime for which I have been convicted before this court, may it rest assured that when my sentence has been completed I will still be moved, as men are always moved, by their conscience; I will still be moved by my dislike of the race discrimination against my people when I come out from serving my sentence, to take up again, as best I can, the struggle for the removal of those injustices until they are finally abolished once and for all. . . .

I have done my duty to my people and to South Africa. I have no doubt that posterity will pronounce that I was innocent and that the criminals that should have been brought before this court are the members of the government.

When I had finished, the magistrate ordered a ten-minute recess to consider the sentence. I turned and looked out at the crowd before exiting the courtroom. I had no illusions about the sentence I would receive. Exactly ten minutes later, in a courtroom heavy with tension, the magistrate pronounced sentence: three years for inciting people to strike and two years for leaving the country without a passport; five years in all, with no possibility of parole. It was a stern sentence and there was wailing among the spectators. As the court

rose, I turned to the gallery and again made a clenched fist, shouting *"Amandla!"* three times. Then, on its own, the crowd began to sing our beautiful anthem, *"Nkosi Sikelel' iAfrika."* People sang and danced and the women ululated as I was led away. The uproar among the gallery made me forget for a moment that I would be going to prison to serve what was then the stiffest sentence yet imposed in South Africa for a political offense.

Downstairs, I was permitted a brief good-bye to Winnie, and on this occasion she was not at all grim: she was in high spirits and shed no tears. She seemed confident, as much a comrade as a wife. She was determined to brace me. As I was driven away in the police van I could still hear the people outside singing *"Nkosi Sikelel' iAfrika."*

▼   ▼   ▼   ▼   ▼

Prison not only robs you of your freedom, it attempts to take away your identity. Everyone wears the same uniform, eats the same food, follows the same schedule. It is by definition a purely authoritarian state that tolerates no independence or individuality. As a freedom fighter and as a man, one must fight against the prison's attempt to rob one of these qualities.

From the courthouse, I was taken directly to Pretoria Local, the gloomy red-brick monstrosity that I knew so well. But I was now a convicted prisoner, not an awaiting-trial prisoner, and was treated without even that little deference that is afforded to the latter. I was stripped of my clothes and Colonel Jacobs was finally able to confiscate my kaross. I was issued the standard prison uniform for Africans: a pair of short trousers, a rough khaki shirt, a canvas jacket, socks, sandals, and a cloth cap. Only Africans are given short trousers, for only African men are deemed "boys" by the authorities.

I informed the authorities that I would under no circumstances wear shorts and told them I was prepared to go to court to protest. Later, when I was brought dinner, stiff cold porridge with a half teaspoonful of sugar, I refused to eat it.

▼ ▼ ▼ ▼ ▼

At midnight, I was awake and staring at the ceiling—images from the trial were still rattling around in my head—when I heard steps coming down the hallway. I was locked in my own cell, away from the others. There was a knock at my door and I could see Colonel Aucamp's face at the bars. "Mandela," he said in a husky whisper, "are you awake?"

I told him I was. "You are a lucky man," he said. "We are taking you to a place where you will have your freedom. You will be able to move around; you'll see the ocean and the sky, not just gray walls."

He intended no sarcasm, but I well knew that the place he was referring to would not afford me the freedom I longed for. He then remarked rather cryptically, "As long as you don't make trouble, you'll get everything you want."

Aucamp then woke the others, all of whom were in a single cell, ordering them to pack their things. Fifteen minutes later we were making our way through the iron labyrinth of Pretoria Local, with its endless series of clanging metal doors echoing in our ears.

Once outside, the seven of us—Walter, Raymond, Govan, Kathy, Andrew, Elias, and myself—were handcuffed and piled into the back of a police van. It was well after midnight, but none of us was tired, and the atmosphere was not at all somber. We sat on the dusty floor, singing and chanting, reliving the final moments of the trial. The warders provided us with sandwiches and cold drinks and Lieutenant Van Wyck was perched in the back with us. He was a pleasant fellow, and during a lull in the singing, he offered his unsolicited opinion on our future. "Well," he said, "you chaps won't be in prison long. The demand for your release is too strong. In a year or two, you will get out and you will return as national heroes. Crowds will cheer you, everyone will want to be your friend, women will want you. Ag, you fellows have it made." We listened without comment, but I confess his speech cheered me considerably. Unfortunately, his prediction turned out to be off by nearly three decades.

▼ ▼ ▼ ▼ ▼

We were departing quietly, secretly, under a heavy police escort, in the middle of the night, and in less than half an hour we found ourselves at a small military airport outside the city. We were hustled onto a Dakota, a large military transport plane that had seen better days. There was no heat, and we shivered in the belly of the plane. Some of the others had never flown before and they seemed more anxious about our voyage than our destination; bumping up and down in a plane at fifteen thousand feet seemed far more perilous than being locked in a cell behind high walls.

After about an hour in the air, dawn lightened the terrain below. The plane had portholes, and as soon as we could see in the half-light, my comrades pressed their faces to the glass. We flew southeast, over the dry, flat plains of the Orange Free State and the green and mountainous Cape peninsula. I, too, craned to see out the portholes, examining the scenery not as a tourist but as a strategist, looking for areas where a guerrilla army might hide itself.

There had been a running argument since the formation of MK as to whether the countryside of South Africa could support a guerrilla army. Most of the High Command thought that it could not. When we flew over a wooded, mountainous area called Matroosberg in the Cape, I yelled to my colleagues that here was terrain where we could fight. The men became excited and craned to get a better look, and indeed, the heavily forested area appeared as though it could shelter a nascent guerrilla force.

Minutes later we approached the outskirts of Cape Town. Soon, we could see the little matchbox houses of the Cape Flats, the gleaming towers of downtown, and the horizontal top of Table Mountain. Then, out in Table Bay, in the dark blue waters of the Atlantic, we could make out the misty outline of Robben Island.

We landed on an airstrip on one end of the island. It was a grim, overcast day, and when I stepped out of the plane, the cold winter wind whipped through our thin prison uniforms. We were met by guards with automatic weapons; the atmosphere was tense but quiet, unlike the boisterous reception I had received on my arrival on the island two years before.

We were driven to the old jail, an isolated stone building, where we were ordered to strip while standing outside. One of the ritual indignities of prison life is that when you are transferred from one prison to another, the first thing that happens is that you change from the garb of the old prison to that of the new. When we were undressed, we were thrown the plain khaki uniforms of Robben Island.

Apartheid's regulations extended even to clothing. All of us, except Kathy, received short trousers, an insubstantial jersey, and a canvas jacket. Kathy, the one Indian among us, was given long trousers. Normally Africans would receive sandals made from car tires, but in this instance we were given shoes. Kathy, alone, received socks. Short trousers for Africans were meant to remind us that we were "boys." I put on the short trousers that day, but I vowed that I would not put up with them for long.

The warders pointed with their guns where they wanted us to go, and barked their orders in simple one-word commands: "Move!" "Silence!" "Halt!" They did not threaten us in the swaggering way that I recalled from my previous stay, and betrayed no emotion.

The old jail was only temporary quarters for us. The authorities were in the process of finishing an entirely separate maximum-security structure for political prisoners. While there, we were not permitted to go outside or have any contact with other prisoners.

The fourth morning we were handcuffed and taken in a covered truck to a prison within a prison. This new structure was a one-story rectangular stone fortress with a flat cement courtyard in the center, about one hundred feet by thirty feet. It had cells on three of the four sides. The fourth side was a twenty-foot-high wall with a catwalk patrolled by guards with German shepherds.

The three lines of cells were known as sections A, B, and C, and we were put in Section B, on the easternmost side of the quadrangle. We were each given individual cells on either side of a long corridor, with half the cells facing the courtyard. There were about thirty cells in all. The total number of prisoners in the single cells was usually about twenty-four. Each cell had one window, about a foot square, covered with iron bars. The cell had two doors: a metal gate or grille with iron bars on the inside and a thick wooden door outside of that. During the day, only the grille was locked; at night, the wooden door was locked as well.

The cells had been constructed hurriedly, and the walls were perpetually damp. When I raised this with the commanding officer, he told me our bodies would absorb the moisture. We were each issued three blankets so flimsy and worn they were practically transparent. Our bedding consisted of a single sisal, or straw, mat. Later we were given a felt mat, and one placed the felt mat on top of the sisal one to provide some softness. At that time of year, the cells were so cold and the blankets provided so little warmth that we always slept fully dressed.

I was assigned a cell at the head of the corridor. It overlooked the courtyard and had a small eye-level window. I could walk the length of my cell in three paces. When I lay down, I could feel the wall with my feet and my head grazed the concrete at the other side. The width was about six feet, and the walls were at least two feet thick. Each cell had a white card posted outside of it with our name and our prison service number. Mine read, "N Mandela 466/64," which meant I was the 466th prisoner admitted to the island in 1964. I was forty-six years old, a political prisoner with a life sentence, and that small cramped space was to be my home for I knew not how long.

We were immediately joined by a number of prisoners who had been held in the general section of the prison, a squat brick building not far from Section B. The general prison, known as sections F and G, contained about a thousand mostly common-law prisoners. As many as a quarter of them were political prisoners, and a handful of those men were put with us in Section B. We were isolated from the general prisoners for two reasons: we were considered risky from a security perspective, but even more dangerous from a political standpoint. The authorities were concerned we might "infect" the other prisoners with our political views.

Among the men put with us was George Peake, one of the founders of the South African Coloured People's Organizational, a Treason Trialist, and most recently a member of the Cape Town City Council. He had been sentenced for planting explosives outside a Cape Town prison. Dennis Brutus, another Coloured political activist, was a poet and writer from Port Elizabeth imprisoned for violating his bans. We were also joined by Billy Nair, a longtime member of the Natal Indian Congress, sentenced for sabotage as a member of Umkhonto we Sizwe.

Within a few days we had more company, including Neville Alexander, a prominent

Coloured intellectual and member of the Non-European Unity Movement, who had formed a tiny radical offshoot called the Yu Chi Chan Club in Cape Town, which studied guerrilla warfare. Neville had a B.A. from the University of Cape Town and a doctorate in German literature from Tubingen University in Germany. Along with Neville, there was Fikile Bam, a law student of the University of Cape Town and another member of the Yu Chi Chan Club; and Zephania Mothopeng, a member of the PAC National Executive. Zeph had been a teacher in Orlando, and was a staunch opponent of Bantu Education, and one of the most level-headed of the PAC's leaders. Three aged peasants from the Transkei, sentenced for plotting to assassinate K. D. Matanzima, now the chief minister of the "self-governing" Transkei, were also imprisoned with us.

This became our core group of about twenty prisoners. Some I knew, some I had heard of, while others I did not know at all. Normally, in prison, one of the few festive times is seeing old friends and new faces, but the atmosphere in those first few weeks was so oppressive we were not even able to greet each other. We had as many guards as prisoners, and they enforced every regulation with threats and intimidation.

That first week we began the work that would occupy us for the next few months. Each morning, a load of stones about the size of volleyballs was dumped by the entrance to the courtyard. Using wheelbarrows, we moved the stones to the center of the yard. We were given either four-pound hammers or fourteen-pound hammers for the larger stones. Our job was to crush the stones into gravel. We were divided into four rows, about a yard-and-a-half apart, and sat cross-legged on the ground. We were each given a thick rubber ring, made from tires, in which to place the stones. The ring was meant to catch flying chips of stone, but hardly ever did so. We wore makeshift wire masks to protect our eyes.

Warders walked among us to enforce the silence. During those first few weeks, warders from other sections and even other prisons came to stare at us as if we were a collection of rare caged animals. The work was tedious and difficult; it was not strenuous enough to keep us warm but it was demanding enough to make all our muscles ache.

June and July were the bleakest months on Robben Island. Winter was in the air, and the rains were just beginning. It never seemed to go above forty degrees Fahrenheit. Even in the sun, I shivered in my light khaki shirt. It was then that I first understood the cliché of feeling the cold in one's bones. At noon we would break for lunch. That first week all we were given was soup, which stank horribly. In the afternoon, we were permitted to exercise for half an hour under strict supervision. We walked briskly around the courtyard in single file.

On one of our first days pounding rocks, a warder commanded Kathy to take a wheelbarrow filled with gravel to the truck parked by the entrance. Kathy was a slender fellow unused to hard physical labor. He could not budge the wheelbarrow. The warders yelled: *"Liwt daardie kruiwa loop!"* (Let that wheelbarrow move!) As Kathy managed to nudge it forward, the wheelbarrow looked as if it would tip over, and the warders began to laugh. Kathy, I could see, was determined not to give them cause for mirth. I knew how to maneuver the wheelbarrows, and I jumped up to help him. Before being ordered to sit down, I managed to tell Kathy to wheel it slowly, that it was a matter of balance not strength. He nodded and then carefully moved the wheelbarrow across the courtyard. The warders stopped smiling.

The next morning, the authorities placed an enormous bucket in the courtyard and announced that it had to be half full by the end of the week. We worked hard and succeeded. The following week, the warder in charge announced that we must now fill the bucket three-quarters of the way. We worked with great diligence and succeeded. The next week we were ordered to fill the bucket to the top. We knew we could not tolerate this much longer, but said nothing. We even managed to fill the bucket all the way, but the warders had provoked us. In stolen whispers we resolved on a policy: no quotas. The next week we initiated our first go-slow strike on the island: we would work at less than half the speed we had before to protest the excessive and unfair demands. The guards immediately saw this and threatened us, but we would not increase our pace, and we continued this go-slow strategy for as long as we worked in the courtyard.

▼　▼　▼　▼　▼

Robben Island had changed since I had been there for a fortnight's stay in 1962. In 1962, there were few prisoners; the place seemed more like an experiment than a fully-fledged prison. Two years later, Robben Island was without question the harshest, most iron-fisted outpost in the South African penal system. It was a hardship station not only for the prisoners but for the prison staff. Gone were the Coloured warders who had supplied cigarettes and sympathy. The warders were white and overwhelmingly Afrikaans-speaking, and they demanded a master-servant relationship. They ordered us to call them *"baas,"* which we refused. The racial divide on Robben Island was absolute: there were no black warders, and no white prisoners.

Moving from one prison to another always requires a period of adjustment. But journeying to Robben Island was like going to another country. Its isolation made it not simply another prison, but a world of its own, far removed from the one we had come from. The high spirits with which we left Pretoria had been snuffed out by its stern atmosphere; we were face to face with the realization that our life would be unredeemably grim. In Pretoria, we felt connected to our supporters and our families; on the island, we felt cut off, and indeed we were. We had the consolation of being with each other, but that was the only consolation. My dismay was quickly replaced by a sense that a new and different fight had begun.

From the first day, I had protested about being forced to wear short trousers. I demanded to see the head of the prison and made a list of complaints. The warders ignored my protests, but by the end of second week, I found a pair of old khaki trousers unceremoniously dumped on the floor of my cell. No pin-striped three-piece suit has ever pleased me as much. But before putting them on I checked to see if my comrades had been issued trousers as well. They had not, and I told the warder to take them back. I insisted all African prisoners must have long trousers. The warder grumbled, "Mandela, you say you want long pants and then you don't want them when we give them to you." The warder balked at touching trousers worn by a black man, and finally the commanding officer himself came to my cell to pick them up. "Very well, Mandela," he said, "you are going to have the same clothing as everyone else." I replied that if he was willing to give me long trousers, why couldn't everyone else have them? He did not have an answer.

▼   ▼   ▼   ▼   ▼

At the end of our first two weeks on the island, we were informed that our lawyers, Bram Fischer and Joel Joffe, were going to be visiting the following day. When they arrived, we were escorted to the visiting area to meet them. The purpose of their visit was twofold: to see how we had settled in, and to verify that we still did not want to appeal our sentences. It had only been a few weeks since I had seen them, but it felt like an eternity. They seemed like visitors from another world.

We sat in an empty room, a major just outside supervising the consultation. I felt like hugging them, but I was restrained by the presence of the major. I told them that all of us were well, and explained that we were still opposed to an appeal for all the reasons we had previously enunciated, including the fact that we did not want our appeal to interfere with the cases of other ANC defendants. Bram and Joel seemed resigned to this, though I knew Bram believed we should mount an appeal.

When we were winding up our conversation, I briefly asked Bram about Molly, his wife. No sooner had I pronounced Molly's name than Bram stood up, turned away, and abruptly walked out of the room. A few minutes later, he returned, once again, composed, and resumed the conversation, but without answering my question.

Our meeting ended shortly afterward, and when we were walking back to our cells with the major, he said to me, "Mandela, were you struck by the behavior of Bram Fischer?" I said that I had been. He told me that Molly had died in a car accident the previous week. Bram, he said, had been driving and had swerved to avoid an animal in the road, and the car had plunged into a river. Molly had drowned.

We were devastated by the news. Molly was a wonderful woman, generous and unselfish, utterly without prejudice. She had supported Bram in more ways than it was possible to know. She had been wife, colleague, and comrade. Bram had already experienced disaster in his life: his son had died of cystic fibrosis in adolescence.

The act of turning away when I asked about Molly was typical of Bram's character. He was a stoic, a man who never burdened his friends with his own pain and troubles. As an Afrikaner whose conscience forced him to reject his own heritage and be ostracized by his own people, he showed a level of courage and sacrifice that was in a class by itself. I fought only against injustice, not my own people.

I informed the major that I intended to write Bram a condolence letter, and he responded that I could do so. The rules governing letter-writing were then extremely strict. We were only permitted to write to our immediate families, and just one letter of five hundred words every six months. I was therefore surprised and pleased when the major did not oppose my writing Bram. But he didn't live up to his agreement. I wrote the letter and handed it over to the major, but it was never posted.

Within a few months, our life settled into a pattern. Prison life is about routine: each day like the one before; each week like the one before it, so that the months and years blend into each other. Anything that departs from this pattern upsets the authorities, for routine is the sign of a well-run prison.

Routine is also comforting for the prisoner, which is why it can be a trap. Routine can be a pleasant mistress whom it is hard to resist, for routine makes the time go faster. Watches and timepieces of any kind were barred on Robben Island, so we never knew precisely what time it was. We were dependent on bells and warders' whistles and shouts. With each week resembling the one before, one must make an effort to recall what day and month it is. One of the first things I did was to make a calendar on the wall of my cell. Losing a sense of time is an easy way to lose one's grip and even one's sanity.

Time slows down in prison; the days seem endless. The cliché of time passing slowly usually has to do with idleness and inactivity. But this was not the case on Robben Island. We were busy almost all the time, with work, study, resolving disputes. Yet, time nevertheless moved glacially. This is partially because things that took a few hours or days outside would take months or years in prison. A request for a new toothbrush might take six months or a year to be filled. Ahmed Kathrada once said that in prison the minutes can seem like years, but the years go by like minutes. An afternoon pounding rocks in the courtyard might seem like forever, but suddenly it is the end of the year, and you do not know where all the months went.

The challenge for every prisoner, particularly every political prisoner, is how to survive prison intact, how to emerge from prison undiminished, how to conserve and even replenish one's beliefs. The first task in accomplishing that is learning exactly what one must do to survive. To that end, one must know the enemy's purpose before adopting a strategy to undermine it. Prison is designed to break one's spirit and destroy one's resolve. To do this, the authorities attempt to exploit every weakness, demolish every initiative, negate all signs of individuality—all with the idea of stamping out that spark that makes each of us human and each of us who we are.

Our survival depended on understanding what the authorities were attempting to do to us, and sharing that understanding with each other. It would be very hard if not impossible for one man alone to resist. I do not know that I could have done it had I been alone. But the authorities' greatest mistake was keeping us together, for together our determination was reinforced. We supported each other and gained strength from each other. Whatever we knew, whatever we learned, we shared, and by sharing we multiplied whatever courage we had individually. That is not to say that we were all alike in our responses to the hardships we suffered. Men have different capacities and react differently to stress. But the stronger ones raised up the weaker ones, and both became stronger in the process. Ultimately, we had to recreate our own lives in prison. In a way that even the authorities acknowledged, order in prison was preserved not by the warders but by ourselves.

As a leader, one must sometimes take actions that are unpopular, or whose results will not be known for years to come. There are victories whose glory lies only in the fact that they are known to those who win them. This is particularly true of prison, where one must find consolation in being true to one's ideas, even if no one else knows of it.

I was now on the sidelines, but I also knew that I would not give up the fight. I was in a different and smaller arena, an arena for whom the only audience was ourselves and our oppressors. We regarded the struggle in prison as a microcosm of the struggle as a whole. We would fight inside as we had fought outside.

The racism and repression were the same; I would simply have to fight on different terms.

Prison and the authorities conspire to rob each man of his dignity. In and of itself, that assured that I would survive, for any man or institution that tries to rob me of my dignity will lose because I will not part with it at any price or under any pressure. I never seriously considered the possibility that I would not emerge from prison one day. I never thought that a life sentence truly meant life and that I would die behind bars. Perhaps I was denying this prospect because it was too unpleasant to contemplate. But I always knew that someday I would once again feel the grass under my feet and walk in the sunshine as a free man.

I am fundamentally an optimist. Whether that comes from nature or nurture, I cannot say. Part of being optimistic is keeping one's head pointed toward the sun, one's feet moving forward. There were many dark moments when my faith in humanity was sorely tested, but I would not and could not give myself up to despair. That way lay defeat and death.

Questions

1. Why did Mandela wear his native Xhosa kaross instead of a suit and tie to the courtroom and why did the officials object?

2. What is the main argument Mandela used in his self-defense at his trial?

3. What behavior did Mandela follow from the beginning of his arrival on Robben Island and how did that enable him to survive twenty-seven years in prison?

Recommended Reading

Mandela, Nelson. *Nelson Mandela Speaks: Forging a Democratic, Nonracial South Africa.* New York: Pathfinder, 1993.

Sampson, Anthony. *Mandela: The Authorized Biography.* New York: Knopf, 1999.

Woods, Donald. *Biko,* 2d ed. New York: Henry Holt & Co., 1987.

Film

The Long Walk to Freedom

CHAPTER 5

John Lewis

John Lewis was born in February 1940 in Troy, Alabama and grew up on a farm. He received a Bachelor of Arts in Philosophy and Religion from Fisk University and also attended the American Baptist Theological Seminary in Tennessee. While a student, he became interested in the issues of civil rights and began organizing others to have peaceful "sit-ins" at segregated lunch counters in Nashville, Tennessee. Quite often in these sit-ins, students were beaten and arrested, but they were not defeated. In 1961 Lewis joined the Freedom Riders a group of young men and women who decided that they would challenge segregation in the South by attempting to use segregated facilities at bus stations. Frequently the students were beaten violently by opponents of integration, including the local police, and soon the events in Tennessee were being discussed and debated by college students in campuses across the nation. Though he had been beaten numerous times, John Lewis did not give up. He and others soon formed a new organization, the Student Nonviolent Coordinating Committee (SNCC). This group hoped to win over young people committed to nonviolent methods of ending racial injustice. Although other groups, such as Dr. Martin Luther King's Southern Christian Leadership Conference (SCLC) already existed, SNCC hoped to attract a younger group of supporters. John Lewis became the Chairman of SNCC during the most important years of its activity, from 1963–1966. He was one of the organizers of and speakers at the March on Washington in August 1963, which brought over 100,000 people to the nation's capital to demand peacefully that the national government begin enforcing the civil rights guaranteed to all in the Constitution.

In 1964 Lewis and other leaders in SNCC decided to organize Mississippi Freedom Summer, a program to bring students from all over the country to Mississippi, Alabama, and Georgia to work on voter registration, to help the local black community in community projects, and to set up Freedom Schools for children. As the Program began in the summer of 1964, three civil rights workers, Chaney, Goodman and Schwerner, went missing in Mississippi as they investigated the bombing of a church. SNCC decided to continue with the program nonetheless, even after their missing bodies were found. When the summer ended many students remained in the South continuing their work with voter registration and various community projects. In the spring of 1965 Lewis and another SNCC leader Hosea Williams attempted to lead a peaceful march in Selma, Alabama across the Edmund Pettus Bridge. Alabama state troopers met the marchers with horses and clubs; John Lewis himself was beaten badly. That day, March 7, 1965, came to be known as Bloody Sunday, and is discussed in the chapter below. Once again, media coverage of the violent beatings of peaceful demonstrators led to nationwide outrage and a second march was organized from Selma to the capital Montgomery. People by the thousands came to Selma; by the time the marches had ended, two people had been killed. Nonetheless in the following months, Congress passed the Voting Rights Act of 1965.

John Lewis remained active in SNCC until 1966. By late 1965 SNCC members became divided between advocates of black nationalism, of a violent rebellion, and those who wanted to keep SNCC as it had been formed originally, a nonviolent organization, open to all races. For the next years Lewis remained very active in voter registration activities, holding many important positions of leadership, including the Director of the Voter Education Project. In 1977 President Jimmy Carter appointed him director of ACTION, a federal volunteer agency. In 1981 he was elected to the Atlanta City Council and after five years of service, decided to run for Congress in 1986. He is currently serving his eighth term as Congressman from Georgia's fifth Congressional District. He has won the respect and trust of all for his honest and direct approach. In the chapter below, Lewis portrays the events surrounding Bloody Sunday and the march to Montgomery.

Bloody Sunday

I've been back to Selma many times since that fateful Sunday afternoon. Normally I'm with a large crowd, gathered for one anniversary or another of that '65 march. The town is alive with noise and excitement on such days, but the rest of the time it remains today what it was back then: a sleepy dying little Southern community. Many of the storefronts along its downtown Broad Street are boarded up, with handwritten FOR LEASE signs taped on the windows. The businesses that are left—Rexall Drugs, the El Ranchero cafe, Walter Craig Sportsman's Headquarters ("TONS OF GUNS" is its slogan—point more to the past than they do to the future.

The Dallas County Courthouse is still there, its steps that same pale green, though the building itself has now been painted the color of cream. Brown's Chapel, of course, still stands as well, with the same arched white-washed ceiling inside, the same rows of folding, theater-style seats up in its U-shaped balcony.

There's a monument in front of the church, a bust of Dr King, which, on my most recent visit there, was coated with a thin dusting of snow. The unlikely snowfall had brought out children by the dozen in the dirt yards of the Carver projects, across the street from the church. They were hooting and hollering, trying valiantly to make snowmen out of the sprinkling of powder that lay on the ground. A couple of them were having a snowball fight, hiding from one another behind the streetside markers that commemorate the history that was written here in 1965.

None of those children were alive back then, but most of them know better than any historian the details of what happened on March 7 of that year. They've heard the story so many times, from parents and grandparents, from neighbors and friends—from the people who were there.

How could anyone ever forget a day like that?

It was brisk and breezy, a few puffs of purplish clouds scattered across the clear blue sky. By the time I arrived at Brown's Chapel, about half past noon, there were already close to five hundred marchers gathered on the ballfield and basketball courts beside and beyond the church. Some of the SCLC staffers were holding impromptu training sessions, teaching the people to kneel and protect their bodies if attacked.

Hosea and Bevel were off to the side, huddled with Andy Young, the three of them talking animatedly, as if something was wrong. And there was something wrong. Dr King, it turned out, had decided late the day before to postpone the march until Monday. He'd missed too many preaching commitments at his church in Atlanta, he explained. He needed to deliver his sermon that weekend. The march from Selma, he decided, would have to wait a day. That was the message Andy Young had been sent to deliver.

Hosea was clearly upset. So was Bevel. The people were here, and they were ready. There was no way to turn them back home now.

This was the first I'd heard of this news. Later I would learn that there were other factors that had affected Dr King's decision, the most serious being a death threat, of which there had been several during the previous two months. Dr. King was initially leaning toward still coming, but his staff talked him out of it.

Or so the story goes. There is still disagreement and speculation today among many people about King's decision not to march that day. There is still resentment among a lot of people, especially SNCC members, who saw this as nothing but abandonment, a cop-out.

I don't feel that way. First of all, I can't imagine anyone questioning the courage of Martin Luther King Jr. Beyond that, in terms of the specific circumstances of that Sunday, no one in SNCC was in any position to criticize Dr. King. As far as I was concerned, they had lost the right to pass judgment of any kind on this march the moment they decided not to take part in it.

After seeing that the march could not be stopped, Andy Young went inside the church and called Dr. King in Atlanta. They talked over the situation and King instructed Andy to choose one among them—Andy, Hosea or Bevel—to join me as co-leader of the march. The other two would remain behind to take care of things in case there was trouble.

Andy returned with that news, and the three of them proceeded to flip coins to see who would join me. The odd man would march; the other two would stay.

The odd man turned out to be Hosea, and so that little slice of history was settled—by the flip of a quarter.

It was mid-afternoon now, and time to assemble. A team of doctors and nurses from a group called the Medical Committee for Human Rights had arrived the day before on a flight from New York and set up a makeshift clinic in the small parsonage beside the church. We expected a confrontation. We knew Sheriff Clark had issued yet another call the evening before for even more deputies. Mass arrests would probably be made. There might be injuries. Most likely we would be stopped at the edge of the city limits, arrested and maybe roughed up a little bit. We did not expect anything worse than that.

And we did *not* expect to march all the way to Montgomery. No one knew for sure, until the last minute, if the march would even take place. There had been a measure of planning, but nowhere near the preparations and logistics necessary to move that many people in an orderly manner down fifty-four miles of highway, a distance that would take about five days for a group that size to cover.

Many of the men and women gathered on that ballfield had come straight from church. They were still wearing their Sunday outfits. Some of the women had on high heels. I had on a suit and tie, a light tan raincoat, dress shoes and my backpack. I was no more ready to hike half a hundred miles than anyone else. Like everyone around me, I was basically playing it by ear. None of us had thought much further ahead than that afternoon. Anything that happened beyond that—if we were allowed to go on, if this march did indeed go all the way to Montgomery—we figured we would take care of as we went along. The main thing was that we *do* it, that we march.

It was close to 4 P.M. when Andy, Hosea, Bevel and I gathered the marchers around us. A dozen or so reporters were there as well. I read a short statement aloud for the benefit of the press, explaining why we were marching today. Then we all knelt to one knee and bowed our heads as Andy delivered a prayer.

And then we set out, nearly six hundred of us, including a white SCLC staffer named Al Lingo—the same name as the commander of Alabama's state troopers.

We walked two abreast, in a pair of lines that stretched for several blocks. Hosea and I led the way. Albert Turner, an SCLC leader in Perry County, and Bob Mants were right behind us—Bob insisted on marching because I was marching; he told me he wanted to be there to "protect" me in case something happened.

Marie Foster and Amelia Boynton were next in line, and behind them, stretching as far as I could see, walked an army of teenagers, teachers, undertakers, beauticians—many of the same Selma people who had stood for weeks, months, *years,* in front of that courthouse.

At the far end, bringing up the rear, rolled four slow-moving ambulances.

I can't count the number of marches I have participated in in my lifetime, but there was something peculiar about this one. It was more than disciplined. It was somber and subdued, almost like a funeral procession. No one was jostling or pushing to get to the front, as

often happened with these things. I don't know if there was a feeling that something was going to happen, or if the people simply sensed that this was a special procession, a "leaderless" march. There were no big names up front, no celebrities. This was just plain folks moving through the streets of Selma.

There was a little bit of a crowd looking on as we set out down the red sand of Sylvan Street, through the black section of town. There was some cheering and singing from those onlookers and from a few of the marchers, but then, as we turned right along Water Street, out of the black neighborhood now, the mood changed. There was no singing, no shouting—just the sound of scuffling feet. There was something holy about it, as if we were walking down a sacred path. It reminded me of Gandhi's march to the sea. Dr. King used to say there is nothing more powerful than the rhythm of marching feet, and that was what this was, the marching feet of a determined people. That was the only sound you could hear.

Down Water Street we went, turning right and walking along the river until we reached the base of the bridge, the Edmund Pettus Bridge.

There was a small posse of armed white men there, gathered in front of the *Selma Times-Journal* building. They had hard hats on their heads and clubs in their hands. Some of them were smirking. Not one said a word. I didn't think too much of them as we walked past. I'd seen men like that so many times.

As we turned onto the bridge, we were careful to stay on the narrow sidewalk. The road had been closed to traffic, but we still stayed on the walkway, which was barely wide enough for two people.

I noticed how steep it was as we climbed toward the steel canopy at the top of the arched bridge. It was too steep to see the other side. I looked down at the river and saw how still it was, still and brown. The surface of the water was stirred just a bit by the late-afternoon breeze. I noticed my trench coat was riffling a little from that same small wind.

When we reached the crest of the bridge, I stopped dead still.

So did Hosea.

There, facing us at the bottom of the other side, stood a sea of blue-helmeted, blue-uniformed Alabama state troopers, line after line of them, dozens of battle-ready lawmen stretched from one side of U.S. Highway 80 to the other.

Behind them were several dozen more armed men—Sheriff Clark's posse—some on horseback, all wearing khaki clothing, many carrying clubs the size of baseball bats.

On one side of the road I could see a crowd of about a hundred whites, laughing and hollering, waving Confederate flags. Beyond them, at a safe distance, stood a small, silent group of black people.

I could see a crowd of newsmen and reporters gathered in the parking lot of a Pontiac dealership. And I could see a line of parked police and state trooper vehicles. I didn't know it at the time, but Clark and Lingo were in one of those cars.

It was a drop of one hundred feet from the top of that bridge to the river below. Hosea glanced down at the muddy water and said, "Can you swim?"

"No," I answered.

"Well," he said, with a tiny half smile, "neither can I."

"But," he added, lifting his head and looking straight ahead, "we might have to."

Then we moved forward. The only sounds were our footsteps on the bridge and the snorting of a horse ahead of us.

I noticed several troopers slipping gas masks over their faces as we approached.

At the bottom of the bridge, while we were still about fifty feet from the troopers, the officer in charge, a Major John Cloud, stepped forward, holding a small bullhorn up to his mouth.

Hosea and I stopped, which brought the others to a standstill.

"This is an unlawful assembly," Cloud pronounced. *"Your march is not conducive to the public safety. You are ordered to disperse and go back to your church or to your homes."*

"May we have a word with the major?" asked Hosea.

"There is no word to be had," answered Cloud.

Hosea asked the same question again, and got the same response.

Then Cloud issued a warning: *"You have two minutes to turn around and go back to your church."*

I wasn't about to turn around. We were there. We were not going to run. We couldn't turn and go back even if we wanted to. There were too many people.

We could have gone forward, marching right into the teeth of those troopers. But that would have been too aggressive, I thought, too provocative. God knew what might have happened if we had done that. These people were ready to be arrested, but I didn't want anyone to get hurt.

We couldn't go forward. We couldn't go back. There was only one option left that I could see.

"We should kneel and pray," I said to Hosea.

He nodded.

We turned and passed the word back to begin bowing down in a prayerful manner.

But that word didn't get far. It didn't have time. One minute after he had issued his warning—I know this because I was careful to check my watch—Major Cloud issued an order to his troopers.

"Troopers," he barked. *"Advance!"*

And then all hell broke loose.

The troopers and possemen swept forward as one, like a human wave, a blur of blue shirts and billy clubs and bullwhips. We had no chance to turn and retreat. There were six hundred people behind us, bridge railings to either side and the river below.

I remember how vivid the sounds were as the troopers rushed toward us—the clunk of the troopers' heavy boots, the whoops of rebel yells from the white onlookers, the clip-clop of horses' hooves hitting the hard asphalt of the highway, the voice of a woman shouting, "Get 'em! *Get* the niggers'"

And then they were upon us. The first of the troopers came over me, a large, husky man. Without a word, he swung his club against the left side of my head. I didn't feel any pain, just the thud of the blow, and my legs giving way. I raised an arm—a reflex motion—as I curled up in the "prayer for protection" position. And

then the same trooper hit me again. And everything started to spin.

I heard something that sounded like gunshots. And then a cloud of smoke rose all around us.

Tear gas. I'd never experienced tear gas before. This, I would learn later, was a particularly toxic form called C-4, made to induce nausea.

I began choking, coughing. I couldn't get air into my lungs. I felt as if I was taking my last breath. If there was ever a time in my life for me to panic, it should have been then. But I didn't. I remember how strangely calm I felt as I thought, This is it. People are going to die here. *I'm* going to die here

I really felt that I saw death at that moment, that I looked it right in its face. And it felt strangely soothing. I had a feeling that it would be so easy to just lie down there, just lie down and let it take me away.

That was the way those first few seconds looked from where I stood—and lay. Here is how Roy Reed, a reporter for *The New York Times,* described what he saw:

> The troopers rushed forward, their blue uniforms and white helmets blurring into a flying wedge as they moved.
>
> The wedge moved with such force that it seemed almost to pass over the waiting column instead of through it. The first 10 or 20 Negroes were swept to the ground screaming, arms and legs flying, and packs and bags went skittering across the grassy divider strip and on to the pavement on both sides.
>
> Those still on their feet retreated.
>
> The troopers continued pushing, using both the force of their bodies and the prodding of their nightsticks.

A cheer went up from the white spectators lining the south side of the highway.

The mounted possemen spurred their horses and rode at a run into the retreating mass. The Negroes cried out as they crowded together for protection, and the whites on the sidelines whooped and cheered.

The Negroes paused in their retreat for perhaps a minute, still screaming and huddling together.

Suddenly there was a report like a gunshot and a grey cloud spewed over the troopers and the Negroes.

"Tear gas!" someone yelled.

The cloud began covering the highway. Newsmen, who were confined by four troopers to a corner 100 yards away, began to lose sight of the action.

But before the cloud finally hid it all, there were several seconds of unobstructed view. Fifteen or twenty nightsticks could be seen through the gas, flailing at the heads of the marchers.

The Negroes broke and ran. Scores of them streamed across the parking lot of the Selma Tractor Company. Troopers and possemen, mounted and unmounted, went after them.

I was bleeding badly. My head was now exploding with pain. That brief, sweet sense of just wanting to lie there was gone. I needed to get up. I'd faded out for I don't know how long, but now I was tuned back in.

There was mayhem all around me. I could see a young kid—a teenaged boy—sitting on the ground with a gaping cut in his head, the blood just gushing out. Several women, including Mrs. Boynton, were lying on the pavement and the grass median. People were weeping. Some were vomiting from the tear gas. Men on horses were moving in all directions, purposely riding over the top of fallen people, bringing their animals' hooves down on shoulders, stomachs and legs.

The mob of white onlookers had joined in now, jumping cameramen and reporters. One man filming the action was knocked down and his camera was taken away. The man turned out to be an FBI agent, and the three men who attacked him were later arrested. One of them was Jimmie George Robinson, the man who had attacked Dr. King at the Hotel Albert.

I was up now and moving, back across the bridge, with troopers and possemen and other retreating marchers all around me. At the other end of the bridge, we had to push through the possemen we'd passed outside the *Selma Times-Journal* building.

"Please, no," I could hear one woman scream.

"God, we're being *killed!*" cried another.

With nightsticks and whips—one posseman had a rubber hose wrapped with barbed wire—Sheriff Clark's "deputies" chased us all the way back into the Carver project and up to the front of Brown's Chapel, where we tried getting as many people as we could inside the church to safety. I don't even recall how I made it that far, how I got from the bridge to the church, but I did.

A United Press International reporter gave this account of that segment of the attack:

> The troopers and possemen, under Gov. George C. Wallace's orders to stop the Negroes' "Walk for Freedom" from Selma to Montgomery, chased the screaming, bleeding marchers nearly a mile back to their church, clubbing them as they ran.

Ambulances screamed in relays between Good Samaritan Hospital and Brown's Chapel Church, carrying hysterical men, women and children suffering head wounds and tear gas burns.

Even then, the possemen and troopers, 150 of them, including Clark himself, kept attacking, beating anyone who remained on the street. Some of the marchers fought back now, with men and boys emerging from the Carver homes with bottles and bricks in their hands, heaving them at the troopers, then retreating for more. It was a scene that's been replayed so many times in so many places—in Belfast, in Jerusalem, in Beijing. Angry, desperate people hurling whatever they can at the symbols of authority, their hopeless fury much more powerful than the futile bottles and bricks in their hands.

I was inside the church, which was awash with sounds of groaning and weeping. And singing and crying. Mothers shouting out for their children. Children screaming for their mothers and brothers and sisters. So much confusion and fear and anger all erupting at the same time.

Further up Sylvan Street, the troopers chased other marchers who had fled into the First Baptist Church. A teenaged boy struggling with the possemen, was thrown through a church window there.

Finally Wilson Baker arrived and persuaded Clark and his men to back off to a block away, where they remained, breathing heavily and awaiting further orders.

A crowd of Selma's black men and women had collected in front of the church by now, with SNCC and SCLC staff members moving

through and trying to keep them calm. Some men in the crowd spoke of going home to get guns. Our people tried talking them down, getting them calm. Kids and teenagers continued throwing rocks and bricks.

The parsonage next to the church looked like a MASH unit, with doctors and nurses tending to dozens of weeping, wounded people. There were cuts and bumps and bruises, and a lot of tear gas burns, which were treated by rinsing the eyes with a boric acid solution.

Relays of ambulances sent by black funeral homes carried the more seriously wounded to Good Samaritan Hospital, Selma's largest black health-care facility, run by white Catholics and staffed mostly by black doctors and nurses. One of those ambulance drivers made ten trips back and forth from the church to the hospital and to nearby Burwell Infirmary, a smaller clinic. More than ninety men and women were treated at both facilities, for injuries ranging from head gashes and fractured ribs and wrists and arms and legs to broken jaws and teeth. There was one fractured skull—mine, although I didn't know it yet.

I didn't consider leaving for the hospital, though several people tried to persuade me to go. I wanted to do what I could to help with all this chaos. I was so much in the moment, I didn't have much time to think about what had happened, nor about what was yet to come.

By nightfall, things had calmed down a bit. Hosea and I and the others had decided to call a mass meeting there in the church, and more than six hundred people, many bandaged from the wounds of that day, arrived. Clark's possemen had been ordered away but the state troopers were still outside, keeping a vigil.

Hosea Williams spoke to the crowd first, trying to say something to calm them. Then I got up to say a few words. My head was throbbing. My hair was matted with blood clotting from an open gash. My trench coat was stained with dirt and blood.

I looked out on the room, crammed wall to wall and floor to ceiling with people. There was not a spot for one more body. I had no speech prepared. I had not had the time or opportunity to give much thought to what I would say. The words just came.

"I don't know how President Johnson can send troops to Vietnam," I said. "I don't see how he can send troops to the Congo. I don't see how he can send troops to *Africa,* and he can't send troops to Selma, Alabama."

There was clapping, and some shouts of "Yes!" and "Amen!"

"Next time we march," I continued, "we may have to keep going when we get to Montgomery. We may have to go on to *Washington.*"

When those words were printed in *The New York Times* the next morning, the Justice Department announced it was sending FBI agents to Selma to investigate whether "unnecessary force was used by law officers and others." For two months we'd been facing "unnecessary force," but that apparently had not been enough.

This, finally, was enough. Now, after speaking, it was time for me to have my own injuries examined. I went next door to the parsonage, where the doctors took one look at my head and immediately sent me over to Good Samaritan. What I remember most about arriving there was the smell in the waiting room. The chairs were jammed with people from the march—victims and their families—and their clothing reeked of tear gas. The bitter, acrid smell filled the room.

The nurses and nuns were very busy. Priests roamed the room, comforting and calming people. When one of the nurses saw my head, I was immediately taken through and X-rayed. My head wound was cleaned and dressed, then I was admitted. By ten that night, exhausted and groggy from painkillers, I finally fell asleep.

It was not until the next day that I learned what else had happened that evening, that just past 9:30 P.M., ABC Television cut into its Sunday night movie—a premiere broadcast of Stanley Kramer's *Judgment at Nuremberg,* a film about Nazi racism—with a special bulletin. News anchor Frank Reynolds came on-screen to tell viewers of a brutal clash that afternoon between state troopers and black protest marchers in Selma, Alabama. They then showed fifteen minutes of film footage of the attack.

The images were stunning—scene after scene of policemen on foot and on horseback beating defenseless American citizens. Many viewers thought this was somehow part of the movie. It seemed too strange, too ugly to be real. It *couldn't* be real.

But it was. At one point in the film clip, Jim Clark's voice could be heard clearly in the background: "Get those goddamned niggers!" he yelled. "And get those goddamned *white* niggers."

The American public had already seen so much of this sort of thing, countless images of beatings and dogs and cursing and hoses. But something about that day in Selma touched a nerve deeper than anything that had come before. Maybe it was the concentrated focus of the scene, the mass movement of those troopers on foot and riders on horseback rolling into and over two long lines of stoic, silent, unarmed people. This wasn't like Birmingham, where chanting and cheering and singing preceded a wild stampede and scattering. This was a face-off in the most vivid terms between a dignified, composed, completely nonviolent multitude of silent protesters and the truly malevolent force of a heavily armed, hateful battalion of troopers. The sight of them rolling over us like human tanks was something that had never been seen before.

People just couldn't believe this was happening, not in America. Women and children being attacked by armed men on horseback—it was impossible to believe.

But it had happened. And the response from across the nation to what would go down in history as Bloody Sunday was immediate. By midnight that evening, even as I lay asleep in my room over at Good Samaritan, people from as far away as New York and Minnesota were flying into Alabama and driving to Selma, forming a vigil of their own outside Brown's Chapel. President Johnson, who had been contacted by the Justice Department almost immediately after the attack, watched the ABC footage that evening. He knew he would have to respond. Dr. King, too, was informed of what had happened as soon as the President—Andy Young called King in Atlanta, and the two agreed that now there *would* be a march. They made plans to file a request the first thing

in the morning, asking for a federal injunction barring state interference in a massive Selma-to-Montgomery march.

That request arrived the next morning, Monday, in Montgomery, on the desk of Federal District Judge Frank Johnson—the same judge who had issued the injunction four years earlier providing us with safe passage out of Montgomery during the Freedom Ride.

Banner headlines, with four-column photographs—many showing the trooper clubbing me as I lay on the ground with my arm upraised—appeared that Monday morning in newspapers around the world. By midday I was receiving telegrams and cards and flowers from total strangers. A wreath arrived from an elderly woman in Southern California: "A FORMER ALABAMIAN," the card read. "WE ARE WITH YOU."

Dr. King and Ralph Abernathy came to see me. They told me what was going on outside, that people all across the country were with us, that they were going to have this march. "It's going to happen, John," Dr. King told me. "Rest assured it is going to happen."

John Doar, from the Justice Department, came to interview me about the attack, to take a deposition of sorts. The federal government was now very involved in this thing.

The hospital staff kept the press away from my room, except for a UPI photographer, who was allowed in to shoot a picture, I saw no reporters at all.

I was in a lot of pain that day. And I felt very strange lying in that bed. With all my arrests and injuries over the years, I had never actually been admitted to a hospital before. I'd been treated, but never admitted. And I did

not like it. I felt very restless and a little bit
frightened. Maybe it was the drugs, but I had
visions of someone slipping into the room and
doing something to me. I felt vulnerable, helpless.

Worst of all, though, was the sense of
being cut off. I was hearing about everything
secondhand, if at all. It was killing me not to
know what was going on outside that hospital,
because I knew there was plenty going on.

And I was right.

Several carloads, and a truckload as well, of
SNCC field workers from Mississippi had
rushed in that day, along with a chartered plane
of staff people from Atlanta—Forman and
others. All told, more than thirty SNCC
people had arrived in Selma by that afternoon.

They came with a mixture of hurt and outrage and shame and guilt. They were concerned for the local people of Selma, and also
for one of their own. I had been hurt, and they
didn't like it. It made them mad. It got them
excited, too. This was an emergency, a crisis,
something to *respond* to. It was like firemen
who hadn't had a fire to put out in a long time.
Now everyone wanted to be the first to get to
the blaze.

None of them came to see me in the hospital, except for Lafayette Surrney, whose purpose was to collect information for a press
release. I really wasn't hurt about that. I
guessed that they were probably very busy.

And I was right. Word came from Judge
Johnson that Monday afternoon that he would
not grant an injunction without a hearing, and
he would not be able to hold a hearing any
sooner than Thursday That evening the SCLC
and SNCC leadership—Dr. King, Andy Young

and others of the SCLC; Forman, Willie Ricks
and Fay Bellamy of SNCC, along with Jim
Farmer, who'd come on the scene to represent
CORE—argued over whether they should risk
losing the judge's support by staging a march
before getting his approval, or risk losing cred-
ibility and momentum by waiting patiently
until he issued his injunction.

Unlike two days earlier, when he had been
dead set against SNCC's participation, Forman
was now pushing hard to march, and to march
now. Hosea was with him, as was Farmer. Most
of the others leaned toward accepting Judge
Johnson's terms. If I had been there, I would
have said we should march and let the courts
do what they would—what they *should*. I
wouldn't have gone as far as Forman, who was
furious that this judge was telling us to wait—
he called Judge Johnson's offer "legal black-
mail"—but I would have said this was no time
to stop and sit still.

Our SNCC people were even more fed up
with the SCLC than they had been two days
before. King's staff had prepared a fund-raising
ad to be placed in *The New York Times*, showing a photograph of me being beaten on the
bridge. That really bothered a lot of our
people. The way Julian later put it to one
reporter, "It was *our* chairman who was leading the march. . . . SCLC was hogging all the
publicity and all the money and doing very little to deserve it. . . . We just resented SCLC's
ability to capitalize on things we thought we
were doing."

I understood that resentment. But again, I
felt that SNCC had lost the upper hand completely, along with any right to complain, by
not being part of that march. When Julian said

it was "our chairman" leading the march, he was ignoring the fact that our leadership had pointedly decided the night before that I would march not as the chairman of SNCC but as myself. There was something wrong with trying to have it both ways now. I had played the role of a go-between up until this point, bridging my roles with both SNCC and the SCLC, but clearly that was going to be harder to do from here on out.

The final decision at that Monday night meeting was left up to Dr. King, and he decided there would be no march on Tuesday. Then he left with the others to attend a rally at Brown's Chapel. The place was packed; the atmosphere was overwhelmingly emotional, and apparently it overwhelmed Dr. King as well, who stunned everyone who had been at that meeting by announcing to the crowd that there *would* be a march the next day.

Late that night and on into the next morning, the SNCC and SCLC leaders met at the home of a local black dentist, Dr. Sullivan Jackson, to hash out the plans for the Tuesday march. State and federal authorities had issued official statements forbidding it. George Wallace actually claimed he had "saved lives" by having Lingo and Clark and their men stop us that Sunday afternoon—the counties ahead, the places we would have to pass through to get to Montgomery said the governor, were much more dangerous than anything we faced in Selma. Those same dangers, he now claimed, were too great to allow us to march on this day.

Dr. King and the others were up until 4 A.M. trying to work out some sort of compromise with government officials in the face of a restraining order against this march issued by Judge Johnson. King spoke by phone early that morning with Attorney General Katzenbach in Washington. Then, after a few hours' sleep, King met with several federal officials, including John Doar and former Florida governor LeRoy Collins, who was now director of the Justice Department's Community Relations Service and who had been sent by President Johnson to mediate this situation. After Collins met with King that morning, he went to talk to state and local officials, including Lingo and Clark, who were once again stationed with their troops at the east end of the bridge.

No one besides Dr. King and a few of his closest staffers knew exactly what was decided by those early-morning phone calls and meetings. When a column of two thousand marchers led by Dr. King left Brown's Chapel early that afternoon, walking the same route toward the same bridge we'd tried to cross that Sunday, they all assumed they were headed for Montgomery. When they were stopped at the bridge by a U.S. marshal who read aloud Judge Johnson's order against this march, they assumed this was just a formality. And when Dr. King then led the column over the crest of the bridge to the bottom of the other side, where the armed troopers were massed once again, the marchers steeled themselves for another attack.

This time, though, the troopers stood still and simply watched as Dr. King brought the column to a halt and led the marchers in prayer. Then they sang "We Shall Overcome." And then, as the troopers moved aside to open the way east to Montgomery, Dr. King turned around and headed *back* to the church.

The marchers were shocked and confused. They had no idea what was going on. They had come to put their bodies on the line, and now they were backing down, retreating, going home. They followed Dr. King—what else could they do? But they were disappointed. Many were openly angry.

Jim Forman was absolutely livid. When he—and everyone else—learned that Dr. King had made an agreement with federal officials that morning to march only to the bridge, as a symbolic gesture, and then to turn back and await Judge Johnson's hearing later that week, he exploded, denouncing Dr. King's "trickery" and saying that this was the last straw. SNCC had had enough. There would be no more working with the SCLC. There would be no waiting for any judge's injunction. SNCC was finished with waiting, finished with Selma. It was time to do something on our own, said Forman. Within twenty-four hours he shifted our manpower and focus from Selma to the streets of Montgomery, where SNCC-led student forces, from Tuskegee Institute and Alabama State University began laying siege to the state capitol with a series of demonstrations more overt and aggressive than anything seen in Selma. Taunting, provoking, clashing with mounted policemen—the SNCC protests that week in Montgomery would prove to be nothing like our non-violent campaign in Selma.

All this news hit me like a windstorm when I was released from the hospital that Tuesday night. I was still in great pain—my head was pounding. My skull was fractured. I'd had a serious concussion. The doctors told me I needed more treatment and suggested I see some specialists up in Boston. But there was no way I was going to Boston. There was no time. I'd already lain in that hospital long enough. It was driving me crazy

One good thing about the three days I spent in that hospital bed was that it gave me a lot of time to think, to reflect. I had every reason to be discouraged. My feelings and philosophy about the movement, about our strategies and tactics, my commitment to nonviolence, my loyalty to Dr King were all increasingly putting me at odds with many of my SNCC colleagues. We even differed about the events of that Tuesday, about Dr. King's "double-dealing," as some of them called it. I had no problem with what Dr. King did. I thought it was in keeping with the philosophy of the movement, that there comes a time when you must retreat, and that there is nothing wrong with retreating. There is nothing wrong with coming back to fight another day. Dr. King knew—we all knew—that Judge Johnson was going to give us what we were asking for if we simply followed procedure, followed the rules.

But I was in the minority. Most of the people in SNCC were sick of procedure, sick of the rules. Some were sick of me. By all rights, I should have been despondent when I came out of that hospital, but I wasn't. Quite the opposite. I guess I've always been a person who looks at the big picture rather than focusing on little details. That's probably a curse as much as it is a blessing. But that's what I saw that Tuesday night as I emerged from that hospital—the big picture. And it looked wonderful. I was convinced now more than ever that we would prevail. The response we had gotten nationally in the wake of that Sunday attack was so much greater than anything I'd seen since I'd become a part of the movement for civil rights. It was greater than the Freedom Rides, greater than the March on Washington, greater than Mississippi Summer. The country seemed truly aroused. People were really moved. During the first forty-eight hours after Bloody Sunday there were demonstrations in more than eighty cities protesting the brutality and urging the passage of a voting rights act. There were speeches on the floors of both houses of Congress condemning the attack and calling for voting rights legislation. A telegram signed by more than sixty congressmen was sent to President Johnson, asking for "immediate" submission of a voting rights bill.

Yes, we had serious problems within SNCC. They would have to be worked out, and I had no doubt they would be. But meanwhile, the movement had an incredible amount of momentum. When I came out of the hospital that Tuesday night, despite all the buzz among my SNCC colleagues about the "betrayal" that afternoon, I was exhilarated.

There was a rally that night at Brown's Chapel, and I was overjoyed to be there. People in the press were pushing and pushing about the "split" between SNCC and the SCLC. They asked me openly about it. I told them, no, there was no split. How could there be a split, I said, between two groups that have never pretended to be one?

"I am not going to engage in any public discussion of organizational problems," I stated. "SCLC is not the enemy. George Wallace and segregation are the enemy."

Ivanhoe Donaldson put it a different way. "Within the movement," he told one reporter, "we are a family. Arguments take place in any family."

He couldn't have put it any better. And the wisest families, he might have added, keep their arguments to themselves. Yes, we had problems among ourselves and with the SCLC, but I wasn't about to discuss them with the press.

That night, after the rally at Brown's, I went home with one of the families in the Carver project, the Wests, and slept like a baby. It was not until the next morning that I heard what had happened while I was asleep.

More than four hundred out-of-town ministers—most of them white—had taken part in the march that afternoon. After the rally that evening, three of them went and had dinner at Walker's Cafe, the diner that was such a favorite among movement people. After their meal, as they walked back toward the church, they lost their way and wound up passing through a poor white section of town. As they went by a little bar called the Silver Moon, a crowd from inside the bar came out and surrounded them. Before they knew what was happening, one of the three, a thirty-eight-year-old Unitarian minister from Boston named James J. Reeb, was clubbed in the head by a full baseball-style swing of a bat. He was so badly injured that the local emergency room staff put him in an ambulance and sent him on to Birmingham University Hospital, where he was listed Wednesday morning in critical condition with a large blood clot in his brain.

Thursday, with the Reverend Reeb's condition headlined in the newspapers, I went to Montgomery for the beginning of the federal court hearing on the SCLC request for an injunction to block state interference and allow a Selma-to-Montgomery march. Walking back into Frank Johnson's courtroom, where I'd testified four years earlier during the Freedom Ride, felt familiar in some ways, but different in one hugely important one. Four years earlier, the governor of Alabama was John Patterson. He was the figure of state authority who was squared off against the federal figure, Judge Johnson. Now the governor was George Wallace, a man whose clashes with Judge Johnson went back for years and years.

Frank Johnson and George Wallace had been classmates at the University of Alabama in the 1930s, but other than that they had next to nothing in common. While Wallace was from the same southeastern, deeply Confederate part of the state as I, Johnson grew up in north Alabama, near Tennessee, in a county that had actually sided with the Union during the Civil War. Early in his career Johnson established a reputation for fairness and reason in the face of racists. During the Montgomery bus boycott he was a member of a three-judge panel that handed down a decision in favor of desegregation. Later, he sat on another panel that struck down Alabama's poll-tax law. In 1958 he ordered the voter registration records of Barbour County to be turned over to the U.S. Civil Rights Commission. The Barbour County circuit judge who held those records refused to give them up. Only after Johnson threatened him with a contempt charge did the circuit judge relent and give up the records. That judge was George Wallace.

In the wake of that episode, Wallace famously called Johnson an "integrating, carpetbagging, scalawagging, race-mixing, bald-faced liar." Now, seven years later, the two were squaring off again, this time with Wallace sitting in the governor's mansion.

We had spent several days meeting with our lawyers—Fred Gray, Arthur Shores, Orzell Billingsley and J. L. Chestnut—preparing our case, which was to establish that our rights had been repeatedly violated during our two-month campaign in Selma, often through violent means, and that this march, as a method of demonstrating our *right* to those rights, should be allowed.

We expected the hearing to extend over several days, which it did. I testified, describing in detail my experience the Sunday of the attack on the Edmund Pettus Bridge. The FBI agents who witnessed that attack also testified. A film clip of the attack—three minutes of footage shot by Larry Pierce for CBS—was shown, and when the courtroom lights were turned back on, Judge Johnson stood silently, shook his head, straightened his robe and called for a recess. He was visibly disgusted.

On the third day of the hearing Colonel Lingo testified and indicated that the order to use force that day came straight from George Wallace. He didn't come right out and say it then, but years later, when Lingo was running for sheriff of Jefferson County he was explicit. "I was ordered to cause the scene that the troopers made," he said. "Who ordered me? The governor! Governor George C. Wallace ordered me to stop the marchers even if we had to use force, to bring this thing to a halt. He said that we'd teach other niggers to try to march on a public highway in Alabama. He said that he was damned if he would allow such a thing to take place."

Whether Wallace actually ordered it or not, he certainly condoned the attack that took place that Sunday. And he never criticized it. In fact, even as Judge Johnson's hearing was moving into its third day, Wallace was on his way to Washington to meet with President Johnson and try to convince the President to step in and stop us from marching. That meeting wound up backfiring on Wallace. Not only did Johnson not agree to help Wallace, but he emerged from the meeting and made a stunning announcement to the reporters waiting outside:

The events of last Sunday cannot and will not be repeated, but the demonstrations in Selma have a much larger meaning. They are a protest against a deep and very unjust flaw in American democracy itself.

Ninety-five years ago our Constitution was amended to require that no American be denied the right to vote because of race or color. Almost a century later, many Americans are kept from voting simply because they are Negroes.

Therefore, this Monday I will send to the Congress a request for legislation to carry out the amendment of the Constitution.

That was Saturday, March 13. The Reverend Reeb had passed away two nights earlier, prompting even more demonstrations across the country in support of our efforts in Selma. That Sunday, Forman and I flew to New York for a march in Harlem protesting the events in Alabama. Several thousand people, most of them black, a great many dressed in white Masonic uniforms, paraded, then listened as I told them what had happened and what was going to happen in Selma.

Meanwhile, down in Montgomery, as well as in cities across the country, SNCC-led demonstrations were heating up. There were sit-ins at the Justice Department and protests outside the White House. I heard later that President Johnson actually complained at a meeting that Sunday night that his daughter Luci couldn't study because of all the noise outside.

The next day, Monday, I was back in Montgomery for the fourth day of the hearing. It was clear now that Judge Johnson was going to give us the injunction we wanted. He asked us that day to submit a plan for the march we wanted to make. We went back that afternoon—Andy Young, Hosea Williams, Jack Greenberg, who was head of the NAACP's Legal Defense Fund, several other SCLC people and I—to the Albert Pick Motel in Montgomery and drew up details of the number of people we expected to march, the route we would follow and the number of days it would take.

Then I headed back to Selma, where a rally was held that afternoon in honor of the Reverend Reeb. More than two thousand people marched through downtown Selma to the courthouse steps, where Dr. King led a twenty-minute service, with Jim Clark's deputies looking on but doing nothing to stop it.

I was in Selma that night when I got word that there had been an outburst of violence earlier that afternoon in Montgomery, where several hundred SNCC demonstrators—mainly the Tuskegee Institute and Alabama State students organized by Forman—had clashed with police and mounted deputies who tried to stop them from demonstrating. When the police began pushing in and physically shoving the students aside, some of the students responded by throwing rocks, bricks and bottles. That brought the mounted possemen forward, swinging clubs and whips. When the students ran, the possemen chased them on horseback, actually riding up onto the porches of private homes. At least one glass door was broken by the charge of a deputy on horseback.

I was horrified to hear this. It was almost surreal. The violence seemed to be getting wilder and wilder each day. I talked to Forman early that evening on the phone and agreed that we should stage a march the next day to protest the extremity of the possemen's attack. I had the final day of Judge Johnson's hearing to attend in the morning, but I would be there for the march after that.

After talking with Forman, I settled in that night at the home of Dr. Jackson, the Selma dentist, to watch President Johnson make a live televised address to Congress. Dr. King and several SCLC staffers were also squeezed into Dr. and Mrs. Jackson's small living room. The President had invited Dr. King and me to come up to Washington that night and join the audience for his speech, but we decided the place for us to be was Selma.

And so, along with 70 million other Americans who watched the broadcast that evening, we listened to Lyndon Johnson make what many others and I consider not only the finest speech of his career, but probably the strongest speech any American president has ever made on the subject of civil rights. It began powerfully:

At times history and fate meet at a single time in a single place to shape a turning point in man's unending search for freedom. So it was at Lexington and Concord. So it was a century ago at Appomattox. So it was last week in Selma, Alabama.

It moved toward a climax with a focus on voting rights:

Rarely in any time does an issue lay bare the secret heart of America itself. . . . The issue of equal rights for American Negroes is such an issue. And should we defeat every enemy and should we double our wealth and conquer the stars and still be unequal to this issue, then we will have failed as a people and as a nation.

And it peaked with the President citing our favorite freedom song, the anthem, the very heart and soul, of the civil rights movement:

Even if we pass this bill, the battle will not be over. What happened in Selma is part of a far larger movement which reaches into every section and state of America. It is the effort of American Negroes to secure for themselves the full blessings of American life.

Their cause must be our cause too. Because it is not just Negroes, but really it is all of us who must overcome the crippling legacy of bigotry and injustice.

And we *shall* overcome.

All told, the speech was forty-five minutes long. It was interrupted forty times by applause, twice by standing ovations. I was deeply moved. Lyndon Johnson was no politician that night. He was a man who spoke from his heart. His were the words of a statesman and more; they were the words of a poet. Dr. King must have agreed. He wiped away a tear at the point where Johnson said the words "We shall overcome."

Predictably, not everyone was so moved. I was not surprised to hear Jim Forman attack the speech. The President's reference to our anthem was a "tinkling empty symbol," Forman told one reporter. "Johnson," he later said to another writer, "spoiled a good song that day."

We never did have time to discuss the speech, Forman and I. Events were tumbling much too swiftly The next morning I was back in Montgomery, watching our attorneys hand Judge Johnson the plans for our march. The hearing was now over. Johnson would make his decision by the following day.

That afternoon—gray overcast, with a steady rain drizzling down—I joined Forman, Dr. King and others at the front of a group of six hundred people marching from the state capitol to the Montgomery County Courthouse to protest the violence of the day before. To this day photos from that day's march, showing us wearing ponchos and raincoats, are mistakenly presented as if they were taken during the march from Selma to Montgomery, which they were not. That march was yet to come.

That evening, at a rally called by SCLC officials, with Dr. King and Abernathy in the audience, along with dozens of middle-class, mainstream black ministers, Forman stunned everyone with one of the angriest, most fiery speeches made by a movement leader up to that point.

> There's only one man in the country that can stop George Wallace and those posses.
>
> These problems will not be solved until the man in that shaggedy old place called the White House begins to shake and gets on the phone and says, "Now listen, George, we're coming down there and throw you in jail if you don't stop that mess." . . .
>
> I said it today and I will say it again. If we can't sit at the table of democracy, we'll knock the fucking legs *off!*

The fact that he quickly caught himself and muttered the words "Excuse me" was lost on almost everyone there. This was a church. Not only were those pews filled with ministers, but there were women and children in the audience, too. They were shocked. I was not. I'd heard Forman use that kind of language many times at SNCC meetings. But I was dismayed. That was not the language of the nonviolence movement. That was not the *message* of the movement, at least not of the movement I was a part of. And that was what was most significant to me about that speech, not the fact that Forman's words were so bold and profane, but the fact that they pointed the way down a road SNCC was headed that I knew I would not be able to travel.

Even Dr. King, when he stepped to the podium after Forman was finished, had trouble restoring calm. People were visibly upset. Several had already gotten up to leave. Then, as if on some sort of cue, one of Dr. King's staffers arrived, approached the podium and had a word with King, who nodded, smiled and waved everyone quiet.

Judge Johnson, Dr. King announced, had issued his ruling. The march from Selma to Montgomery would be allowed.

The judge's written order, officially released the next morning, beautifully and succinctly summarized what we had been through in Selma, and *why* we had gone through it:

The evidence in this case reflects that . . . an almost continuous pattern of conduct has existed on the part of defendant Sheriff Clark, his deputies, and his auxiliary deputies known as "possemen" of harassment, intimidation, coercion, threatening conduct, and, sometimes, brutal mistreatment toward these plaintiffs and other members of their class. . . . .

The attempted march alongside U.S. Highway 80 . . . on March 7, 1965, involved nothing more than a peaceful effort on the part of Negro citizens to exercise a classic constitutional right: that is, the right to assemble peaceably and to petition one's government for the redress of grievances.

. . . it seems basic to our constitutional principles that the extent of the right to assemble, demonstrate and march peaceably along the highways and streets in an orderly manner should be commensurate with the enormity of the wrongs that are being protested and petitioned against. In this case, the wrongs are enormous. The extent of the right to demonstrate against these wrongs should be determined accordingly.

We had told the judge the march would begin on Sunday, March 21. This was Wednesday. That gave us five days to prepare. And this time, as compared to our small, spontaneous effort on Bloody Sunday, there would *be* preparation, as well as the full participation of SNCC, the SCLC, the NAACP, the Urban League and every other civil and human rights organization in the United States. In many ways, this event promised to be as big as the March on Washington. The numbers would be nowhere near that many, of course, but unlike the demonstration in Washington, which was a rally more than an actual march, this was literally going to be a mass *movement* of people, thousands and thousands of them, walking down a highway, cutting through the heart of the state of Alabama.

The next five days were a swirl of activity, much like preparing an army for an assault. Marchers, not just from Selma but from across the nation, were mobilized and organized, route sections and schedules were mapped out, printed up and distributed, tents big enough to sleep people by the hundreds were secured. Food. Security. Communications. There were thousands of details to take care of, and thousands of dollars, most of it raised by the SCLC, to be spent. Just a quick scan of the records from that week indicates both the enormity and the tediousness of this undertaking:

- 700 air mattresses at $1.45 each
- 700 blankets donated by local churches and schools
- Four carnival-sized tents rented for $430 apiece
- 17,000 square feet of polyethylene for ground cloth, at a cost of $187
- 700 rain ponchos
- Two 2,500-watt generators for lighting campsites
- 2,000 feet of electrical wiring

Walkie-talkies, flashlights, pots and pans and stoves for cooking . . . the list went on and on. And so did the manpower. A crew of twelve ministers—we called them the "fish and loaves committee"—was responsible for transporting food to each campsite each evening. Ten local women cooked the evening meals in church kitchens in Selma. Ten others made sandwiches around the clock. Squads of doctors and nurses from the same Medical Committee for Human Rights that had provided the physicians who tended the wounded on Bloody Sunday now geared up for a different kind of casualty, with dozens' of cases of rubbing alcohol and hundreds of boxes of Band-Aids, for the marchers' sore muscles and blistered feet.

Meanwhile, state and federal authorities were doing their part to prepare. The two westbound lanes of Highway 80 between Selma and Montgomery would be closed off for the five days of the march—all traffic in both directions would be routed onto the eastbound lanes. At the order of President Johnson, more than 1,800 armed Alabama National Guardsmen would line the fifty-four-mile route, along with two thousand U.S. Army troops, a hundred FBI agents and a hundred U.S. marshals. Helicopters and light planes would patrol the route from the air, watching for snipers or other signs of trouble, and demolition teams would clear the way ahead of us, inspecting bridges and bends in the road for planted explosives.

That Saturday night, the evening before the march would begin, more than two hundred people came to spend the night in Brown's Chapel. We all made short speeches—Bevel and Diane, Andy Young and I. Dick Gregory couldn't help working a little routine into his speech. "It would be just our luck," he said, looking ahead to our arrival in Montgomery, "to find out that Wallace is colored."

When we awoke Sunday morning, more than three thousand people had gathered outside the church. Dr. King greeted them with a speech intended to make the local Selmans among them comfortable with the middle-class professionals and out-of-town celebrities who

had arrived to join them. We were all very sensitive about this, about keeping the focus as much as possible on the people who had brought this historic day about, the everyday men and women of Selma. We made a point to put them at the front of the march, right behind the row that led the way.

That row included Dr. King and his wife, Coretta, A. Philip Randolph, Ralph Bunche, Ralph and Juanita Abernathy, Andy Young, Hosea, me, Forman, Dick Gregory and Rabbi Abraham Heschel of the Jewish Theological Seminary of America, a biblical-looking man with a long, flowing white beard. 'When he walked up to join us, one onlooker shouted out, "There goes *God!*"

Someone arrived with an armful of Hawaiian leis, which were placed around each of our necks. Abernathy stepped forward and announced, "Wallace, it's all over now."

And then we stepped off, 3,200 people walking in a column that stretched a mile long. Ahead of us rolled a television truck, its lights and cameras trained on Dr King's every step.

Behind us walked an unimaginable cross section of American people.

There was a one-legged man on crutches—Jim Leatherer, from Saginaw, Michigan—who answered each person who thanked him for coming by thanking them in return. "I believe in you," he said over and over again. "I believe in democracy."

There was a couple from California pushing a baby in a stroller.

Assistant Attorneys General John Doar and Ramsey Clark were both there, walking among the crowd like everyone else.

Cager Lee, Jimmie Lee Jackson's elderly grandfather, who had been wounded the night Jimmie Lee was killed, was with us. It was hard for him to do even a few miles a day, but Mr. Lee was bound and determined to do them. "Just got to tramp some more," he said, nodding his head and pushing on.

Ministers, nuns, labor leaders, factory workers, schoolteachers, firemen—people from all walks of life, from all parts of the country, black and white and Asian and Native American, walked with us as we approached the same bridge where we'd been beaten two weeks before. The same troopers were there again, but this time National Guardsmen were there as well, and we passed over the river without incident, trailed by two truckloads of soldiers and a convoy of Army jeeps.

And now we were out of the city, the pebble-and-tar pavement of Highway 80 carrying us on into the countryside, through swampy marshland, past mossy Spanish oaks, rolling red clay farmland, and small, twisting creeks and rivers.

There was some jeering from occasional white onlookers gathered here and there along the shoulder of the road. Profanities from passing traffic were pretty constant. A man in a car with the words "Coonsville, USA" painted on doors drove beside us for several days. And a private plane passed over the first day dropping a small snowstorm of hate leaflets. But other than a couple of small incidents—one white marcher was hit in the face when he walked over to a filling station for a Coke, and bricks were thrown into a campsite one night injuring several sleeping marchers—there was no actual violence.

We covered seven miles the first day, accompanied by the constant clicking of cameras as dozens of photographers and reporters circled us all the way. We stopped that night at a prearranged site, as spelled out in the plans we had given Judge Johnson. A man named David Hall, who worked for the Carver housing project as a maintenance manager and who owned an eighty-acre farm east edge of Dallas County, offered his land for us to pitch our tents that first night. The father of eight children, Mr. Hall, who was black, was asked whether he feared retaliation from the white community for doing us such a favor. "The Lord," he answered simply, "will provide."

That was basically the same answer a seventy-five-year-old woman named Rosa Steele gave when asked how she felt about letting us stay our second night on her 240-acre farm in Lowndes County. "I'm not afraid," said Mrs. Steele. "I've lived my three score and ten."

It was cold that first evening, below freezing as a matter of fact. More than two thousand of the marches bedded down beneath three large tents. In the morning they would have to head back to Selma—Judge Johnson's order included a stipulation that we limit the number of marchers the second day to three hundred, since we'd be passing through a section of Lowndes County where the road narrowed from four to two lanes. The marchers that night made the most of their evening together. They clapped hands, built huge fires, sang and soaked in that Freedom High until they finally fell asleep.

The other thousand or so people who had walked with us that day were driven back to Selma that night in a caravan of cars and trucks.

I was among them. Before allowing me to make this march at all, my doctors insisted that I sleep in a bed each evening. They did not want me spending the nights on hard ground, out in the cold. My head was still bothering me badly enough that I agreed with them. I would walk that entire fifty-four-mile route, but I spent each night back in Selma, with a doctor nearby in case something went wrong with my head.

That Monday, the second day, I rejoined the group and put on an orange vest, which we had decided each of the three hundred people chosen to march that day would wear for identification. We moved much more swiftly that day, covering sixteen miles by nightfall. Dr. King left that evening to fulfill a speaking engagement in Cleveland. He would be back two days later for the last leg of the march.

Tuesday the number of marchers swelled back to three thousand as the road widened back to four lanes and we were allowed to lift the limitation. The skies darkened early, and a torrential downpour began that lasted all day. To beat back the rain, we started a song, a little chant written by a guy named Len Chandler:

> *Pick 'em up and lay 'em down,*
> *All the way from Selma town.*

The weather was miserable, but no one complained. No one got tired. No one fell back. To me, there was never a march like this one before, and there hasn't been one since. The incredible sense of community—of *communing*—was overwhelming. We felt bonded with one another, with the people we passed, with the entire nation. The people who came out of their homes to watch as we passed by—

rural people, almost all of them black, almost all of them poor—waved and cheered, ran into their kitchens and brought us out food, brought us something to drink. More than a few of them put down what they were doing and joined us.

We covered eleven miles that day as well, and sixteen the next. And now we were just outside Montgomery. We were sunburned, windburned, weary looking like the "last stragglers of a lost battalion," as one reporter described it. Our final stop was a place called the City of St. Jude, a Catholic complex of a church, a hospital and a school located two miles from Montgomery, operated through charity to serve the black community. Dr. King was there when we arrived, along with a crowd of 1,500 people that swelled by the hundreds every hour, as night fell and the scene turned into a celebration, a festival.

Dozens of celebrities arrived for a massive outdoor concert organized by whom else?— Harry Belafonte. The entertainers included Tony Bennett, Sammy Davis Jr., Billy Eckstine, Shelley Winters, Ossie Davis, Leonard Bernstein, Nina Simone, Odetta, Johnny Mathis, Nipsey Russell, Peter, Paul and Mary, the Chad Mitchell Trio, Anthony Perkins, Elaine May, George Kirby, Joan Baez and Dick Gregory. They all performed that evening on a makeshift stage fashioned from stacks of coffins loaned by a local black funeral home. Yes, *coffins.*

It was a spectacle, a salute to Selma, with more than 20,000 people gathered under the stars for four hours of songs, speeches and sketches. At one point a reporter asked Elaine May if she thought this show and all these celebrities were turning this serious march into a circus. She snapped back, "The only real circus is the state of Alabama and George Wallace."

The next morning—a spectacularly sunny day—we went to see Governor Wallace, 50,000 of us. It was six miles from St. Jude's to the state capitol building. There had been yet another death threat made on Dr. King, and so, as a precaution, several ministers were dressed in the same blue suit he wore that day and marched beside him, to confuse any would-be snipers.

Into downtown we came, around the fountain on Court Square, where slaves had watered their owners' horses in antebellum times, up Dexter Avenue past the church where Dr. King preached when he was a minister in Montgomery and finally out onto the open square in front of the sun-drenched silver-and-white state capitol building. I could see the Alabama state flag flying high above the rotunda dome, along with the flag of the Confederacy. But the American flag was nowhere in sight. Neither was George Wallace, though we learned later that he watched the entire afternoon, peeking out through the drawn blinds of the governor's office.

A podium had been set up on the trailer of a flatbed truck, along with a microphone and loudspeakers. Peter, Paul and Mary sang. Then came the speakers: Ralph Bunche, Roy Wilkins, Jim Farmer, Whitney Young, Rosa Parks, Ralph Abernathy, Fred Shuttlesworth, Jim Bevel, Bayard Rustin and I. And then, finally, Dr. King stepped up to deliver one of the most important speeches of his life. Again, as in Washington, he rose to the occasion:

I know some of you are asking today, "How long will it take?" I come to say to you this afternoon however difficult the moment, however frustrating the hour, it will not be long, because truth pressed to the earth will rise again.

How long? Not long, because no one can live forever.

How long? Not long, because you will reap what you sow.

How long? Not long, because the arm of the moral universe is long but it bends toward justice.

How long? Not long, because mine eyes have seen the glory of the coming of the Lord, trampling out the vintage where the grapes of wrath are stored. He has loosed the faithful lightning of his terrible swift sword. His truth is marching on.

Glory hallelujah! *Glory hallelujah!*

Four and a half months after that day, on August 6, after a long, weaving journey through both houses of Congress, the 1965 Voting Rights Act was signed into law by Lyndon Johnson during a nationally televised midday ceremony at the U.S. Capitol. Earlier that morning I was invited to meet privately with the President in the Oval Office. Jim Farmer was there, along with a military officer—a black Army major named Hugh Robinson. This was my first visit to the White House since the March on Washington, and my first one-on-one visit with a president.

Johnson dominated the conversation, his legs propped on a chair, his hands folded back behind his head. We talked for about twenty minutes, and near the end of the meeting the President leaned forward and said, "Now John, you've got to go back and get all those folks registered. You've got to go back and get those boys by the *balls*. Just like a bull gets on top of a cow. You've got to get 'em by the balls and you've got to *squeeze,* squeeze 'em till they *hurt*."

I'd heard that Lyndon Johnson enjoyed talking in graphic, down-home terms, but I wasn't quite prepared for all those bulls and balls.

The signing that afternoon in the President's Room of the Capitol—the same room in which Abraham Lincoln signed the Emancipation Proclamation—was a powerfully moving moment for me. This law had teeth. Among its provisions were:

- the suspension of literacy tests in twenty-six states, including Alabama, Georgia and Mississippi, which had been the focal points of so much of our work
- the appointment of federal examiners to replace local officials as voter registrars
- authorization for the attorney general to take action against state and local authorities that use the poll tax as a prerequisite to voting

"The vote," President Johnson declared that day, "is the most powerful instrument ever devised by man for breaking down injustice and destroying the terrible walls which imprison men because they are different from other men."

After signing the bill, Johnson gave pens to Dr. King, Rosa Parks and several other civil rights "leaders," including me. I still have mine

today, framed on the wall of my living room in Atlanta, along with a copy of the bill itself.

That day was a culmination, a climax, the end of a very long road. In a sense it represented a high point in modern America, probably the nation's finest hour in terms of civil rights. One writer called it the "nova of the civil rights movement, a brilliant climax which brought to a close the nonviolent struggle that had reshaped the South."

It was certainly the last act for the movement as I knew it. Something was born in Selma during the course of that year, but something died there, too. The road of nonviolence had essentially run out. Selma was the last act. Even that climactic day at Montgomery, at the end of the march from Selma, was darkened a few hours after Dr. King spoke by the murder of Viola Gregg Liuzzo, a thirty-nine-year-old white housewife from Detroit who had come down as a volunteer for the march. She was driving her Oldsmobile sedan back to Montgomery that night after transporting some marchers home to Selma after the march when she was shot to death on a lonely stretch of Highway 80 in Lowndes County—a stretch of road we had triumphantly walked over just days earlier. Four Klansmen were eventually arrested, tried and, not surprisingly, found "not guilty" of Mrs. Liuzzo's murder. The same four men were later tried on civil rights charges in Judge Johnson's courtroom and were convicted and sentenced to ten years in prison, but that was little consolation to Mrs. Liuzzo's family or to the many people in the movement—especially the younger ones—who saw her death as just one more reason to give up on this notion of nonviolence.

How could I blame them? As I later explained to a writer from *The New York Times* who asked me how I felt looking back on the campaign at Selma:

> We're only flesh. I could understand people not wanting to get beaten anymore. The body gets tired. You put out so much energy and you saw such little gain. Black capacity to believe white would really open his heart, open his life to nonviolent appeal, was running out.

It had been Selma that held us together as long as we did. After that, we just came apart.

Questions

1. Is there anything in Lewis's descriptions of the marches in Alabama in the spring of 1965 which were particularly shocking and surprising?

2. Why did John Lewis conclude: "The road to nonviolence had run out. Selma was the last act"?

3. Did President Johnson and the U.S. Congress respond correctly to the events? Why? Why not?

Recommended Reading

Farmer, James. *Lay Bare the Heart: An Autobiography of the Civil Rights Movement.* New York: Arbor, 1985.

Moody, Ann. *The Coming of Age in Mississippi.* New York: Dial, 1968.

Williams, Juan. *Eyes on the Prize: America's Civil Rights Years, 1954–65.* New York: Penguin, 1988.

Film

Eyes on the Prize

Liang Heng and Judith Shapiro

Liang Heng is not a famous human rights activist, but he grew up during the Chinese cultural revolution, and his story vividly describes the impact of the Chinese Communist party's policies on young children. Liang was born in 1954 in Changsa, Hunan Province. His parents considered themselves loyal communists. When he was three years old, his mother was asked to offer a suggestion for improving the conditions where she worked. She made three minor suggestions for improving working conditions, but was then condemned for doing so and accused of being a "rightist." She lost her position and was sent away to be rehabilitated. From that point Liang Heng's life changed. His father, Liang Shan, an intellectual and journalist on the *Hunan Daily*, condemned his wife and forbid his three children from visiting their mother, hoping thereby to defend his children and protect their future. In order to cut off all ties to his wife, he divorced her, took custody of the children, and then remarried. Yet his efforts were virtually in vain; for when the Great Cultural Revolution began in 1966, Liang Shan was also condemned because he was a writer and an intellectual. He was sent off to a rehabilitation camp in the countryside, leaving Liang and his older sisters alone. Nonetheless, in spite of what had happened, Liang and his sisters continued to worship Chairman Mao and the Chinese Communist Party, and tried to do all they could to be good communists. Yet Liang kept observing actions and behavior which made him question government policies and the party. Moreover, since his parents had both been labeled anti-party, he continued to have doors shut in his face, just as his father had feared. The propaganda within China was so overwhelming that it took Liang a long time to realize that something was fundamentally wrong with the entire system.

Liang was exceptionally tall, which led him to become a basketball player, although he was not accepted on to the professional athletic team because of his family's political past. He was admitted to the Hunan Teachers' College. It was there that he met Judith Shapiro, an American who had come to China to teach American literature. It was 1979, Mao had died three years earlier, and the relationship between Communist China and the United States had recently improved. Chinese were for the first time officially allowed to marry foreigners. Although they faced initial resistance to their marriage, both from school officials and Liang's family, and had to go through much bureaucratic red tape, Liang Heng and Judith Shapiro were finally married when the new head of China, Deng Xiaoping, granted permission. After Liang graduated, the couple emigrated to the United States, where he continued his education at Columbia University. He is currently working as the editor-in-chief of a Chinese language quarterly, *The Chinese Intellectual*. Judith Shapiro writes on Chinese society and also works as an interpreter and consultant on Chinese affairs.

This selection from the autobiography takes place when Liang was 12 years old before his father was arrested. It was the beginning of the Cultural Revolution in China when young people were encouraged to rise up and condemn those "enemies of the people" who would be arbitrarily and unjustly condemned for not being sufficiently loyal to the state. Mao counted on the enthusiasm and obedience of teenage boys and girls to help him carry out a wide-sweeping purge of the population which led to the arrest of millions. Rather than admit that China's economic and social programs had failed because of ill-conceived government planning, the Communist Party had chosen to blame their own mistakes on innocent citizens, claiming they had sabotaged the system, and not worked hard enough to fulfill the communist goals. The truth was that since the Communist revolution of 1949, the party had failed to provide the Chinese population with a decent standard of living and any of the basic freedoms of speech, press, or thought. In the conclusion to his book, Liang wrote that the greatest tragedy was that the Chinese people had "blind obedience" to the government. Although he knew that his parents' generation no longer had the strength, he believed that his own generation had learned to see the world critically and therefore offered great promise for China's future.[1]

---

[1] Liang Heng and Judith Shapiro, *Son of the Revolution*, 292.

"Are You a Bloodsucker?"

By the time I graduated from primary school—in May of 1966 when I was just twelve—the Cultural Revolution was already approaching. The newspapers were full of criticism of the "Three-family Village," a group of writers whose works they called "poisonous weeds." After I had been at home only two weeks, I was summoned back to school for a meeting just like a real grownup. This was the first time my classmates and I participated in what came to be known as "political study," an activity now as integral to urban Chinese life as lining up at the dining hall for a breakfast of rice gruel and *mantou*.

Our teacher read to us from the newspapers about how our class enemies were working from within to deliberately attack and smash the Party and Socialism. These "enemies" had derided the Great Leap Forward of the late fifties as "just a lot of boasting." They had slandered the dictatorship of the proletariat, and even told our great Party to "take a rest." Our teacher explained that workers, peasants, and soldiers must join together to fight against these insidious "black" intellectuals, and not be taken in by their devious and subtle methods. Even though we were still small, he said, we too had a part to play. We should begin by writing compositions denouncing our enemies. We should take out our notebooks and "open fire."

I didn't really know what to write, but I found several phrases that sounded right to me and set them down carefully:

The Three-family Village is evil. They attack the Party and Socialism. Down with the Capitalist elements! Down with Wu Han! Down with Deng Tuo! Down with Liao Mo-sha!

I felt extremely busy and important, and after the meeting I hurried home to tell my sisters everything. But they were just as excited as I was, having been through the same things in their own schools. Liang Fang put me in my place. "Everyone is denouncing those people. What makes you think you're so special?"

On the next two days we learned songs and dances with simple lyrics like "Down with the Three-family Village! Workers, peasants, and soldiers unite! Angrily open fire on the Black Gang!" There was also a pageant in which three students imitated the writers. One, bent over and gnarled, pointed upward and said, "The sun is black," while a second chortled evilly and agreed. "Not all flowers are red!" The rest of us were workers, peasants, and soldiers, and wielded huge cardboard pencils like bayonets, shouting, "Angrily open fire!"

Such activities were a lot of fun, and a welcome break from the aimless life at home in the newspaper compound. I was sorry when our meetings were over. In Changsha city, though, the wave of criticism was still mounting, and we heard more and more about a "Great Proletarian Cultural Revolution" that was to expose the Reactionary Capitalist stand of the academic authorities who opposed the Party and Socialism. It was all extremely confusing, so one rare evening when Father was at home reading his newspaper under the hanging lightbulb, I asked him what he thought.

He sighed pensively and began to reminisce, as he often did when he wanted to teach me something. "You know, before Liberation I suffered terribly. After your grandfather died, my mother couldn't feed my brother and sisters and me, so she put us in an orphanage. The rest had already died. Then after the orphanage was bombed by the Japanese, I was lucky if I could get even one bowl of rice to eat every day. Fortunately some relatives helped me go to a school, and while I was there I joined the KMT's Youth League, thinking they had the way to save China. Then in Kunming I met some Party members working underground. They taught me about Revolution and gave me books to read. I gradually understood how important Socialism was for our people, and began to participate in Party activities. I wrote poems and articles for them, and eventually they trained me to become a reporter. I was lucky enough to help found the *Hunan Daily* when Changsha was liberated. Did you know I helped to edit the very first issue ever printed? We took over the old KMT *Central Daily* and called it the *New Hunan News*. And the calligraphy for our masthead was written by Chairman Mao himself. Those were exciting days!"

I had heard these things many times before, but I loved hearing them again. It was just like the old days when Father used to tell us stories. I sat very still hoping he would continue.

"The Party saved me, and I have always believed that the Party understands far more than we ordinary people ever can what is right for our country. My greatest dream is that someday I'll fulfill the conditions and be accepted as a Party member, for there could be no greater honor for a writer on this earth. But meeting the requirements is no easy matter. Sometimes we have to struggle with ourselves. The Anti-Rightist Movement was a terrible test for me, but I conquered myself and supported the Party. It makes me very sad to see that some people have Capitalist ideas and want to oppose the only system that can build China. They're not bad men, but we should help them see their errors. You should help them, too, and at the same time you can learn for yourself about how important it is always to support the Party. You can learn about principles of Revolution so you will never make political mistakes the way they have."

My father's words filled me with pride, because he was talking to me about his own thoughts almost like a grownup. I felt I understood better why he had been so strict with Liang Fang on the question of breaking with our mother, and why she had tried so hard to reform her thought and join the League. Now I knew why Father was always asking us to study the works of Chairman Mao and write self-examinations when we had done something wrong. Although I had heard many of the same words from my teachers, coming from him they had much more impact, and I was filled with a sense of great responsibility to the Party. I resolved that I would always try to make Father proud of me, and actively help the Party to fight against Capitalism.

But it seemed I was to have no chance because the criticism movement appeared to be over. Liang Fang told me it was because Work Teams had been sent to all the schools to supervise the Cultural Revolution, but instead of helping to carry out the movement, they were upholding the leaders' conservative views and holding back the eager students. They were even collecting information about the more radical students, and labeling them counter-revolutionaries and "small Rightists" because they had gone to present petitions at the Municipal and Provincial Party Committees. Liang Fang had been an activist, and was furious. "We thought the Work Teams would support us," she said. "But instead they organized student spies to gather 'black materials' about us, and they claim *we're* obstructing the Cultural Revolution! They call us 'monsters and demons' and want to 'sweep us away,' when they're the ones who are counterrevolutionary. Everything's backwards. Well, we'll see who's right. We'll see who's doing the obstructing!"

For a while it seemed that Liang Fang was wrong. The Work Teams had control. The situation was quiet the way hot water is when the fire is down low, merely simmering. But when, on July 16, 1966, Chairman Mao swam for an hour in the Yangtze River, it boiled.

I will always remember that event, partly because it was the first occasion on which the newspaper was printed in red ink. (Later, it happened often; in fact, the printing color became an issue of unusual Revolutionary sensitivity. Once, when black ink was used when it should have been red, there were demonstrations for days.) The issue was also distributed free of charge, so the lines of people waiting for their copies stretched way down the street.

The whole nation rejoiced because our beloved leader had battled the waves for so long at the age of more than seventy, turning his feat inevitably into a metaphor. "The current of the Yangtze is strong and there are many waves, but if a person is not afraid to struggle he will overcome all difficulties," he said. His swim celebrated his strength and the strength of his policies; it was another spur in the side of Revolution.

Great congratulatory festivities were held in every unit, and the streets shook with drums and firecrackers. Changsha looked just like it did on National Day, with red flags in a row over the gateway to every unit and special red lanterns glowing at night. I felt close to this great leader who had always been a little mysterious to me. I understood swimming. I knew what it was like to feel tired after being in the water for a long time. I was twelve years old and very strong, but I doubted that I could swim for as long as Chairman Mao had. At last I knew that Chairman Mao was made of human flesh and blood, and at the same time I was moved with an even greater respect. I resolved once again to serve him with all my heart.

A little more than a week after the swim, Liang Fang came home flushed and ecstatic. "We've won," she announced. "The Work Teams are being withdrawn. The 'black materials' that they collected will be burned, the students' 'caps' will be taken off, and everybody will go home and write self-criticisms!"

Father arrived soon after, and he knew more; through the newspaper he often heard things before everyone else. He told us how while Chairman Mao had been away from

Peking in recent months, the Central Committee had taken a Revisionist line, stifling the Cultural Revolution while pretending to support it. As soon as Chairman Mao returned to the capital after his swim in the Yangtze, he held a lot of meetings, and the Cultural Revolution Directorate ordered the withdrawal of the Work Teams. Suddenly Father lowered his voice, as if he couldn't quite believe his own words. "Even Chairman Liu was criticized, and will have to write a self-examination. It's amazing." He shook his head and paused. "You'd better not tell anyone, because it's still 'internal' information."

I felt a thrill of pride that my father knew so much, and was bursting with the desire to tell my friends. But my excitement was tempered by the fact that Father was obviously troubled by the news, as if he couldn't quite accept the idea that there was conflict within the Party. I realize now that his faith was being challenged for the first time.

The secret was out soon enough, for on August 5 Chairman Mao put up his famous BOMBARD THE HEADQUARTERS poster. He criticized leaders "from the Central down to the local levels," accusing them of "suppressing Revolutionaries" and "juggling black and white." His major targets were obviously Liu Shao-qi, Chief of State and Vice-Chairman of the Communist Party; Deng Xiao-ping, General Secretary of the Central Committee Secretariat; and Tao Zhu, Secretary of the Central South Party Committee. Soon the whole city was transformed into a circus of posters. New Work Teams appeared at the *Hunan Daily*, and within a day posters went up on the modern Soviet-style office building.

Unlike the general denunciations of the past, they were now pointed attacks against specific individuals. One of the first to go was Senior Assistant Editor Meng.

I read about him with amazement. First of all, the posters said, he had willfully obstructed the Cultural Revolution. Second, he had pretended great Revolutionary purity in order to hide his landlord background. Third, his personal life was immoral and suspicious, for when his wife died, he took her older sister as his second wife. The death had been far too convenient, and the posters demanded to know who was really responsible. I felt a thrill of fear. That familiar, pompous official who had given my father the *Chairman Mao's Selected Works* as a wedding gift was a secret criminal!

Another victim was a typesetter in his fifties, a man on good terms with my family who had invited Father to his home several times. He had been a cavalry officer for the KMT, and photographs of him on his horse in all his military splendor were taken from his file and prominently displayed on the office building wall. He had of course discussed his past with the Party before, and given them everything they asked for, including the pictures. I was fascinated to discover this grizzled neighbor transformed into a grand military officer with a gleaming sword, and wondered which of my other neighbors would prove to have extraordinary alter egos.

All this was an exciting process which none of us dared to question. It seemed that every day good people were exposed as evil ones lurking behind Revolutionary masks. Friendly people were hidden serpents, Revolutionaries became counter-revolutionaries, and officials who usually rode cars to meetings might actually be murderers. It was confusing because the changes came so fast, and we used to joke with each other saying, "They dug somebody else up today," meaning that, as the newspapers liked to put it, "The telescope of Chairman Mao Thought has been used to enlarge our enemies and reveal them in their original states." Still, most people felt that the Cultural Revolution was a wonderful thing, because when our enemies were uncovered China would be much more secure. So I felt excited and happy, and wished I could do something to help.

Then one morning when I was sitting at home with nothing special to do, Little Li walked in. He was the smartest of my playmates and my good friend, and I was pleased to see him. He sat down with his customary seriousness on the edge of the bed and said, "You know, everyone has been quoting Chairman Mao, saying, 'There is no wrong in Revolution; it is right to rebel.' We should do something too. There are a lot of Capitalist tendencies in our old primary school. Remember, how Teacher Luo was always quoting the Russians? We should organize the other students and launch a Cultural Revolution there, too."

I thought this was a great idea. We would be following Chairman Mao just like the grownups, and Father would be proud of me. I suppose too I resented the teachers who had controlled and criticized me for so long, and I looked forward to a little revenge.

As it turned out, so did many of the other students, and they were delighted to be able to use Chairman Mao's stamp of approval to do what before they could only do under the cover of darkness with a slingshot and a window. Our unity was instantaneous, and we met at Little Li's apartment that evening. We had the place to ourselves because his mother lived at her own unit and his father was a proofreader who worked the night shift.

Little Li went to the newspaper to get some paper and ink and returned with his arms full.

"They support us!" he told us excitedly. "They say we can have all the supplies we need, and maybe later even an office!"

This was more than we had dared to dream of. We divided up the paper happily, one sheet for each person and a pile for me since I was to draw satirical cartoons. But then, faced with the vast open spaces before us, we suddenly discovered we didn't know what Capitalism and Revisionism really were. Little Li was the only one able to come up with anything, and he painted with a flourish ANGRILY OPEN FIRE ON THE *HUNAN DAILY'S* ATTACHED PRIMARY SCHOOL'S CAPITALIST REVISIONIST LINE!!! We all thought this was just fine, but it was obviously not enough, and we sat in worried silence until my friend Gang Di's older brother, Gang Xian, made a good suggestion. "Why don't we go out to the street and see what other people have written?"

That was the first time in my life I didn't go home to bed. We spent half the night wandering around writing down the words on the big character posters. The low gray buildings along Changsha's main streets were literally white with paper, shining in the dull yellow lamplight. The glass shop windows were unrecognizable, and posters even hung from between the parasol trees, rustling like ghosts in the night. Even at that hour people were rushing about shouting and putting up new posters, as if all the grievances that had been suppressed for so many years were coming out at once, shaking the city.

I suppose the workers felt somewhat the way we did, and were using the Cultural Revolution to get back at their superiors for everything from tiny insults to major abuses of policy. The posters on the Sun Yat-sen Road Department Store attacked the leaders for allowing the workers no freedom of discussion and willfully speaking for all. They accused the leaders of taking home government property and using influence to get scarce goods and special privileges. They denounced one leader for insulting women by touching their shoulders when he spoke to them, and another for wearing slippers to work and taking off his shirt in the office.

The leaders of the Grass Pavilion Street Residence Committee were attacked for sitting around in their offices reading newspapers and playing mah-jongg instead of resolving the people's problems, those at the car repair factory for caring more for dancing than administration and for delivering reports while dressed in their shorts. Leaders at the North District Party Committee were guilty of all of these abuses and more, including taking up the Revisionist ways of the departed Soviet experts by living in their abandoned guest houses. The lists of crimes went on and on, and it was clear to us that everything was fair game. It was hard to sort it all out, but by the time we returned to Little Li's house at 1 A.M., we knew what to write.

Gang Di denounced the music teacher for her high heels and coquettish voice. Little Monkey said Teacher Chen used a Capitalist teaching method by always telling us stories for ten minutes before class to calm us down. The son of a press photographer wrote about how the math teacher wore perfume in the summertime. Gang Xian had once been harshly punished for farting in class; he criticized the hygiene teacher for making us sit with our arms behind us and our hands on our elbows, a criticism that we all applauded heartily. But best of all was Little Li's criticism of Teacher Luo, in which his boasts of using advanced Soviet teaching methods were used as proof of his surrender to the USSR. I illustrated this with a picture of a man with a shiny bald head standing before a blackboard with a piece of chalk in one hand and a Soviet flag in the other.

I also drew Teacher Chen holding a baby with twenty heads in her arms, and the math teacher with a bottle of perfume held to her armpit and a swarm of flies buzzing around her head. ("Why does it stink?" the caption read. "It is the stink of Capitalism!") Everybody liked my cartoons very much, and we decided our work was so good that we should post it in a prominent place where everyone in the newspaper could see it.

It was near dawn when we went to put up our masterpieces on the old brick dining hall. As we scooped the messy paste out of our basin with our hands, we imagined how everyone would praise us as Revolutionary Pathbreakers. At last we put up a blank sheet and all of us signed our names. Then we separated. I went home with Little Li and didn't wake up until noon the next day.

My friend was very excited, for he had already been to the dining hall. Many grownups were crowded around our posters, praising us and saying we were very brave. I imagined the great respect we would now enjoy, so I hurried eagerly home to listen to Father's compliments.

He was there waiting for me, but he didn't look happy. "Well," he said sarcastically. "So the Revolutionary Pathbreaker is home. Did you break a path to anything to eat?"

His words stung me and I didn't answer, going to the table and picking up a cold *mantou* left over from breakfast.

"Put that down." He was very fierce. "Sit down, I want to talk to you."

Suddenly I wanted to rebel at home, too. I was tired of being controlled so tightly. Between home and school I felt I could barely move. I yelled, "It's right to rebel, it's right to rebel, it's right to rebel." I found myself stamping my feet and flailing my arms in rhythm.

"You should see how stupid you look," commented my father dryly.

"Cursing a Revolutionary Pathbreaker is what's stupid," I returned. I grabbed a piece of paper and my father's writing brush. "We'll see who needs posters," I said.

"Put down that brush," he commanded. "You never touch my brush, understand?"

I shrugged and picked up a pen and wrote in big characters, IT'S RIGHT TO REBEL! LIANG SHAN SAYS A REVOLUTIONARY PATHBREAKER IS STUPID. IF HE DOESN'T ADMIT HIS WRONGS, LIANG HENG WILL OPEN FIRE ON HIM!! I marched into his bedroom and stuck my poster on the foot of his bed with a thumbtack.

But Father was only amused. "If Chairman Mao knew, I wonder what he'd think of you?" he asked.

"Chairman Mao wants us to rebel," I answered immediately.

"Calm down now, why don't you. Sit down," he said gently. "Let's talk together."

Unfortunately, my experiences as a Rebel were only an evening long, so in the end I sat down, my self-righteous passion transformed into the apprehension of a small boy.

Father said, "Last night you did an unglorious thing. You thought you were really something, didn't you, with so many people looking at your cartoons? But why did you want to be so disrespectful to your teachers? Don't you understand how disgraceful your behavior is?"

It was unbearable to be lectured after I had expected so much glory. I answered bravely, "Doesn't Chairman Mao want us to criticize Capitalist thought? If teachers have Capitalist thought shouldn't they be criticized? Didn't you tell me yourself that we must obey the Party and carry out the Cultural Revolution?"

"Capitalist thought?" he exclaimed. "Do you think the things you drew pictures of were Capitalist thought? Your teachers were so good to you, giving you knowledge when you were still so small, training you, caring for you. And then not only don't you thank them, you insult and humiliate them. Of course it's right to heed Chairman Mao's call, but the purpose of this movement is to ferret out our enemies, not to attack our friends. Now I want you to take a book of quotations from Chairman Mao and study it carefully. Find out what he really wrote." Father went into his bedroom and study, where there were bookcases with several hundred volumes, and returned thumbing through a precious copy of the *Quotations of Chairman Mao,* the "Little Red Book" that as yet had been distributed only to high-ranking cadres and newspapermen. "Look here," he said. "Chairman Mao may have said, 'It's right to rebel,' but he also said, 'Among Revolutionary comrades, one should not use a rough manner.'"

I took the book and looked at the place Father *had* marked, and my heart hesitated because he was right. Chairman Mao had said those words. "Eat now," Father said, "and think about it. This afternoon you can study the *Quotations,* and when you have finished you can write a self-examination for me."

It was 2 p.m., and my father went to work. I was miserable. I knew I had been wrong. "Although the teachers have Capitalist tendencies," I wrote, "they are still Revolutionary comrades. We should help them, not insult them. I think I was wrong . . ."

When Father returned after five he held out his hand for my paper. I gave it to him and he read it carefully. "Good," he said finally. "But I think you need to do one more thing, because what you did was very wrong. You should go to your teachers' houses and apologize."

My heart sank. What would my classmates say? That I was a coward? A traitor? But Father stood there smoking, and his eyes bored through his glasses and deep into me as if they saw everything. I moved reluctantly through the door.

It must have taken me a full half hour to walk to the Attached Primary School, which was really just ten minutes from our house. I found new alleyways among the brick buildings and lingered at the basketball court, always imagining how angry the teachers must be, and wondering whether they would ignore me or yell at me. When I finally came to Teacher Luo's dormitory I was in such a state that I would have run home if a cat had darted out of the bushes.

Teacher Luo's wife was taking the laundry in from the balcony. "Liang Heng!" she cried, and it was too late to escape. Then she called inside. "Luo Qing-guang! Liang Heng is here!"

Teacher Luo came out immediately, and to my utter shock, he was smiling and nodding as if he hadn't seen me for a long time. "Liang Heng! Come right upstairs and have some tea. We'll have a talk."

When I was uncomfortably seated with a dish of candy before me and a cup of tea at my elbow, Teacher Luo said, "Your father came to see me this afternoon." He continued gently, "It doesn't matter, it all belongs to the past."

I said, "Teacher Luo, please pardon me. I'm very sorry."

He said, "Forget about it. If you ever have any question about your schoolwork, you're always welcome here."

A very special feeling choked me, and I got up in confusion and nodded and ran out the door so he wouldn't see me crying, nearly knocking over the dish of candy as I went. How could he be so kind to me after what I had done to him? Didn't he remember that I had painted him with the Soviet flag in his hand?

Father had been to see all the other teachers, too, and they all treated me kindly and accepted my apologies. But as I walked home, I was in a panic for fear one of my classmates would see me and ask where I'd been. I would never tell them what I had done. From then on I would choose my methods more carefully, so that I would never again be placed in such an ignoble position.

Of course, I had no intention of giving up rebellion, not when the whole country was involved in the Cultural Revolution. The next step was to give our Rebel group a more formal status. Little Li organized us, about thirty young teenage boys from the newspaper, and after much discussion we chose the name Criticize Revisionism Struggle Team. I did not speak so loudly as before my apology to the teachers, but I certainly was an active member. We announced ourselves on red paper one sunny afternoon, all thirty of our names painted in black ink. The *Hunan Daily* Cultural Revolution Committee gave us an unbelievably big two-room office, a printing press and paper, blankets, and a red flag. No one could have been prouder than Little Li and I as we surveyed our new domain.

But the next morning, as Little Li, Gang Di, Gang Xian, and I were writing our blackboard newspaper, the photographer's son ran up gasping, "Something terrible, something terrible. They don't want to be in our organization anymore."

Little Li's eyebrows were as straight as a sword across his square face as he demanded, "Who doesn't want to be in our organization?"

"All of them. They've taken their names away."

We ran over to the dining hall and were dumbfounded. Twenty-three names had been inked out, and our red poster now looked like a slice of watermelon full of black pits. The seven remaining names were all those of the sons of intellectuals: editors, reporters, the photographer and the art editor.

We stood looking at each other. Finally Little Li spoke what was in our minds "Well, we'll keep going anyway. We'll protect Chairman Mao's struggle to the death." His words were the same as those we heard on broadcasts, but braver and more inspiring. We nodded our heads resolutely.

But before we'd recovered from our shock, something even worse happened. One of our ex-comrades walked by and sneered at us and then spat on the cement at our feet. "You sons of Reactionary Capitalist stinking intellectuals. Run and look at your fathers' big character posters. Then hurry home and criticize *them*, why don't you."

I was simply unable to comprehend his words. My father wasn't a powerful official, had never accepted bribes or used public furniture, had never used power to criticize a worker unfairly. He was just a low-ranking cadre working for a Party newspaper, and no one in the whole world loved Chairman Mao better than he. How could there be posters about him? How could anyone say he had Capitalist thought?

As in a dream, we hurried to the office building. There had been a lot of new activity. Now the posters stretched all the way up to the fourth floor, and ropes hung with still more had been strung from one wing of the *L* to the other. To get through, you had to push posters aside like hanging curtains. We began the painful search for our fathers' names. What would have been a game the day before was now a nightmare. We found Little Li's father first. PUBLICLY EXPOSE THE KMT SPY LI XIAO-XIONG!!! the poster cried.

> Although Li Xiao-xiong is an old Party member, he wears his Party cloth to disguise his true mission. Before Liberation, he was an active reporter for the KMT's *Central Daily,* and he volunteered to stay behind as a spy when we routed Chiang Kai-shek's dogs and they fled to Taiwan. Every day he gathers information for them, and works against us from within. As a proofreader, he has had many opportunities to show his hatred of the Party, as on the occasion when he deliberately turned the character "ten thousand" upside down. But our Great Leader Chairman Mao will live ten thousand and ten thousand years despite such pernicious spies. Down with Li Xiao-xiong!!!!!

I couldn't believe it. Little Li had told me so many times about his father's glorious career as an underground Party member before Liberation. At times I had even been envious, wishing I could be as proud of my own father. This was like seeing him in a distorting mirror. Could Little Li have been lying to me? I turned to look at my friend. He was staring like a statue and biting his lower lip, while two tears rolled down his motionless face.

Then Gang Di pulled me by the sleeve. He had found my father's posters. I followed him numbly through the gaily painted paper, still believing there had been a mistake. But then I saw the terrible words, burning characters on brilliant yellow paper. EXPOSE THE PLOT OF THE REACTIONARY SCHOLAR LIANG SHAN TO THE LIGHT OF DAY!!!!!

There were too many sheets, maybe ten or more, each as tall as a man. And every word

engraved itself on my heart with a blazing knife, every phrase struck me with a blow that was even greater than terror. I would never believe the ground was steady again.

> Liang Shan is a thoroughly Capitalist newsman, our newspaper's Three-family Village. He has used the knowledge given to him by the Party to attack the Party, writing many Reactionary articles. In one of them, an essay about the growth of a sunflower, he dared to fart that the flower relies on its own lust for life. How evil, how poisonous! The Three-family Village said the sun had dark shadows, meaning the Party has made errors. But Liang Shan says the sunflower doesn't need the sun, at all! His insidious idea is that China can be strong without the Communist Party. Isn't this singing the same tune as Capitalist KMT Reactionary Revisionism? Liang Shan is worse than Capitalism, fiercer than the KMT, more dangerous than Revisionism. Down with Liang Shan!!!!!

The poster went on to a second topic, STRIP AWAY LIANG SHAN'S SKIN!!!!!

> That Liang Shan opposes the Party and Socialism is only natural. Let's investigate his history. His father was a doctor who came from Zhejiang to Hunan through tricking his "private patients" out of their money. So Liang Shan learned this skill from his family. When he was young, he eagerly entered the KMT's Youth League. His ex-wife is a Rightist, and she certainly became a Rightist under his influence. Then he saw by what happened to her that it won't do to oppose the Party openly, and he used articles and poetry to try to undermine it secretly. So his injury to the Revolution is even greater than his wife's. Chairman Mao teaches us, "Sham is sham, and the mask must be stripped off." Now the Great Proletarian Cultural Revolution is stripping off Liang Shan's skin to reveal his true appearance!!!!!

The third section went:

LIANG SHAN IS A BLOODSUCKER!!!!!

Liang Shan has not only failed to make a contribution to the Revolution, but has stolen a lot away. Although in the past he gave up a level of his salary, that was his pretense of progress! In fact, he earned a lot of extra money for his articles. Every penny he earned was the blood of the people. He used the blood he sucked away to fatten himself up, and what did he give the people? Not artwork, but shit, garbage, poisonous weeds!!!!!

The fourth section:

WHAT DID LIANG SHAN ACTUALLY DO?

For many years Liang Shan edited a magazine called *Correspondent* for our young newspapermen, and his sole purpose was to propagandize the Capitalist news viewpoint and to instruct our young reporters in Western news techniques. He said news should be "true," and to him this meant it should attack the Party's faults, and even slander our Party. He said, "A reporter should have power, and when he needs information he should use his courage and ingenuity to get it by any means possible." Isn't his meaning clear? He wants intellectuals to lead the country! Moreover, he used the magazine to gild Western writers. In all those years, he used only one quotation from Chairman Mao, but hundreds from Tolstoy, Balzac, Shakespeare, Mark Twain. . . . Liang Shan! Your eyes are blind. Go for a walk on Wall Street, why don't you? Here, you will bump into things until your head is bloody. Are you Chinese or a foreigner's dog? You have given our young reporters too many poisonous ideas. We now order Liang Shan to confess his crimes, or else we will break his dog's head!!!!!

There was more, but the words wouldn't stay still. I was trembling all over. The bright paper posters floating about me had become walls of iron, the unknown sandaled feet glimpsed beyond them those of enemies. Everything was backwards, distorted, corrupted, insane. I didn't know if I was dreaming or if my life at home was a dream. I hugged myself, pinching my arms, but I didn't wake up. I closed my eyes and opened them but the words were still there. My Revolutionary father was an enemy. My father whose dream it was to join the Party was a Capitalist. How had things been ruined? Why had he ruined things? I didn't know where to put my misery and my hatred. I would never trust my perception of reality again.

Then I discovered the press photographer's son standing a few feet away from me crying softly. Dazed, we turned back toward our headquarters, equally silent, equally miserable, equally afraid to see anyone, equally afraid to go home. Little Li and the Gang brothers were already there, ashen and waiting. It was almost as if an instinct bred in us through our short careers in Chairman Mao Thought told us to return to our Revolutionary base, to turn automatically toward the Revolution for security when our homes fell away beneath us. We had no words for each other, but we felt tremendously close. And we knew that even though our fathers were now Capitalists and spies, we must go on rebelling. What we did not yet understand was that from that day forth we had lost the right to express our love and our loyalty; Revolutionary fervor would no longer be permitted to us. But we did have some kind of premonition that our office would be taken away.

Sure enough, near dinnertime a worker in glasses named Zhou Sa-wu arrived with about ten of our classmates at his heels. He didn't have much to say. "This is no place for you, stinking intellectuals' sons. Get out."

Then the other children grabbed our writing materials and pushed us out. Someone kicked me hard in the back of the leg. The door slammed sharply behind us.

We stood for a long time in the courtyard hugging trees and looking up at our old headquarters. At last we began to cry.

When the signal for dinner sounded, there was nothing to do but walk slowly home. We set off in our various directions, hating ourselves and the world, envying our Revolutionary classmates, afraid of the knowledge that something terrible had begun, not yet comprehending its magnitude. I barely registered the loudspeaker's announcement that there would be an important radio broadcast that evening, and I passed the basketball court without really seeing the people preparing drums, flags, blank red posters, and fresh white paint for the parade. I was no longer part of that world. I had been kicked off the team. I was an outcast.

Someone had taken the lock off our door, but it was shut tight. Our home presented a peculiar, sad, unfriendly appearance, which only deepened my misery. I pushed my way in and discovered Father sitting in a dense cloud of cigarette smoke, which he was concentrating on making thicker, the butts lying on the wooden floor like wreckage after some disaster. He barely moved when I came in. It hurt me to look at him, so I headed toward the drawer where the meal tickets were kept. My hand shook on the handle.

Then it was as if something swept over me, and I found myself swinging around, screaming out the question in my heart. "Father, is it true that you're a bloodsucker?" Suspicion, love, anger, sympathy, and hatred struggled against one another. I felt as if I would explode.

Father was silent, signaling that he had heard me only by crushing out his cigarette and lighting a new one. I stared at the stub on the floor, long, white, and barely smoked.

"Tell me," I demanded. "Tell me, you should tell me. I have to know."

He remained silent, not meeting my eyes.

I wanted to shake him. "Why won't you say anything?"

He finally spoke, in what was close to a whisper. "You should always believe the Party and Chairman Mao."

He hadn't answered my question, and I stood staring and waiting.

He made another effort. "The Cultural Revolution is a mass movement. The people who criticized me have deep proletarian feelings and a great love for Chairman Mao." I could hardly believe my ears. It was all true, then. Father continued, "I've made a lot of mistakes. I should examine myself thoroughly. But as long as I'm faithful to the Party and Chairman Mao, it won't be long before I mend my errors."

I was scarcely listening. I could only repeat his crimes numbly, as if reciting a lesson. "Is it true you said China can be strong without the Party? Is it true you used articles and poems to undermine it secretly? What about how you tried to teach Capitalist news reporting? How do you explain those things?"

My father's hand trembled as he struck another match. Then in the silence we heard a great clattering on the stairs, and Liang Fang and Liang Wei-ping burst into the room. They were both crying; and they ran directly to their bed and threw themselves onto it, hugging the pillows. Their sobs were terrible in the silence.

Soon Liang Fang started accusing Father. "I'm so miserable being born into a family like this. First I had a mother who prevented me from joining the League. Now that I'm finally accepted as a Revolutionary, you have to ruin everything. Look," she cried, taking out a piece of paper. "Tonight I was supposed to be a marshal at the parades. This was the plan for the march. Do you think I can possibly face anyone now?" With a wail, she ripped her map into little pieces.

Father sat by the table with his head in his hands, passively accepting Liang Fang's fury as if he deserved it. He reached automatically for his pack of cigarettes, but it was empty. Liang Wei-ping, always the gentlest of us, nudged Liang Fang as if asking her to control herself and went into the other room and got another pack. As she handed it to Father I asked him, "Do you know what they called us today? 'Sons of Capitalist Reactionary stinking intellectuals.' They've cut us out of all their activities, kicked us out of the office. They won't let us do anything anymore."

Father raised his head and repeated, "You should believe the Party. Believe Chairman Mao." His words sounded like a prayer, a principle kept in his heart to invoke in times of trouble. They had been the key to his spirit for the past twenty years.

But Liang Fang raged. "Others don't believe *you*! They say you're a Capitalist, a bloodsucker, a foreigner's dog!"

Then my father stood up, his face white, his words tumbling out in one breath. "It's because I'm none of those things that I believe the Party and Chairman Mao. I've done nothing to wrong you. You can continue to participate in the Revolution. If you want to, you can break off with me. Go live at school if you like. But I'll tell you one thing. No matter how you hate me, I've always been loyal to Chairman Mao. And I've always supported the Party and Socialism."

"If I have to go, I'll go!" she shouted, grabbing at her bedding and clothing. "I don't want this counterrevolutionary family. I don't need this counterrevolutionary father and mother!"

Liang Wei-ping followed her older sister's lead. "I'm going too," she said with resignation. "Maybe it's better that way." She stood up and started gathering her things.

Father's eyes were red. "Go, go, all of you go. I won't blame you. I don't want to hold you back."

I don't know how the evening would have ended if the loudspeaker hadn't sounded outside our window. "The Red radio waves have happy news. Everyone please tune in and listen carefully. Everyone please tune in."

From force of habit cultivated only over the last few months, we rushed to the tiny transistor on the table. We arranged ourselves around it and laid our heads down so we could concentrate. Crackling from the radio came, "The August 8th Decision of the Central Committee of the Chinese Communist Party Concerning the Great Proletarian Cultural Revolution."

It seemed that one of the purposes of the statement was to clarify the targets of the

Cultural Revolution. And as we listened the heavy stone that we bore on our backs became lighter and lighter, especially when we heard the Fifth Article.

> Who are our enemies and who are our friends? . . . The main target of the present movement is those within the Party who are in authority and are taking the Capitalist road. The strictest care should be taken to distinguish between the anti-Party, anti-Socialist Rightists and those who support the Party and Socialism but have said or done something wrong or have written bad articles or other works. . . .

When all "Sixteen Articles" were finished, there were tears of joy in Father's eyes and he said triumphantly, "See, your father is no counterrevolutionary. I'm the third type of cadre, someone who has made serious mistakes but is not an anti-Party anti-Socialist Rightist."

My sisters smiled and looked embarrassed at having been so upset; I felt ashamed that I had thought so harshly of Father. We began to discuss the posters calmly and decided that since he had already talked with the Party about his membership in the KMT Youth League and about our mother, those problems wouldn't be regarded as serious crimes. His failure to quote Chairman Mao frequently in his writings would be considered a matter for education. The foul language and abuse in the posters merely showed the passion of the people and were not to be taken seriously.

Just as we were enjoying our renewed intimacy, we heard a blast of firecrackers and drums like an earthquake under our feet. Liang Fang jumped up as if she had forgotten something. "The parade!" she cried. "Oh

Father, I *do* want to go live at school, but that's just for convenience in the Revolution, not because I want to move away from home."

So Father helped her to pack her bag, and tucked some cakes and sugar in the side to show he had forgiven her. She left in a great hurry because she was late, and we stood on the balcony and watched her go. From then on, she was always off making Revolution somewhere, and never really lived at home again.

Liang Wei-ping went into the kitchen to cook noodles because we had been so upset we had missed going to the dining hall. I sat and talked with Father. I was still in shock because of what had happened to me that afternoon.

Father comforted me. "Don't be discouraged. Even if you don't participate in their group, your thought can follow the Cultural Revolution and you can still learn from it. Every day you can read the newspapers, and you and I will have our own study class, and make a plan for reading the whole of Chairman Mao's works. We'll sit together in the evenings and discuss them." I felt a lot better, because I loved reading with my father. Still, nothing could make up for being excluded by my classmates.

After dinner, Father suddenly said, as if just struck by the idea, "Maybe we should look through our things and see if we have anything that's not so good. If we get rid of it now, it might save us a lot of trouble later on. Remember how when China and Russia broke relations I had to get rid of all my books about the Soviet Union?"

So we went into the large inner room and looked through his books. He selected only a few, pulling them out with regret; they included Liu Shao-qi's famous *Discussion on the Training of a Communist Party Member.* I knew the earnest way my father always read everything, underlining and annotating; every book represented hours of labor and thought. We went through the magazines, too, where I came on a picture of Liu Shao-qi standing with Chairman Mao. "What about this one?" I asked. "Should we throw away the part with Chairman Liu on it?"

"Oh no, better not do that. We'd better turn it in to the Work Team," my father answered. (At the time, I thought he was being overcautious, but as it turned out, his political experience saved us from disaster. Our downstairs neighbors cut Liu Shao-qi out of the picture, and they were denounced for deliberately ruining a photograph of Chairman Mao. This kind of thing happened so often that eventually a rule was established that whenever someone wanted to replace an old picture of Chairman Mao with a new one, he had to notify the leaders of his unit and get their permission.)

The books and pictures made a small pile on the table, and with them as reminders of his crimes, Father sat down with his brush and ink to criticize himself. When I woke up in the middle of the night to go to the bathroom he was writing, his normally well-groomed hair in disorder, concentrating so hard that he didn't even hear me get up.

Questions

1. Why did Liang Heng and his classmates condemn their teachers?

2. Why did his father, Liang Shan, object to their actions?

3. How do Liang Heng and his sisters react to the Communist Party's condemnation of their father?

4. What does this chapter reveal about the impact on the family of the Communist Party's policies?

Recommended Reading

Wei Jingsheng. *The Courage to Stand Alone: Letters from Prison and other Stories.* New York: Viking Penguin, 1997.

Chang, Jung. *Wild Swans: Three Daughters of China.* New York: Doubleday, 1992.

Films

Wild Swans
Farewell My Concubine

CHAPTER 7

Andrei Sakharov

Andrei Sakharov was born on May 21, 1921, in Moscow. He received a doctorate in physics at the age of 26 and soon began doing research leading to the development of the first Soviet hydrogen bomb. Sakharov was given recognition and material rewards for his scientific work. Concerned over the deaths caused by radioactive fallout from the testing of the hydrogen bomb in the early 1960s, he wrote an essay calling for the end of nuclear tests and reductions in nuclear arms. While remaining loyal to the Soviet system, he hoped that the Cold War conflict could be gradually reduced through concerted efforts working toward peaceful coexistence. During the early 1960s other Soviet citizens had begun to protest violations of civil rights, and Sakharov soon became involved in the dissident movement. When the Soviet government invaded Czechoslovakia in 1968 to crush the reform movement and prevent Czechoslovakia from breaking away from the Soviet bloc, Sakharov and other dissidents protested. In 1970 he founded the Committee for Human Rights.

In 1975 the Soviet government signed the Helsinki Accords, declaring that they would uphold certain human rights principles. Soviet dissidents, including Sakharov, decided to challenge their government's violation of these principles, bringing attention to it in the international press. The dissidents also called for the right of emigration. Immediately, Sakharov's activities drew the attention of Soviet authorities and he lost his position, his access to scientific laboratories, and his material perks. They even refused to permit him to accept the Noble Peace Prize in 1975; his wife, Elena Bonner, went to Stockholm to accept it on his behalf.

With the Soviet invasion of Afghanistan in 1979, Sakharov immediately condemned the war and called for an immediate withdrawal. To silence him, Soviet authorities sent him to live in internal exile in the city of Gorky. For the next six years, he lived in Gorky but continued to communicate with the outside world with the help of his wife Elena Bonner. To bring attention to his cause, he also engaged in several protest hunger fasts, a tactic used by Gandhi and other human rights activists.

When Mikhail Gorbachev came into power in 1985, he immediately embarked upon a policy of reform, known as restructuring and openness. Soon thereafter he telephoned Sakharov and invited him to return to Moscow, ending his exile. In 1989, the first free elections were held in the Soviet Union, and Sakharov was elected to the Soviet parliament or Duma. Nonetheless he did not cease speaking out and in his last speech to the Duma, he condemned the Soviet government's violent treatment of peaceful demonstrators in the republic of Georgia. He died several days later on December 14, 1989. Many Soviet citizens view Sakharov as one of the key figures in bringing about the disintegration of the former Soviet Union and the creation of a new democratic Russia.

1968
The Prague Spring.
Reflections on Progress, Peaceful Coexistence, and Intellectual Freedom

By the beginning of 1968, I felt a growing compulsion to speak out on the fundamental issues of our age. I was influenced by my life experience and a feeling of personal responsibility, reinforced by the part I'd played in the development of the hydrogen bomb, the special knowledge I'd gained about thermonuclear warfare, my bitter struggle to ban nuclear testing, and my familiarity with the Soviet system. My reading and my discussions with Tamm (and others) had acquainted me with the notions of an open society, convergence, and world government (Tamm was skeptical about the last two points). I shared the hopes of Einstein, Bohr, Russell, Szilard, and other Western intellectuals that these notions, which had gained currency after World War II, might ease the tragic crisis of our age. In 1968, I took my decisive step by publishing *Reflections on Progress, Peaceful Coexistence, and Intellectual Freedom.*

My work on *Reflections* happened to coincide with the Prague Spring. A year earlier, I'd finally bought a short-wave receiver, and I listened once in a while to the BBC and Voice of America, especially to programs on the Six Day War. In 1968, I began tuning in regularly to the news from Czechoslovakia,

and heard Ludvík Vaculík's stirring manifesto, "2,000 Words"—and much more besides. Zhivlyuk and Roy Medvedev supplied additional details during their increasingly frequent visits.

What so many of us in the socialist countries had been dreaming of seemed to be finally coming to pass in Czechoslovakia: democracy, including freedom of expression and abolition of censorship; reform of the economic and social systems; curbs on the power of the security forces, limiting them to defense against external threats; and full disclosure of the crimes of the Stalin era (the "Gottwald era" in Czechoslovakia). Even from afar, we were caught up in all the excitement and hopes and enthusiasm of the catchwords: "Prague Spring" and "socialism with a human face."

Events in the Soviet Union echoed those in Prague, but on a much reduced scale. In the campaign in defense of Ginzburg, Galanskov, and Lashkova [who were tried in January 1968], more than a thousand signatures—an extraordinary number under Soviet conditions—were collected, mainly from the intelligentsia. A few years earlier, no one would have dreamed of publicly defending such "hostile elements." Later, after 1968, when everyone understood the consequences for himself and his family, even sympathetic people refused to lend their names to such initiatives. The signature campaign and other similar efforts were harbingers of the human rights movement, a sort of Prague Spring in miniature. They frightened the KGB into taking tough counter-measures: firing, blacklisting, public reprimand, expulsion from the Party.

To my shame, I must admit that the signature campaign simply passed me by at the time, just as had the 1964 banishment of Joseph Brodsky from Leningrad and the 1965 arrests of Sinyavsky and Daniel. For some reason, Roy Medvedev and Zhivlyuk delayed telling me about the campaign until it was over.

Sometime around the end of January 1968, Zhivlyuk suggested that I write an article on the role of the intelligentsia in today's world. The idea appealed to me, and I soon set to work. I did most of my writing at the Installation after working hours, from seven to midnight, and brought the draft home with me when I visited Moscow. Klava's attitude toward my project was ambivalent: she knew full well what I was doing and the potential consequences for our family, but she allowed me complete freedom of action. By this time her health was beginning to deteriorate, draining more and more of her physical and emotional energy.

The title I gave my essay, *Reflections on Progress, Peaceful Coexistence, and Intellectual Freedom*, seemed appropriate in tone for a non-specialist inviting his readers to join him in a discussion of public issues. Its scope far exceeded Zhivlyuk's original suggestion, encompassing virtually the entire range of my future public activities and laying a theoretical foundation for them. I wanted to alert my readers to the grave perils threatening the human race—thermonuclear extinction, ecological catastrophe, famine, an uncontrolled population explosion, alienation, and dogmatic distortion of our conception of reality. I argued

for convergence, for a rapprochement of the socialist and capitalist systems that could eliminate or substantially reduce these dangers, which had been increased many times over by the division of the world into opposing camps. Economic, social, and ideological convergence should bring about a scientifically governed, democratic, pluralistic society free of intolerance and dogmatism, a humanitarian society which would care for the Earth and its future, and would embody the positive features of both systems.

I went into some detail on the threat posed by thermonuclear missiles—their enormous destructive power, their relatively low cost, the difficulty of defending against them. I wrote about the crimes of Stalinism and the need to expose them fully (unlike the Soviet press, I pulled no punches), and about the vital importance of freedom of opinion and democracy. I stressed the value of progress, but warned that it must be scientifically managed and not left to chance. I discussed the need for substantive changes in foreign policy. My essay outlined a positive, global program for mankind's future; I freely acknowledged that my vision was somewhat Utopian, but I remain convinced that the exercise was worthwhile.

Later on, life (and Lusia) would teach me to pay more attention to the defense of individual victims of injustice, and a further step followed: recognition that human rights and an *open society* are fundamental to international confidence, security, and progress.

I prefaced *Reflections* with an epigraph taken from Goethe's *Faust*:

He alone is worthy of life and freedom
Who each day does battle for them anew!

The heroic romanticism of these lines echoes my own sense of life as both wonderful and tragic, and I still consider them a fitting choice for my essay. Years later I learned that Lusia, who then knew nothing about me, was captivated by the youthful and romantic spirit of this verse, and it established a spiritual bond between us before we ever met.

Another aspect of the truth that I prize and that complements Goethe's metaphor is contained in the following lines by Alexander Mezhirov:

I lie in a trench under fire.
A man enters his home, from the cold.

Mezhirov understands that struggle, suffering, and heroic exploits are not ends in themselves, but are worthwhile only insofar as they enable other people to lead normal, peaceful lives. Not everyone need spend time in the trenches. The meaning of life is life itself: that daily routine which demands its own form of unobtrusive heroism. Goethe's lines are often read as an imperative call to revolutionary struggle, but that seems to me unjustified; there is nothing peremptory or fanatical in them once they are stripped of their poetic imagery. *Reflections* rejected all extremes, the intransigence shared by revolutionaries and reactionaries alike. It called for compromise and for progress moderated by enlightened conservatism and caution. Marx notwithstanding, evolution is a better "locomotive of history" than revolution: the "battle" I had in mind was nonviolent.

I rewrote *Reflections* several times, and did, I feel, finally achieve a logical and coherent presentation of my thoughts. But the essay's literary quality leaves a lot to be desired; it suffered from my inexperience and lack of editorial counsel and, in some sections, from a lack of literary taste.

By mid-April, the essay was almost completed. Zhores Medvedev has written that I tried to keep its contents a secret by having several different secretaries type *Reflections,* and Solzhenitsyn has unfortunately repeated this fiction as evidence of my supposed naïveté.[1] The manuscript was in fact typed by a single secretary who had secret clearance. I realized that a copy might well end up in the KGB's ideological department, but I had no wish to lay myself open to allegations of engaging in covert activities. In my situation, any attempts along these lines were bound to be uncovered, and I have always shunned clandestine behavior as a matter of principle.

As far as I know, the KGB did not intervene until *Reflections* began to circulate in Moscow. Before that, it's probable that only the counterintelligence department knew of the manuscript's existence, and they didn't care At the end of May, however, the KGB was alerted at the Installation and customs control was reinforced in Moscow. I've been told that two KGB divisions (this may well be an exaggeration) were involved in "Operation Sakharov," the fruitless attempt to prevent the circulation of *Reflections.* But I'm getting ahead of my story.

On the last Friday in April, I flew to Moscow for the holidays, bringing a typed copy of the essay in my briefcase. Roy Medvedev came to see me that evening, and I exchanged *Reflections* for the final chapters of his book on Stalin.

Medvedev claimed that Sergei Trapeznikov, head of the Central Committee's science department, was exerting a negative influence on Brezhnev and through him on domestic and foreign policy in general. I was persuaded to include a reference to Trapeznikov in *Reflections;* I now regret this personal attack, which was entirely out of character for me and alien to the style and spirit of an essay calling for reason, tolerance, and compromise. Moreover, my comments were based on uncorroborated hearsay; ever since meeting Trapeznikov in 1970, I have found it difficult to believe that he could have played a significant political role.

Medvedev came back a few days later. He had shown my essay to friends (which I had given him permission to do); they considered it a historic document and he passed on some of their written comments. (These were unsigned, but the authors probably included Evgeny Gnedin, Yuri Zhivlyuk and Eugenia Ginzburg, plus a few Old Bolsheviks and writers.) After adding the new paragraphs on Trapeznikov, and making a few other changes and corrections, I gave the manuscript back to Medvedev. He was going to produce a dozen or more carbon copies. Some of these, he warned me, might end up abroad. I replied that I had taken that into account. (We were communicating in writing to foil eavesdroppers.)

On May 18, I paid a call on Khariton at his dacha. In the course of our conversation, I mentioned that I was writing an essay on war and peace, ecology, and freedom of expression. Khariton asked what I intended to do with it. "I'll give it to samizdat," I answered. He became excited and said: "For God's sake, don't do that." "It's too late to stop it now," I confessed. Khariton became even more agitated and changed the subject. Later he pretended that this conversation never took place, which was fine from my point of view.

Early in June (probably on the 6th), I traveled with Khariton to the Installation in his personal railroad car, which contained a spacious compartment for him, a compartment for guests, the conductor's compartment, a kitchenette, and a lounge which could sleep several persons on folding cots (I often slept there myself). After the waitress had cleared the supper dishes and left the lounge, Khariton broached a subject that was plainly difficult for him: "Andropov called me in. His agents have been finding [in the course of clandestine searches] copies of your essay all over the place—it's circulating illegally, and it will cause a lot of harm if it gets abroad. Andropov opened his safe and showed me a copy. [From the way Khariton said this, it was obvious that he hadn't been allowed to examine the copy—hardly the way to treat a three-time Hero of Socialist Labor.] Andropov asked me to talk to you. You ought to withdraw your manuscript from circulation."

"Why don't you take a look at the copy I've got with me?" I suggested.

Khariton retired to his compartment, where he had a desk and a table lamp. I fell right to sleep in the guest compartment, despite the stuffiness of that prerevolutionary railroad car.

In the morning we met again.

"Well, what do you think?" I inquired.

"It's awful."

"The style?"

Khariton grimaced. "No, not the style. It's the *content* that's awful!"

"The contents reflect my beliefs. I accept full responsibility for circulating my essay. It's too late to withdraw it."

For the rest of June, I continued to tinker with the essay, but succeeded only in making it longer, not better. I sent a copy of the slightly revised version to Brezhnev, and showed another copy to Boris Efimov, who preferred the first version. I was unaware that an attempt had already been made to send my essay abroad through a *New York Times* correspondent; he had refused, fearing a provocation.

In mid-June, Andrei Amalrik gave a copy of *Reflections* to Karel van het Reve, a Dutch correspondent.

On July 10, a few days after returning to the Installation and exactly seven years after my clash with Khrushchev, I tuned in the BBC (or VOA?) evening broadcast and heard my name. The announcer reported that on July 6, the Dutch newspaper *Het Parool* had published an article by A. D. Sakharov, a member of the Soviet Academy of Sciences who, according to Western experts, had worked on the Soviet hydrogen bomb. Sakharov called for rapprochement between the USSR and the West, and for disarmament; warned of the dangers of thermonuclear war, ecological catastrophe, and world famine; condemned dogmatism, terror, and Stalin's crimes; and urged democratization, freedom of conscience, and convergence as the way to escape universal destruction. (I don't now recall the broadcast's exact words, but this is the gist of what I hope I heard, and in any case did read

later in a number of well-informed reviews of my essay.)

The die was cast. That evening I had the most profound feeling of satisfaction. The following day I was due to fly to Moscow, but stopped at my office at nine in the morning and noticed Khariton at his desk.

"Foreign stations announced yesterday that my article's been published abroad."

"I knew it would happen" was all Khariton could say. He looked crushed.

Two hours later, I left for the airfield. I was never to set foot in my office again.

Toward the end of July, Slavsky summoned me to the Ministry. A translation of *Reflections* from the Dutch newspaper lay on his desk. Your article?" he asked. I glanced through it and answered in the affirmative.

"Is it the same one you sent to the Central Committee?"

"Not quite, I revised it a bit."

"Give me the new text. Will you protest publication abroad of a preliminary draft without your permission?"

"No, I won't do that. I take full responsibility for the article as published, since it faithfully reflects my opinions."

Slavsky obviously wanted me to make some protest, if only about minor editorial details, but I didn't fall into that trap.

Clearly disappointed, Slavsky made no effort to hide his displeasure: "We won't discuss your opinions today. Party secretaries have been calling from all over the country, demanding firm measures to put a stop to counterrevolutionary propaganda in my ministry. I want you to think about what you've done to us and to yourself. You've got to disown this anti-Soviet publication. I'll read your revised version. Come back three days from now at the same time."

Three days later, Slavsky continued the lecture:

"I've taken a look, and the two versions are practically the same. It's a dangerous muddle. You write about the mistakes of the personality cult as though the Party had never condemned them. You criticize the leaders' privileges—you've enjoyed the same privileges yourself. Individuals who bear immense responsibilities, difficult burdens, deserve *some* advantages. It's all for the good of the cause. You pit the intelligentsia against the leadership, but aren't we, who manage the country, the real intelligentsia of the nation?

"What you wrote about convergence is Utopian nonsense. Capitalism can't be made humane. Their social programs and employee stock plans aren't steps toward socialism. And there's no trace of state capitalism in the USSR. We'll never give up the advantages of our system, and capitalists aren't interested in your convergence either.

"The Party has condemned the cult of personality, but without a strong hand, we could never have rebuilt our economy after the war or broken the American atomic monopoly—you yourself helped do that. You have no moral right to judge our generation—Stalin's generation—for its mistakes, for its brutality; you're now enjoying the fruits of our labor and our sacrifices.

"Convergence is a dream. We've got to be strong, stronger than the capitalists—then there'll be peace. If war breaks out and the imperialists use nuclear weapons, we'll retaliate

at once with everything we've got and destroy their launch sites and every target necessary to ensure victory."

My understanding then and my recollection now is that Slavsky was speaking only about a *retaliatory* strike, but our response would be an immediate, all-out nuclear attack on enemy cities and industry as well as on military targets. The most alarming thing was that he completely ignored the question of what, other than military force, might prevent war. In a world where contradictions, conflicts, and mistrust are rife, and where each side has an arsenal of awesome weapons at its disposal, brute force alone cannot be relied upon to guarantee the peace. As for my suggestions for an open society and for replacing confrontation with rapprochement, Slavsky evidently considered them too foolish to discuss, and simply skipped over them.

I pointed out to him that *Reflections* warned against exactly the kind of approach he was taking, in which life-and-death decisions are made behind the scenes by people who have usurped power (and privilege) without accepting the checks of free opinion and open debate. Then I raised the issue of Czechoslovakia: was there any guarantee against Soviet intervention there? For that would be a tragedy.

Slavsky said the matter was under discussion in the Central Committee, and that armed intervention had been ruled out, provided there was no overt counterrevolutionary violence such as occurred in Hungary. Words alone would not bother us, he added. (On August 21, this turned out to be untrue, but the decision to invade may have been made after our meeting; in any case, it's unlikely that

Slavsky would have been privy to discussions at the very top.)

I've reproduced this conversation in some detail because it's virtually the only serious discussion I've ever had with anyone in authority about *Reflections* or any other statement of mine on public issues.

A couple of weeks after this, Khariton asked me to stop by his home. Slavsky, he told me, opposed my return to the Installation. I asked why.

"Efim Pavlovich [Slavsky] is afraid there might be a provocation against you."

"That's absurd—who would organize it?"

"Those are Efim Pavlovich's orders. You're to remain in Moscow for the time being."

This was tantamount to being fired, and there was nothing I could do about it. I stayed in Moscow, which had been our family's permanent home since 1962. Klava and the children normally joined me at the Installation for the summer, but they were still in Moscow when I was suspended.

On July 22, *Reflections* was published in the *New York Times*. After it was reprinted in August at several American universities, a flood of publications and reactions burst forth. (To my regret, I managed to collect and save only a small fraction of them.) The International Publishers Association released statistics showing that in 1968–1969 more than eighteen million copies of my essay were published around the world, in third place after Mao Zedong and Lenin, and ahead of Georges Simenon and Agatha Christie.

Reflections was well received by liberal intellectuals abroad. The views I had expressed—the threat of thermonuclear war, the value of democracy and intellectual freedom, the need to provide economic assistance to developing countries, the recognition of merit in socialism and capitalism, etc.—coincided in large part with theirs. More important, I represented a vindication of their hopes: a kindred voice had reached them from behind the Iron Curtain and moreover, from a member of a profession which in America was dominated by "hawks." There were even some—mainly journalists—who saw my essay as a trial balloon launched by a Soviet government eager to reduce the risk of war; in this scenario, I was being used as a quasi-official spokesman. On the other hand, my criticism of Soviet society appealed to conservative circles, and everyone seemed pleased by my comments on the environment, my humanitarian concerns, and my scenarios for the future. For all the essay's shortcomings, the publication of *Reflections* was an event, and it had a considerable impact on public opinion in the West.

It circulated widely in the USSR as well—samizdat was flourishing—and the response was enthusiastic. Pyotr Grigorenko's letter has stuck in my mind: he praised my essay as "handy as a spoon at dinnertime." Solzhenitsyn sent me a lengthy critique, anticipating the comments he was to make when we met in person for the first time (see below). I deeply regret that many people were punished for circulating *Reflections*. I know the names of a few: Vladlen Pavlenkov, Sergei Ponomarev, Anatoly Nazarov.[2]

I was particularly gratified by a letter I received from the eminent theoretical physicist Max Born, which was accompanied by a very handsomely inscribed copy of his memoirs in German. Born wrote that he admired my courage and shared most of my ideas, but felt I overrated socialism, which he had always considered a creed for idiots. Nonetheless, he admitted that he had voted Labour while living in England. When Born's memoirs were published posthumously in the USSR, the chapter on his social, ethical, and philosophical views was left out, without any caveat to the Russian reader. Born was criticized for returning to Germany in 1953, but he'd missed the linden trees of his native Rhineland. I also recall a letter from Georges Pire, the Belgian Dominican priest who won the 1958 Nobel Peace Prize. Vladimir Poremsky sent an interesting letter and Western press clippings about my essay, including his own article."[3]

During the first months following publication of my essay, I received quite a few letters by ordinary mail, although they were probably only a fraction of those that had been sent.

On August 21 I went out to buy a newspaper. According to a front-page article, Warsaw Pact troops had entered Czechoslovakia at the request of Party and government officials (unnamed, of course) and were "fulfilling their international duty." The invasion had begun. The hopes inspired by the Prague Spring collapsed. And "real socialism" displayed its true colors, its stagnation, its inability to tolerate pluralistic or democratic tendencies, not just in the Soviet Union but even in neighboring countries. Two natural and rational reforms—the abolition of censorship and free elections to a Party Congress—were regarded as too risky and contagious.

The international repercussions of the invasion were enormous. For millions of former supporters, it destroyed their faith in the Soviet system and its potential for reform.

By coincidence, Anatoly Marchenko's trial opened the day Czechoslovakia was invaded.

Marchenko had been a young worker in Kazakhstan in 1958 when he was first sentenced to labor camp for a barracks brawl with some Chechens. He wasn't guilty of any crime, but judges aren't overly scrupulous in such cases and ethnic politics may have influenced the verdict. Marchenko escaped from his labor camp and in 1960 was caught trying to cross the Iranian frontier. This time he was sent to a Mordovian camp for political prisoners to serve a six-year sentence. His whole life changed after Yuli Daniel arrived in the camp in 1966; influenced by him, Marchenko chose a new tack of rigorous self-examination, nonconformity, social activism, and struggle, which led to his eventual martyrdom. His distinguishing feature was his absolute honesty, a determination to stick to principle that was often mistaken for sheer obstinacy.

Following his release in November 1966, Marchenko drew on his considerable experience of prison and camp life to write *My Testimony*, a powerful and graphic description of the barbaric penal system that replaced Stalin's Gulag.[4]

He was arrested again in July 1968 and tried for a technical violation of passport regulations: spending more than three days in Moscow without permission. This law was enforced only selectively, but the KGB hated Marchenko's independent attitude and his book, which was popular with human rights activists in the USSR and had been published abroad in many languages. Marchenko received a one-year camp sentence, but that didn't satisfy the KGB. He was tried again while in confinement and sentenced to two additional years for slander; when another prisoner asked him why he was so thin, he allegedly answered: "Because the Communists have drunk my blood."

On the morning of August 21, Marchenko's friends were greeted at the courthouse by Pavel Litvinov, who announced: "Our tanks are in Prague!"[5]

Four days later, at noon on Sunday, August 25, Litvinov and Larisa Bogoraz, along with Konstantin Babitsky, Vadim Delone, Vladimir Dremlyuga, Viktor Fainberg, and Natasha Gorbanevskaya, went out onto Red Square to protest the Soviet invasion of Czechoslovakia. With this bold action—many people were punished just for refusing to attend the innumerable official meetings held in support of the intervention—Litvinov, Bogoraz, and their comrades restored our country's honor. They managed to sit for a minute by Lobnoe Mesto, a traditional place of execution in prerevolutionary Russia, and then KGB agents began beating them and tore up their signs reading "Hands Off Czechoslovakia." All seven were arrested, but their protest had broken a shameful silence. Minutes later, cars carrying Dubček, Smrkovsky, and the other Czechoslovak leaders brought to Moscow by force, shot out of the Kremlin's Spassky Gate and raced across Red Square.

I had no advance notice of the demonstration. One of the participants came to see me on the 24th, but I was out and he didn't tell Klava the reason for his visit. It is possible that my absence was arranged. Zhivlyuk had arrived half an hour earlier and urged: "Andrei Dmitrievich, we have to go see Vuchetich right away. He's waiting for you. He's got access to 'himself' [Brezhnev]; who knows whose idea this meeting is. It could help a lot of people."

I had nothing to lose, so I went. I knew little about artistic circles, and had no clear idea what to expect. (Evgeny Vuchetich had unquestioned talent as a sculptor, but politically he was far to the right.)

On the way, Zhivlyuk told me: "You'll meet Fyodor Shakhmagonov, I gave you his manuscript."

Zhivlyuk had in fact brought me the typescript of a short story by Shakhmagonov about a retired KGB officer, praising it as more courageous and profound than Solzhenitsyn's work, a gross exaggeration.

Vuchetich *was* waiting for us. A man of average height with a loud voice and aggressive manner, he was still suffering from the aftereffects of a recent stroke. Shakhmagonov arrived a few minutes later; he embraced Vuchetich, kissing him three times in Russian fashion.

Vuchetich showed me around his studio, pointing out works he'd done "for the money" and others done "for my soul." An enormous female figure symbolizing the Motherland had been commissioned for the Stalingrad memorial.

'The bosses ask me why her mouth is open; it doesn't look pretty. I tell them: She's shouting 'For the Motherland, you mother-f— ers!' That shuts them up."

The memorial for the Battle of the Kursk Salient captured the charm of youth and, at the same time, the horror of war and death, in the bent head of a dying tank soldier.

"For the soul" Vuchetich had portrayed Lenin in his last years, lost in deep and painful thought.

I never saw Vuchetich again. I've since heard that he carved a bust of me using photographs and his memory of our meeting.

Of Shakhmagonov I was told that he had served as Mikhail Sholokhov's secretary and had written Sholokhov's horrifying address to the Twenty-third Party Congress. Shakhmagonov is rumored to be a KGB general. In 1969, he suggested that I write an essay along the same lines as *Reflections* for the Sovetskaya Rossiya publishing house. The article would have to be "publishable"—i.e., acceptable to the Soviet censors. This may have been an attempt to "tame" me. I left an outline of my proposed article at the publisher's office, and Shakhmagonov phoned a few days later to say that there was no sense in going any further: even the essay's title, which included the word "democratization," seemed "provocative." To whom? To the KGB?

The day after visiting Vuchetich, I had my first meeting with Alexander Solzhenitsyn. Tamara Khachaturova, a widow who worked in FIAN's library and was a friend of Solzhenitsyn's first wife, had passed on his suggestion that we meet. Our rendezvous was postponed several times, but finally took place at the apartment of a friend of mine on August 26. (Solzhenitsyn was the first person to tell me about the demonstration the day before on Red Square.)

In *The Oak and the Calf*, Solzhenitsyn writes about the vivid impression I made on him.[6] I can easily return the compliment. With his lively blue eyes and ruddy beard, his tongue-twistingly fast speech delivered in an unexpected treble, and his deliberate, precise gestures, he seemed an animated concentration of purposeful energy.

Before I arrived, Solzhenitsyn had drawn the curtains. He later wrote that our meeting escaped the notice of the KGB. In this I believe he was mistaken, although I don't pretend to be an expert in detecting surveillance. Since I have nothing to hide, I simply ignore our army of highly paid shadows. On this occasion, however, I noted that the taxi driver who picked me up after the meeting made provocative remarks and seemed unusually intent on engaging me in conversation.

I had read almost everything Solzhenitsyn had written and felt enormous respect for him, which has since been reinforced by publication of his epic work, *The Gulag Archipelago*. Real life is never simple, however, and our relations are now difficult—perhaps unavoidably so, since we are not at all alike and differ markedly on questions of principle.

At our first meeting, I listened attentively as he talked away in his usual manner—passionately and with absolute conviction. He began by complimenting me on breaking the conspiracy of silence at the top of the pyramid. Then he voiced his disagreements with me in incisive fashion: Any kind of convergence is out of the question. (Here he repeated Slavsky almost word for word.) The West has no interest in our becoming democratic. The West is caught up in materialism and permissiveness.

Socialism may turn out to be its final ruin. Our leaders are soulless robots who have latched onto power and the good life, and won't let go until forced to do so.

Solzhenitsyn claimed that I had understated Stalin's crimes. Furthermore, I was wrong to differentiate him from Lenin: corruption and destruction began the day the Bolsheviks seized power, and have continued ever since. Changes in scale or method are not changes in principle. According to Professor Kurganov, sixty million people had perished as a result of terror, famine, and associated disease. My figure of ten million deaths in labor camps was too low.

It's a mistake, he continued, to seek a multiparty system; what we need is a nonparty system. Every political party betrays its members in order to serve the interests of the party bosses. Scientists and engineers have a major role to play, but in the absence of an underlying spiritual goal any hope that we can use the tools of science to regulate progress is a delusion that will end in our being suffocated by the smoke and cinders of our cities.

Despite the passage of time, I believe I have faithfully reproduced the gist of Solzhenitsyn's critique.[7]

In response, I acknowledged that there was much truth in his comments. Still, my own opinions were expressed in *Reflections* although in an attempt to make constructive recommendations, I had introduced some simplifications into my argument. My primary aim was to point out the dangers we faced and a possible course of action to avert them. I was counting on people's good will. I didn't expect an immediate response to my essay, but I hoped to influence public thinking over the long term. I might revise it at some future date, but first wanted to think things through.

We went on to discuss the punishment facing the demonstrators who had been arrested in Red Square. A few days later, I phoned Andropov on their behalf. Kurchatov had left instructions that I was to be allowed into the Atomic Energy Institute without a pass or other formalities. I went to the office of Anatoly Alexandrov, then the Institute's director, and used his special telephone to call Andropov. I told him:

"I'm concerned about the people arrested on August 25 on Red Square. Czechoslovakia has become the center of world attention: Communist Parties in the West are following developments, and it will make matters worse if the demonstrators are tried and sentenced."

Andropov said he was preoccupied with Czechoslovakia and had hardly slept all week. The Procurator's Office, not the KGB, was investigating the demonstration. Andropov added, however, that he didn't think the sentences would be severe.

That was my second and last conversation with Andropov.[8]

Freedom of Religion and Freedom of Movement

Not long after these events the trial of Anatoly Krasnov-Levitin drew my attention to the issue of religious freedom. Krasnov-Levitin, a Russian Orthodox believer and former political prisoner, had been arrested in September 1969 on charges of slandering the Soviet system; he was released from detention in August 1970 without a definitive disposition of his case. He found work as a sexton and continued to write about the persecution of believers and about church and monastic affairs.[9]

Krasnov-Levitin was again taken into custody in May 1971. At Chalidze's request, he had spoken out in defense of some elderly women accused of forgery. They had been collecting signatures on a petition to reopen a church in Naro-Fominsk (a town southwest of Moscow) that in the 1930s had been converted into a warehouse—a common practice, but one deeply offensive to believers. For years there had been sporadic efforts to reconsecrate the church; as far as I know, these still continue. There had been no intention to commit forgery; in their simplicity, the old women were convinced that it was all right to sign the petition on behalf of relatives (and, in one instance, for someone who had died). They had collected more than enough signatures without taking these liberties, but the authorities used their mistake to disrupt the campaign and to take the offensive. Chalidze shouldn't have involved Krasnov-Levitin in public statements on this case while he was still formally under investigation.[10]

Krasnov-Levitin was tried on May 19 in Lublino, a suburb of Moscow favored by the authorities for such proceedings, since its remote location discourages the attendance of defendants' family and friends and offers a pretext for barring foreign journalists—there are military installations in the vicinity. (Bukovsky, Tverdokhlebov, Orlov, Osipova, and Velikanova were also tried in Lublino.)

A KGB agent—for some reason I still recall his curly hair—met me outside the courthouse, escorted me to the courtroom, and found me a seat. Later, I realized this courtesy had been designed to prevent me from speaking with any of the dissidents who had gathered in Lublino. I also learned why the KGB goes to great lengths to limit access to such proceedings: not even the most elaborate stage-managing can conceal the fact that the defendants are being tried for their beliefs, and for the public disclosure of information they sincerely believe to be true.

Several incidents at the trial should have given pause to any unprejudiced observer, but despite this, Krasnov-Levitin was sentenced to three years labor camp [for "slandering the Soviet system" and "inciting servants of the church to violate the law on the separation of church and state"]. Just before sentence was pronounced, Vera Lashkova, who had been called as a witness, tossed him a bouquet of red carnations. Krasnov-Levitin rose and bowed with touching, old-fashioned formality. He had made a similar bow when another witness, a young monk, entered the courtroom wearing a black cassock and a pectoral cross. Since his release from labor camp in June 1973 (and his emigration in September 1974), Krasnov-Levitin has continued to champion freedom of conscience in the USSR.

Religious liberty is an important part of the human rights struggle in a totalitarian state. The pervasive, often brutal persecution of churches and religious bodies that characterized the early years of Soviet rule has been replaced by more selective repression directed mainly against those religious institutions of a nonconformist temper, but curbs on worship affect all believers.

Before 1971, I knew little about this subject, but I came to understand the complex and tragic dimensions of religious persecution from Shafarevich's report to the Human Rights Committee on the legal situation of religion in the USSR,[11] from Krasnov-Levitin's studies of church history, from Mikhail Agursky's writing about the antireligious terror of the 1920s, from the *Chronicle of Current Events,* and from personal contact with Baptists, Pentecostals, Seventh Day Adventists, Uniates, and Roman Catholics from the Baltic states.

For me, religious liberty is part of the general issue of freedom of opinion. If I lived in a clerical state, I would speak out in defense of atheists and heretics.

▼   ▼   ▼   ▼   ▼

A second critical problem engaged me at that time—the freedom to choose one's country of residence, with the right both to leave the country and to return. This was, of course, the crux of the Leningrad "skyjacking" case, but it is a mistake to narrow this question to Jewish emigration or even emigration in general.

Early in 1971, a woman who had received permission to leave for Israel came to see me, bringing along her son. She had sold her possessions, but now her ex-husband was objecting to their son's departure, and she refused to go without the boy. She had no money, nowhere to sleep, nothing to eat, and she'd been threatened with having her son removed from her custody. I can't recall what I did to help her, but she did manage to emigrate a few months later.

I have spoken out many times on the subject of the exodus to Israel. It has been fed by Jewish national consciousness, by Zionism (a term I use with no pejorative connotation), by the anti-Semitism that smolders in the Soviet Union and occasionally (as in 1953) bursts into flame, and by a legitimate aspiration to live a life free from discrimination and from the specific constraints peculiar to our country. Jewish emigration won recognition and international support through the efforts of activists such as Shcharansky, Slepak, Nudel, Lerner, and Begun. But the authorities can still open or shut the valve in response to the political situation, since our laws do not guarantee the rights of the individual. Some refuseniks have been waiting for permission to leave since the 1970s. Ironically, exit visas to Israel are sometimes used to rid the country of "undesirables," and many dissidents, both Jews and non-Jews, have left the country by this route. Anatoly Marchenko and others who have refused to play the KGB's game have been cruelly punished.

Would-be emigrants of German descent face even greater obstacles. (Those who want to leave the USSR for reasons not connected with their ethnic ancestry are in the worst situation of all.)

Soon after the founding of the Human Rights Committee in November 1970, Friedrich Ruppel came to see me. The fate of this stocky man of about forty, with a lively, expressive face and curly black hair, was both shocking and typical of hundreds of thousands of Soviet ethnic Germans. In 1941, Ruppel was forcibly deported to Kirghizia. His mother—described by Ruppel as a modest working woman who never opened her mouth in the presence of strangers—was arrested, charged with anti-Soviet agitation, and shot. His father, who was also arrested, returned from the camps after Stalin's death, severely disabled. Some thirty of Ruppel's relatives had been arrested, and most of them died in confinement.

Ruppel himself was arrested in 1941, and thereafter was shunted from one transit prison to another, until two years later he was herded along with a large group of prisoners into a half-ruined church, where they heard their verdicts read out in batches. From the time Ruppel was called up to sign his sentence (ten years), he was a "legal" prisoner—this despite the fact that there had been no investigation, no trial, and no defense. His arrest was evidence enough for the Special Board which convicted him in accordance with the popular maxim: "Show me the man and I'll find the crime."[12]

Ruppel served his term, was released, and became a skilled metalworker. He married. (To my question whether his Russian wife would leave with him, he answered: "The thread follows the needle.") After Ruppel decided to emigrate to West Germany, he set about it with tremendous energy, not only for himself and his family, but for like-minded friends as well. At the same time, he sought posthumous rehabilitation for his mother. Although the case had been an obvious sham, years of effort got him nowhere. Eventually, Ruppel found out that Vorontsov, the judge who had sentenced his mother to death, was now in charge of the review procedure! But his perseverance and courage, together with help from the West German Embassy, German correspondents, and myself, paid off: the matter was taken up by the Western press, pressure was apparently brought to bear on Vorontsov, and Ruppel at long last received a small sheet of paper embel-lished with Vorontsov's signature and an official seal, rehabilitating his mother and dropping all charges "for lack of any evidence that a crime had been committed." In the 1950s, when the rehabilitation campaign was in full swing, thousands, perhaps hundreds of thousands of these certificates were given to relatives of those who had perished. The fact of the matter is, millions should have been issued, since millions died; Ruppel's certificate, however, was one of the last processed before the campaign ended.

Ruppel finally received permission to emigrate in the spring of 1974, and I accompanied him to the Belorus Station to say farewell and to share in the joy of victory. He popped the cork on the bottle of champagne he had brought along; foam overflowed the cut-glass goblets and spilled onto my best suit. Ruppel, unlike many émigré dissidents, succeeded in finding his bearings abroad. He took courses to improve his skills, and now earns a good living despite the fact that German work culture is light-years ahead of ours. And his children followed his good example.

Many ethnic Germans have struggled for years, even decades, to get exit visas. Three generations of one family, the Bergmans, suffered appalling treatment in the course of a fifty-year battle for emigration. Their applications were consistently refused on the grounds that they had no close relatives in Germany. How could they? In the 1970s, Pyotr Bergman was sentenced to three years in labor camp for taking part in a peaceful demonstration, and it wasn't until 1982 that I heard over Deutsche Welle that he'd at last been allowed to go to West Germany.

When Johann Wagner, a worker from Kishinev, applied to emigrate, he was first fired and then brought to trial in the spring of 1978 as a "parasite." He was convicted for "the malicious evasion, by a person leading an antisocial form of life, of an official decision concerning employment and the termination of parasitic existence"—that's the contrived definition in the Criminal Code. (Wagner's thirty-two years as a worker made the charge of parasitism ridiculous on the face of it.) That May, on the eve of Brezhnev's visit to West Germany, I wrote parallel letters to him and to Chancellor Helmut Schmidt, asking them to intercede on Wagner's behalf. This was one of the rare instances when an appeal to higher authority was successful. In August, the Moldavian procurator's office notified me that the case had been reviewed and Wagner released.

Germans who attempt to band together for purposes of mutual aid are severely punished. Dozens have been sentenced to long terms of imprisonment for compiling lists of would-be emigrants, for signing collective petitions, or for taking part in nonviolent demonstrations. Nonetheless, Germans continue to demonstrate in Kazakhstan, in the Baltic states, and in Moscow, and to send their names to the West German Embassy and to foreign correspondents. Ruppel's friends passed on to me lists containing more than 6,000 names. When Senator James Buckley visited me in 1974, I asked him to deliver those precious documents to the West German government, and he did so.

German emigration stems from a natural human desire to return to the land of their forefathers, to share in its culture and language, to enjoy its economic and social achievements. It is understandable that Germans should want to leave a country where they have been victims of appalling injustice—in effect genocide—and where they have been discriminated against in education and employment.

Hundreds of thousands of Soviet citizens of German descent died in labor camps and special resettlement zones, and to this day Germans cannot freely return to their prewar homes in the USSR.[13] A German child is still liable to be branded a Nazi by any classmate who's just been to see a war film!

Why do the Germans' legitimate efforts to emigrate encounter so many difficulties? The main problem is the Soviet authorities' refusal in general to recognize any individual's right to choose his country of residence, whatever his nationality.

Additional factors are also involved. Very few ethnic Germans live in Moscow, and thus their access to foreign correspondents, diplomats, and Soviet agencies is limited. It is a source of satisfaction to me that before my exile to Gorky, I was able to do something about making their plight better known. West German correspondents have always responded favorably to my requests—the majority of them are conscientious journalists, and in contrast to certain of their colleagues from other countries, they do their best to understand matters fully so as not to confuse facts or give a misleading slant to a story. West German diplomats were also sympathetic, but they found it difficult to obtain concessions.

Few ethnic Germans enjoy the benefits of higher education, and this hampers their effort to organize joint actions, to get their stories published, and to cope with shrewd Soviet officials. And then there is the long history of the "German question," carrying, as it does, even more emotional freight than the "Jewish question."

And finally, West German officials and citizens haven't defended the rights of their kinsmen in the USSR with sufficient vigor. I am aware that in saying this I may cause some offense, but I am convinced that Soviet compliance with one of its fundamental obligations under international law should be a prerequisite for détente, trade, and other dealings. All ethnic Germans who want to go to West Germany should be allowed to do so, without invitations from relatives. Few have family there; their relatives live in the Soviet Union or are buried in the resettlement camps of Kazakhstan, Kirghizia, and the Komi Autonomous Republic. Such lame excuses for delay as "knowledge of state secrets" can scarcely apply to the Germans, who are mostly miners, combine operators, and truck drivers. The regime should put an end to serfdom.

In August 1971, I attended the trial of N., a young Russian physicist, and François de Perregaux, a biology teacher and Swiss citizen. At first glance, the defendants looked remarkably alike; on closer examination, however, I realized that de Perregaux might as well have come from another planet.

N., an intriguing fellow who'd been vice-president of an international affairs club at Moscow University, had decided to flee the USSR out of fear of mass repressions in the event of war with China—or at least that's what he told the judge. Following an unsuccessful attempt to cross the Finnish border, he was probably placed under surveillance. He then approached a foreign diplomat involved in his plan, who contacted the Eastern Institute in Switzerland. Sovietologists there came up with de Perregaux, a near-double for N. who was willing to take a risk to save a "dissident" (while enjoying a free trip to the Soviet Union). The plan called for N. to visit de Perregaux's hotel room on some pretext, pour a sleeping powder into his lemonade, steal his identification papers, and use them to fly abroad. The hotel staff would discover the slumbering de Perregaux, the Swiss consul would assist a tourist whose passport had been stolen, and de Perregaux would return safely home. In quest of a nest egg in the West, N. had also tried to send his memoirs ahead through a diplomatic pouch—he anticipated a hefty cash advance from some publisher.

Instead, he was arrested as he went to board his plane, and when de Perregaux awakened, he found himself surrounded by KGB officers instead of hotel staff. N.'s memoirs wound up on the investigator's desk. A plan of such complexity was bound to fail, and the KGB was of course able to outfox the Oriental Institute on what was, after all, its own professional turf. At his trial, N. recanted, explaining that he'd been reading *Pravda* in his prison cell; previously, all his information had come from the BBC. His sentence was reduced from ten to eight years because of his cooperation, and then to six years while he was in labor camp. He emigrated in 1977 and now lives in the U.S.

Why does the West pay more attention to egoistic adventurers than to persons who face danger for the sake of others? I don't understand the Western media's love affair with Soviet citizens who defect while abroad, jeopardizing efforts to establish a firm legal footing for the right to move freely. Some masquerade as conformists in order to get permission to travel abroad; by hoodwinking the Soviet authorities, they only exacerbate official suspicion of others.

I am more kindly disposed toward run-of-the-mill border-crossers who try to leave the country illegally, risking only their own necks. Some of them perform marvels of courage, but the West barely notices them; unfortunately, they lack the glamour of ballet stars and other celebrated defectors.

During a recess, a KGB man walked over to me and asked what I thought of N.'s trial. He added: "You're wasting your time with these drunken dissidents. Riffraff! You can't be sure who's married to whom."

That was the concern of the Civil Registry Office, not of the KGB, I replied, and added that I found the whole trial disgraceful. I had noticed this same KGB man having a word with de Perregaux's father; now, swelling with pride, he told me he'd advised the father that publicly condemning the Eastern Institute could help his son. François de Perregaux was, in fact, released before completing his three-year sentence.

A whole series of events—the complaints of Jewish and German refuseniks; the Leningrad skyjacking case; Simas Kudirka's abortive attempt to defect at sea, the trial of N.; several tragic incidents at the Berlin Wall—moved me, in October 1971, to send the Supreme Soviet my first comprehensive statement on the freedom to choose one's country of residence.[14] I called for legislation which would deal with this question in the spirit of Article 13 of the Universal Declaration of Human Rights.[15] I received no reply.

As I wrote in my appeal: "The freedom to emigrate, which only a few would in fact use, is an essential condition of spiritual freedom;" it influences the level of protection accorded to other civil and political rights and affects international trust and security. Decisions to leave one's country are not made on a whim; vital interests are almost always at stake: to reunite a family; to seek better economic opportunities; to live in freedom; to escape religious, national, or other forms of discrimination; to live with one's "own kind"; or perhaps simply to see other countries and peoples. But whether the motives for departure appear capricious or not, they are not in any case the state's concern. Nor should a decision to leave be irreversible. Only the combination of freedom to emigrate and freedom to return satisfies the right of free choice of residence proclaimed in the Universal Declaration of Human Rights, and reaffirmed by the Covenant on Civil and Political Rights and by the Helsinki Final Act. This and other rights, including the right to exchange information and ideas, religious liberty, freedom of expression, freedom of the press, freedom of association, and the right to strike, constitute the basis for individual liberty and an open, democratic society.

It is a tragedy that citizens of the USSR are denied the right to freely choose their country of residence, official claims to the contrary notwithstanding. It is a tragedy for the hundreds of thousands who have applied to emigrate and then been refused or harassed. It is a tragedy for those who want to return to the USSR. It is a tragedy for those who want to leave but are deterred by the irrevocability of their action or by the hard lot of the refuseniks. It is a tragedy for the entire country, for all citizens, and for international trust, and it is a threat to peace.

Konstantin Zotov, the former head of the Department of Visas and Registration (OVIR), has written:

> There is no social basis for emigration from the Soviet Union. Inasmuch as there is no unemployment, there is no need to leave the country in search of work. Nor do national motivations exist, for all nationalities and ethnic groups in the Soviet Union enjoy full and guaranteed equal rights. Therefore, emigration by Soviet citizens from the Soviet Union is mainly a result of their wish to be reunited with relatives or of marriage to a foreigner.[16]

That's Zotov's pared-down version of the grounds for emigration. And he totally ignores the right to return to one's country. The "competent organs" simply refuse to open a window into our closed society. For decades Soviet citizens have been indoctrinated with the belief that our society, our economic system, our standard of living, our educational and public health systems are superior to anything in the capitalist world. The idea of someone wanting to leave this paradise seems so criminal, so monstrous, that it cannot be uttered aloud. The Soviet authorities will not permit people to travel freely back and forth

and make first-hand comparisons of life in different countries. There's also the mystique of power: our masters cannot allow people to escape their control.

If travel restrictions were lifted, democratic social and economic changes might have to be introduced to keep emigration within bounds. That's what makes the right to choose one's country of residence so important, and why Senator Henry Jackson called this right the "first among equals."

Reducing the whole issue to the particular question of family reunification severely cramps the emigration process. Besides the illegitimate requirement that an invitation from a close relative (even sisters and brothers are sometimes excluded as insufficiently close) be submitted, there is the need to produce a written statement from the applicant's parents waiving any financial claims they may have. This in effect grants parents a veto over the departure of their adult offspring, since there is no legal mechanism for compelling them to furnish the necessary affidavit.

What is more, applications are handled in an arbitrary, secretive manner, and the regulations governing the process have not been published. The most common reasons for refusals are: "insufficient motivation for reunification" and "possession of state or military secrets." No further explanation is usually provided, and appeal procedures are rudimentary at best. All this opens the door to the systematic violation of a fundamental human right. Of those who came to me for help in the 1970s, more than half were seeking to emigrate.

Footnotes

1. *The Oak and the Calf,* pp. 368–369.
2. Vladlen Pavlenkov, a teacher born in 1929, was sentenced in Gorky to seven years in labor camp for circulating anti-Soviet works and planning to found an anti-Soviet organization. Ponomarev, a writer born in 1945, was sentenced as Pavlenkov's code-fendant to five years labor camp. Nazarov, a Dushanbe driver born in 1946, was sentenced to three years labor camp in 1972 for slandering the Soviet system (he mailed Sakharov's essay to a friend).
3. Poremsky's article appeared in *Posev,* Frankfurt, no. 8, August 1968.
4. *My Testimony* (Dutton, 1969).
5. Pavel is the grandson of Maxim Litvinov, an Old Bolshevik who served for many years as Commissar of Foreign Affairs, until he was replaced by Molotov in 1939 to clear the way for rapprochement with Nazi Germany.
6. *The Oak and the Calf,* pp. 369–371.
7. Solzhenitsyn later sent me a written memorandum, entitled "The Agony of Free Speech," repeating and expanding upon his remarks. He published it, with minor revisions and a new title ("As Breathing and Consciousness Return"), in *From Under the Rubble* (Little, Brown, 1975).
8. Dremlyuga was sentenced to three years labor camp; Delone to thirty months labor camp; Litvinov to five years exile; Bogoraz to four years exile; Babitsky to three years exile. Fainberg was sent to a prison psychiatric hospital.
9. Michael Bourdeaux, *Patriarch and Prophets: Persecution of the Russian Orthodox Church Today* (Macmillan, 1969), contains several articles by Krasnov-Levitin.
10. For more on this case, see Chalidze, *To Defend These Rights,* pp.199–208.
11. Igor Chaferévich, *La législation sur la religion en USSR* (Seuil, 1974).
12. Beginning in 1934, the Special Board of the Ministry of Internal Affairs was empowered to imprison or exile persons "deemed to be socially dangerous." Hearings were conducted in secret by three Board members, without defense counsel and often in the absence of the accused. The Special Board was abolished in 1953.
13. The Volga-German Autonomous Soviet Socialist Republic was established in 1924 and abolished in September 1941, and it has never been restored.
14. *Sakharov Speaks,* pp. 160–163.
15. 1. Everyone has the right to freedom of movement and residence within the borders of each state. 2. Everyone has the right to leave any country, including his own, and to return to his country.
16. *Along the Path Blazed in Helsinki* (Progress Publishers, 1980), p. 197.

Questions

1. What was the Soviet government's reaction to the publication of Sakharov's essay, "Reflections on Progress, Peaceful Coexistence and Intellectual Freedom"?

2. What arguments does Sakharov offer to justify freedom of religion, the right to emigrate, the right to return? Have these freedoms been achieved in the new Russia? Have they been achieved in the former Soviet states?

3. Has Sakharov's call for convergence and the peaceful coexistence of socialist and capitalist systems come true?

Recommended Reading

Amalrik, Andrei. *Involuntary Journey to Siberia,* trans. by Manya Harari and Max Hayward. New York: Harcourt, Brace, Jovanovich, 1970.

Sakharov, Andrei. *Sakharov Speaks,* ed. Harrison Salisbury. New York: Knopf, 1974.

Sharansky, Natan. *Fear No Evil.* New York: Random House, 1988.

Films

Sakharov
Burnt by the Sun

CHAPTER 8

Violeta Morales and the Chilean *Arpilleristas*

In the struggle for human rights around the world, there are an infinite number of stories and methods of protest used by people to express their desire for freedom and to protest against oppressive governments. The story of the *arpilleristas* is an unusual one. The name *arpilleristas* describes Chilean women who created a visual story by sewing pieces of material—wool, cotton, and other fabrics—onto square pieces of burlap to create a tapestry explaining what had happened to their sons and daughters, husbands, fathers and brothers and sisters who had been detained and then "disappeared" during the dictatorship of Augosto Pinochet. These brightly colored collage-tapestries are *arpilleras*.

In September 1973 the president of Chile Salvadore Allende was killed during a military coup. General Augosto Pinochet took power, with the help of the United States, and established a dictatorship which lasted for the next twenty years. In the first years of his dictatorship, Pinochet's government arrested, imprisoned, and "disappeared" thousands of people, primarily men, but also women. Those seeking to find information about their family members were ignored, mistreated, and threatened. People went to the detainment centers, to government offices, to prisons in search of their loved ones and during this time met others sharing their problems and grief. In this oppressive environment, people formed numerous organizations to help others find their relatives. As Violeta Morales points out, it was particularly difficult for women and young mothers, accustomed to remaining at home, who found themselves for the first time participating in the larger political sphere.

Violeta Morales is one of the founders of the *Arpilleristas*. In her search for her brother she met other women who shared her plight, and they decided to start sewing these appliqué tapestries, incorporating traditions of the Chilean artist Violeta Parra and embroiderers from Isla Negra in Chile. Soon these women added a political dimension, turning their work into testimonies of what had occurred, visual histories of their experiences in a world in which they could not freely express themselves. With the help of others, they smuggled these tapestries out of Chile and sold them abroad to inform the outside world of what had happened as well as to raise money for support. The women met in workshops on a regular basis, sharing their stories with one another, while they recreated in cloth their stories of the "disappeared," the men whom they had lost but whom they still hoped would return. At the same time, they continued their search, supported their families, and did not give up their hope that one day, justice would prevail. They also formed the Folkloric Troupe of singers and dancers which performed outside of Chile expressing through music and dance the stories they told in their tapestries.

In 1990 Pinochet finally retired as president, and since then he has successfully avoided facing trial on the criminal charges brought against him in international courts for the death of over two thousand people while in power. Today Chile has once again become an open democratic society. The hope of the *arpilleristas* that the oppressive regime would not last forever was not in vain, but few of the disappeared have returned alive, and many women have finally found the bodies of their loved ones in mass graves. This is why Violeta Morales refuses to accept the Final Point Plan offered by the current government to forgive and forget.

The Way to Justice Is Lighted by Truth: Testimony of Violeta Morales, Chilean Arpillerista

I am Violeta Morales, sister of Newton Morales who was arrested and disappeared on August 13, 1974.

Since the military coup of September 11, 1973, we knew that my brother was going to be arrested because he had been a non-commissioned officer in the Chilean Navy. He had retired because the constant trips to the Antarctic had damaged his kidneys. He had never been political nor had participated in political activities. After retiring from the Navy he went to work at the Sumar factory, a polyester plant. There he became a militant of the MIR. With his navy training as an electronics engineer it wasn't difficult for him to soon get the job. Never before had he been politically militant, because while in uniform he always spent long periods on ships and didn't have the opportunity to become affiliated with any group. He never had the connections to become active in the political parties. After working at the plant for a few months, his fellow workers elected him president of the union at the Sumar polyester plant. Because of that we, his family, knew that they would be looking for him. After September 11, 1973, the military junta immediately came out with a decree ordering everyone who was a union leader to report to work. My brother Newton wanted to report because he said, "I haven't

done anything, I'm not afraid." So he was going to report, but we didn't let him. So he stayed home and didn't go to the plant, but he had to keep moving from one family member's house to another. They were searching for him because of his past, because he had been in the military—that was the main reason.

Before the coup, at the Sumar plant, there had been a worker uprising. Troops had surrounded the plant and armed helicopters constantly circled over the plant. During this uprising, some workers shot at one of the helicopters and killed the pilot. After that incident, the government began to look for ex-military employees at the factory in order to arrest them and blame them for the death of the pilot. And because there were several ex-military workers at Sumar, after the coup several workers were arrested, others immediately fled the country and in the case of my brother Newton, we wouldn't let him show up for work. In order to throw them off the trail my brother moved from house to house, and, at the same time, he was helping people to organize. It was difficult for us to watch how my brother gave of himself totally to help others. He didn't even have time to eat, he had to eat on the run. He was always in a hurry and would drop everything to help other people organize against the dictatorship so that it wouldn't become as powerful as he feared it would.

I was alone with my five children—my husband had left me for a woman from another political party. Newton supported us and

From *We, Chile: Personal Testimonies of the Chilean Arpilleristas* by Emma Sepulveda, translated by Bridget Morgan. Used by permission of Azul Editions.

helped us all, including my sister who was then studying journalism at the university and, also, my mother. He helped us with his Navy pension, the salary he received from the Sumar plant, and the little he earned from a construction company where he also worked. He did everything he could to support us. But after the coup he lost everything, the pension and the two factory jobs. Before, we always had food in the cupboards and never lacked for something to eat. My mother ended up selling her jewelry and small valuables, which helped us to last for awhile. With that money we supported ourselves, but eventually that also ran out. I had heard them tell my brother that "life isn't worthwhile if you don't offer it to help your fellow man," and I would ask him, "How can we not care about life if it's the most important thing we have?" Later, with time and struggle, I learned and understood what my brother really meant to say. Living on your knees isn't being human.

Well, getting back to our story, my brother began to live in a clandestine way and it wasn't very hard for him because he had several identification cards showing he was a Navy officer. So he was able to move about freely—when he was out and they'd stop him, he just show them his identification cards and they'd let him through. But then our mother got sick and my brother decided to go see her. They followed him and were waiting for him. The next morning, three men and a female prisoner arrived at my mother's house and they took him away. Later we found out that the woman was Skinny Alexandra.[1] The first time that they came to look for my brother, my mother was alone. The men asked her about my brother and told her they were his associates from work. Later they returned at 9:00 at night. No one else had come home yet. I had left with my children because one of them was having a birthday. They waited for my brother. No one had a chance to warn my brother. The men pretended to be friends from work and my mother believed them. When my brother got to the house, the men took him by the arms and my brother said to my mother who was in the kitchen: "Mama, the DINA are taking me away."[2] My mother didn't understand because she had never been politically active, so she didn't know what was happening. The men tried to calm her down when she grabbed hold of my brother. One of the men took her by the shoulder and said, "Don't worry, Ma'am, he'll be back in ten minutes—we're only going to talk to him because we're friends of his from work." My brother was pale and said nothing, surely so he wouldn't scare my mother. My poor mother believed that they would bring him back soon. After awhile, my sister returned from the university and a neighbor told her that they had taken my brother away in a red van with an antenna. After talking with the neighbors we found out that our entire neighborhood, the Villa Frei in Nuñoa, had been surrounded by armed young couples who pretended they were out on a date. The entire neighborhood was surrounded so that my brother couldn't escape behind the houses. Just as they were taking my brother Newton from the house, my other brother arrived and followed the van with his taxi. After a short distance, he was able to see that they took Newton to a place close to here, near the Church of Saint Francis, to what we now know is London 38.[3]

After our brother disappeared we began, like other families of prisoners, to look for him everywhere. In 1974, in July, DINA had been formed, and it was refining its methods and applying them brutally. We began to make inquiries right away and found out that in the Pro-Peace Committee,[4] that was on Santa Monica Street, they were receiving all kinds of reports of human rights' violations. We also began to look for our brother in the jails, cemeteries, morgues, police stations and wherever there might be a government office. We also went to the courts, and in a lot of those places we were threatened with machine guns for asking questions and looking for disappeared prisoners. We sent thousands of letters to foreign countries, begging for help. We even sent letters to the leaders of the dictatorship, but nothing came of it.

In the Pro-Peace Committee we realized that every day more and more people arrived with the same problems we had. After meeting with so many people, we decided to form a coordinating committee in order to get better organized. Without giving our names, we took turns directing the organization so that we all had a chance to learn and gain experience on how to look for help for our cause. Father Daniel, a French priest who was driven out of Chile and who is now in Peru, together with a nun named María de los Angeles, were the first to help us in the Pro-Peace Committee. They welcomed us, and gave us support and advice during those first moments of desperation and sorrow. My family took turns—my sister, my brother, my mother, and myself—and we went every day to Pro-Peace and everywhere we believed they could help us in the search for my brother. For a long time they followed my mother in the street or came to our house to interrogate us about my brother's activities. My mother became ill, so the doctor recommended that she leave off with everything and go far away to rest in a quiet place. We continued the struggle. My sister dropped out of the university and became part of the daily search with the rest of us. They followed all of us through the streets and stopped us to ask us where we lived and where we worked. They made life impossible for us. In the Pro-Peace committee we began to organize more, and we'd get together in groups to visit other places. One time we went to Puchuncaví, and afterwards they told us that my brother had been taken from London 38 to the Villa Grimaldi. We even went there as a group. After then, we went to 3 Alamos, where they also isolated and tortured political prisoners. One time, my sister went to 3 Alamos and managed to speak with a female prisoner who told her that three people had left from London 38 for 3 Alamos but only one person had arrived, the other two had been dropped off on the way. According to the description, the one who arrived could have been our brother. We were never able to officially confirm the information. We went to 3 Alamos several times. The guards would ask for things to give to our imprisoned family members. Later, the guards would give us back the torn bags—they themselves would eat the food we left. Sometimes they told us that visiting hours were 7:00 in the morning and, when we got to the prison, they would tell us the hours had been changed to 5:00 in the afternoon. We'd go back in the afternoon and they'd tell us that visiting hours were yesterday—they constantly made fun of us. On Christmas Day in 1974, a lieutenant with red eyes, and I mean red eyes because you could see that he was up all night, told us that my brother was famous in that detention center. According to him, they called my brother "Newton the Tough" because he could take the physical punishment, "the Intellectual" because he read a lot, and he also had been given the nickname "Sarge" because he had been in the military. That day, Christmas Day 1974, we asked the red-eyed lieutenant to give us the chance to see our brother and to speak with him, even if just for a few minutes. He went inside and, after awhile, a policeman came out and said, "Newton Morales has never been here." I was with my sister-in-law and she was holding her baby and, because we didn't leave immediately, they put a machine gun to the baby's head and told us that if we didn't go, they would shoot the baby.

Since we were left without any money with which to live, my mother went to the Department of National Defense Funds to ask that they keep giving her my brother's pension. This administrator sent a letter to the administrator of 3 Alamos and, as the letters were going from administrator to administrator, they let my mother enter the precinct for the first time. She went in and says that you could see the barracks where they held the prisoners. In one of the hallways, at a distance, she saw my brother leaning against the wall, wearing dark glasses and hunched over. At that moment they took her arm and made her go into an office. The officer left her there and went to the office next door to prepare a document for signature and, as he was typing, he was saying out loud:

"I, Newton Morales Saavedra confer this power to my mother Regina . . ." Right then, she heard someone enter and say, "What are you doing, officer?" My mother heard the piece of paper being yanked out of the typewriter and the man yell, "Go tell that woman that her son has never been here." The first officer comes back and repeats to my mother that Newton had never been in that prison. Before they took my brother to 3 Alamos, my mother saw him go by in a car with two men, driving through the neighborhood, so that he could help them recognize people that they could arrest. Also, they stopped my mother many times near her house to threaten that if she didn't stop causing trouble by looking for her son, she would lose the rest of her children, too. My other brother lived all the years of dictatorship without work, harassed and without the possibility of leaving the country. My brother Newton didn't even want to leave because he always said, "I am not going into exile. Someone who hasn't done anything, shouldn't be afraid." He never thought that in his country, where even the worst criminals have the right to a hearing, he would end up without justice. He was always sure that if some day they arrested him, he would have the right to a trial and they would see that he was innocent. But here in Chile it wasn't so. There were abuses of power by the military, they eliminated everyone who thought differently from them without a single law that said that to think differently was a crime. They imposed their own laws. And so we struggle on and in order to find our loved ones and fight against the human rights' abuses, we keep on working with Pro-Peace.

In the beginning, we didn't even have the money to pay the bus fare to go to the Pro-Peace offices. Because of that desperation came the idea of making the *arpilleras*. We remembered the activities of the needleworkers of Macul and the works of Violeta Parra, but we wanted to do something different. We didn't want to make something that was only decorative—we wanted something made by hand that would denounce what we and our country were experiencing. We wanted to tell people, with pieces of our very clothing, about our personal experiences. We wanted to sew our history, the hard and sad history of our ruined country. At first we had a problem with sewing materials, the cloth and wool especially. From that came the idea of cutting up our own clothes and unravelling our own sweaters. From those materials came the first *arpilleras*. Our workshop started in 1974 but wasn't made public until 1975. During those years, I took on all responsibility for the search of my brother. My sister had been kidnapped by a taxi driver who questioned her about some names that she recognized. The taxi driver told my sister about her years as a volunteer in working-women's organizations, and he knew all about her activities as a university student. After that incident, my sister began to be afraid to go out in the street to look for our brother. So I assumed all responsibility of the family and the search for my brother Newton. The truth is I was also afraid, we were all afraid to keep asking questions and looking. At that time I devoted myself totally to the *arpillera* workshop—that was what kept me sane at times. There I found other people who were suffering the same experience, and my interest in helping them sometimes made me forget my own tragedy. During those years the "List of the 119" appeared. This list appeared in the newspapers, in the VEA especially, and because of this list and the problem of a certain prisoner who had escaped from Colonel Manuel Contreras, our work became more dangerous. The case of the prisoner was terrible. An arrested man told Colonel Manuel Contreras that he had an informant who was inside the Pro-Peace Committee. One day, troops surrounded the entire sector around the committee's office, and took the prisoner there so that he could help them. The prisoner managed to escape and ran inside the committee office. We (the *arpilleristas*) were there and we helped him. We let him come inside with us and took care of the wounds they had inflicted on him when he was tortured. Colonel Contreras tried to enter the office with soldiers but the committee didn't let them in. There were a lot of churchwomen in that committee and he couldn't attack them. He couldn't get in. That same night, Colonel Contreras met with Pinochet and they decided to shut down the Pro-Peace Committee. At the same time, they expelled the Lutheran bishop and Father Daniel, who had been a great support for us. Soon after that incident, the Chilean cardinal M. Silva Henriquez organized people to form the National Vicariate of Solidarity. So at the end of 1975, beginning of 1976, we sent *arpilleristas* to the Vicariate. In our new "home," we continued fighting by looking for the disappeared and creating more *arpilleras,* out of our own clothes or whatever piece of fabric we could find, so as to continue the denouncement. We channeled the *arpilleras* through the Vicariate for export to other countries, especially Canada, France, and the United States.

Later, they needed people to take charge of the western zone of Santiago. So another volunteer and I went to teach and organize women who were out of work. When we arrived at that center, we were surprised to find that they wouldn't accept women who were family members of disappeared prisoners. It was a great shock for us. They rejected us and called those from the Vicariate "The Political Women." We didn't understand anything about politics—we were used to the fact that here in Chile it was the man who handled political things, we women dedicated ourselves to the home and to the children and that's all. We were used to the husband coming home with a paycheck, or that he would take off with the money, and the woman had to make do as best she could to raise the children. She had to perform miracles to get food, often leaving home to wash other people's clothes. The Pro-Peace Committee had already created shops where women went to wash clothes so they wouldn't die of hunger with their children. Although we had suffered that first violent rejection, we began to organize—as best we could—more workshops for washing clothes, raising rabbits, sewing, making brooms and baking bread. But the favorite workshop was always for arpilleras. More and more, we were teaching and learning the art of creating an *arpillera*. We were the first ones to create the *arpilleras* of denouncement and now, after 20 years, we are still the ones who make the *arpilleras* of denouncement. A lot of things have happened to me because I wanted to

organize the women and distribute our message of denouncement to the whole world. I remember, for example, one morning when I was in a big hurry to take ten *arpilleras* to the center. A lot of times we didn't even have paper with which to wrap them, so we tied them together with rope. That day I had left running from the house, and it seems that I didn't tie them together very well . . . what happened is that when I was passing in front of the guard at the Diego Portales building,[5] I dropped that bundle of *arpilleras* on the ground. The guards came to help me and I grabbed them up as best I could and left walking, very fast, terrified, with the *arpilleras* of denouncement clutched to my chest. On another occasion, a "gringa" who had come to the workshop to buy *arpilleras* tried to leave the country with the *arpilleras* of denouncement and they caught her at the airport. The woman was scared and said that Violeta Morales had sold them to her. I was afraid for some time, it was very difficult, but the Vicariate petitioned for protection and they managed to protect me from arrest. I don't know how they managed it because here, in this country, they don't respect any process of justice, it's a miracle if you're saved. A little while later because of the wide distribution of *arpilleras,* an article came out in the newspaper slandering our work. They blamed a priest who was inciting us, and from then on we began to be persecuted again. They followed us and searched our homes for revolutionary material or *arpilleras*. During that time, I would get up at dawn to keep looking for my brother and I wouldn't return home until nighttime, so my children had to learn to take care of themselves, to cook and clean the house alone. When I arrived home late at night, after my children were asleep, I'd begin to make the *arpilleras* and, at times, I would work through the whole night. That helped calm me down a little, to stop thinking about my fear, and to earn a little extra money so I could feed my children. By making *arpilleras* through the night, I was able to sell them through the Vicariate and earn money for the family. I got used to not sleeping. Sometimes I went more than two nights without sleeping because I was making arpilleras and, during the day, I went out to organize more workshops and to help other women in the search for their sons, husbands, brothers, fathers, etc.

In the same *arpillera* workshops, we began to form instructional groups to teach women their solidarity role with the soup kitchen and other group activities. Sometimes it was hard to instruct the women of the shantytowns because they treated us worse than lepers—they believed that because of our activities of denouncement they would end up in jail or disappeared. It took a lot to get it into their heads that if we don't unite and help each other, we wouldn't be able to do anything. At times, the money we got from the sale of the *arpilleras* went to pay the doctor for a child or for medicine for some family that was part of the workshop. After the first years of dictatorship, the poverty of we poor women of Chile was horrible. In some houses they used furniture to make fires to heat the home or to cook food. Because to that, besides not having work or money to buy food, in most of the houses in the shantytowns the only thing that was there were mattresses thrown on the floor. We *arpilleristas* not only wanted to denounce the

disappearance of our loved ones, but also we wanted people to find out about the poverty in which our compañeras in the shantytowns lived, and the terrible abuses that the military committed in our country. We wanted to shout our outrage to the world about the horrible offenses to humanity and the crimes being committed every day against the basic rights of the individual. Our country had never seen more prostitution than in those years when the poor woman didn't have work or a means to support her family, and went out in the street with her daughters to work as a prostitute. We didn't have any help, we were very alone at that time. It seemed, sometimes, that the whole world had turned its back on us. On this planet there didn't seem to be any politicians, union leaders, or anyone who could help us organize and give us the basic ideas about how to survive the tragedy. I think now, after so many years, that if, back then, we had had leaders, maybe we would have been able to stop the coup before it had done so much damage in our lives. For us women of Chile who were involved in the fight, it was all the more difficult because we realized that our men were so macho . . . instead of helping us during those years they shoved us down. Some women's husbands didn't let them attend the meetings or help in the instruction or the solidarity work. Back then, the man never said, "Compañera, let's go fight together to change the situation of our country." It was the woman who fought, the woman who was raped and beaten, and never received help from her family. During the process of fighting for the liberty of my people I, as a woman, realized that this myth they had put in our heads our whole life—that a man has the power and physical strength to control everything (of course, that is, up to a point)—is very relative and doesn't stop being like all the myths they instill in us women. It was the females, the compañeras, who managed to stop the military nightmare in our country—the woman has the strength that the man never has, or if he ever had it, he lost it. The woman, who always took care of the house, roused herself and didn't bow down again until she had returned liberty to her country and her people. It must be remembered that is was us who organized the first protests.

Some years after organizing the *arpilleristas* in the Vicariate, Father Pepe Aldunate formed a group of laypeople and approached members of our organization, asking that we join them and create the Sebastián Acevedo Group. I joined that organization because it interested me that those people were focusing on the problem of torture. I was the coordinator of the group and worked with a lot of people who were later thrown out of the country. Our group of *arpilleristas* passed out a lot of material in those years. I remember that we gave out, besides the *arpilleras,* doves made from paper and wool, posters, handkerchiefs, or whatever would let people everywhere know of our tragedy.

We were desperate to get our message out, we wanted, like our people had done so many times, to turn to other art forms—we wanted to also express ourselves in our song and dance. We wanted not only to embroider and shout our pain, we also wanted to sing our message of denouncement. So we began to organize people by zones to form song and dance groups. With about 15 people we formed the first folkloric group, and we debuted March 8, 1978, the same day that International Woman's Day was celebrated in Chile. We performed in the Caupolicán Theater with a group formed completely by family members of disappeared prisoners, the same women who we had known for years making *arpilleras.* I remember that, while we were singing in the theater full of people, CNI[6] agents and soldiers with machine guns waited for us in the wings. We will never forget that day because it was historic, a united human mass ready to rise up against the Pinochet's repressive government. We women began that protest that, later on, no one was able to stop until the military fell. We called the group "The Folkloric Group of Families of Disappeared Prisoners." Our uniform changed over the years, and today it is a black skirt and a white blouse. We do a lot of dances, the main ones are the *cueca sola* and the *tonadas.* However, we try to sing the more indigenous rhythms of our national folkloric tradition. For me, personally, the songs I like best are "The Owl" and the *zamba* "They Say That It Isn't Certain" because they speak of the search for a loved one.

When I wasn't working on the *arpilleras,* participating in the coordination of the Sebastian Azevedo Group, or involved in the folkloric group, I spent most of my time looking for my brother and helping with other solidarity tasks with my compañeras. I was very, very discouraged to find out how many compañeras we buried every day who died of cancer. It was hard to stop thinking that with the lives we were leading, that some day it would be another compañera's turn, and we might die without having found our disappeared family members. From 1973 until now, 1994, I have always worked in all the groups that I could, organizing the women of the shantytowns. I put aside my own life. Because for all of us the Pinochet dictatorship forced us to exist but not to live. The dictatorship forced us to give up everything because we had to fight against the torture and the violations of our human rights, and to look tirelessly for our loved ones. I couldn't share those years with my children, with a man, or with the rest of my family. Moreover, after the 17 Day Strike,[7] I began to have health problems. I had constant hemorrhages and, because I came in contact with different gases used by the government defense troops, I developed asthma.

My future doesn't hold much promise, either. I will never have retirement pay or any type of social benefits, because for 20 years I dedicated my life to being a volunteer in constant solidarity work—I gave my life to others, and to the fight against the dictatorship to defend our human rights. Now, after almost 20 years, they offer us the law of the "Final Point," they want to silence our pain, but we will continue as long as we're alive—searching, hoping and asking the four winds . . . "Where are they?" We continue on with the same strength that we began with 20 years ago. We will not accept the Final Point Law or any other law that puts a price on our disappeared sons, husbands or brothers. We will continue making *arpilleras* of denouncement and we will continue protesting. In June 1993 we chained ourselves to another fence, this time it was the new Congress, so that the politicians would listen to us. This year, 1994, we danced the *cueca sola* in front of the Moneda[8] to keep our fight alive. We have to find something, even if it's the bones of our disappeared family members. There is still a lot to do. We will continue with the solidarity that we've always had, hoping for a response from the future governments. It is sad that the organization is getting weaker and we aren't making so many *arpilleras*. I thought that people had generated more political and social awareness, but it seems we haven't learned much. I hope to God that the *arpilleras* remain as a testimony so that other generations, not only in Chile, but also throughout the world, learn much more than what we have learned.

—The Association of Families of the Arrested-Disappeared, Santiago, Chile, January 1994.

Footnotes

1. Skinny Alexandra was supposedly a member of the MIR who, like other prisoners, became a torturer after herself suffering physical and psychological torture. Before the coup she was a student at the University of Concepción. Human rights defense groups have testified about her particular case.

2. DINA was the secret police formed during the military government.

3. London 38 is one of the sites where political prisoners were confined and tortured during the epoch of the dictatorship.

4. The Pro-Peace Committee was formed to aid people that needed help. It was organized by the principal churches.
5. At that time, the Diego Portales building served as the government office of General Augosto Pinochet.
6. The CNI was the Center of National Intelligence at that time.
7. The 17 Day Strike occurred in May 1978, and was the third hunger strike by the arpillera group. In response, Pinochet's government promised that, through the mediation of the Catholic Church, to release information to the families of disappeared prisoners. To date, this promise has not been kept (1994).
8. The Moneda is the governor's palace in Santiago, Chile.

Questions

1. Why was Violeta Morales' brother arrested?

2. How did Violeta Morales' view of the role and potential of women change as a result of her involvement in the search for her brother?

3. What other social and economic changes occurred in Chile during this time?

Recommended Reading

Report of the Chilean National Commission on Truth and Reconciliation, trans. Phillip E. Berryman. 2 vols. Notre Dame, IN: University of Notre Dame Press, 1993.

Agosin, Marjorie and Sepulveda, Emma. *Amigas: Letters of Friendship and Exile,* trans. Bridget Morgan. Austin, TX: University of Texas Press, 2001.

Films

The Missing
Threads of Hope

Aung San Suu Kyi

There is no woman alive in the world today more noted for her human rights work than Aung San Suu Kyi (ASSK) who was just released from her second long-term house arrest in May 2002. Aung San Suu Kyi is the leader of the pro-democracy movement and the head of the National League for Democracy (NLD). She was born in July 1945, the daughter of the national leader of Burma, General Aung San and his wife Khin Kyi. When Aung San Suu Kyi was only two years old, her father was assassinated. At the age of 15 she accompanied her mother to India where her mother served as ambassador. Aung San Suu Kyi attained a B.A.degree in philosophy, politics and economics from Oxford University, England. She held numerous positions, married an Englishman, Dr. Michael Aris, and they had two sons. In 1988 she returned to Burma to care for her ailing mother. Student demonstrations against the current regime had begun, and on August 8, 1988, an uprising broke out against the ruling Burma Socialist Program Party. It was violently crushed by the military forces. In the next months protesters continued to be arrested and killed as the military and the State Law and Order Restoration Council (SLORC) established dictatorial control of the country, which it continues to rule to this day.

From the time of her return to Burma, Aung San Suu Kyi emerged as the leader of the pro-democracy movement and came under the attack of the SLORC. In July 1989 the government placed her under house arrest and she remained under this sentence until her release in 1995. During this period Aung San Suu Kyi went on a hunger strike, and won the support and respect of people around the world. Her party (NLD) the National League for Democracy won 82% of the seats in elections held in 1990, but the ruling SLORC refused to recognize the results of the elections. In 1991 Aung San Suu Kyi won the Noble Peace Prize. She was the recipient of many other awards, including the European Parliament's Sakharov Prize for Freedom of Thought, because of her determined struggle against the oppressive regime. Alan Clements, a Burma expert and former Buddhist monk, conducted this interview with Aung San Suu Kyi in 1995 shortly after her release from house arrest. In 1999 her husband, Dr. Michael Aris, was dying of cancer. The government refused to grant him a visa to visit her, and Aung San Suu Kyi knew that if she left

Burma, she would not be allowed to return. As a result she did not see her husband before his death.

In October 2000 Aung San Suu Kyi was again placed under house arrest for nineteen months. During the fourteen years since she first returned to Burma in 1988, she has spent almost seven of them living under house arrest. This did not prevent her, however, from continuing to study, to write, to publish books, to meet with large groups of people, both from Burma, and most recently from around the world. Since the beginning of 2001, the SLORC government permitted Aung San Suu Kyi to have more contact with visitors from outside Burma, including a human rights inspector from the United Nations, as well as delegates from the European Union and the United States Congress. Economic sanctions against Burma continued to be imposed as a consequence of the government's repression, and beginning in 2001, the SLORC began to loosen their tight reins on the country. The United Nations envoy to Burma, Razali Ismail, has met numerous times in the past year together with Aung San Suu Kyi, other leading members of the League for Democracy and the ruling military junta, to discuss the future of human rights in Burma. The recent release of Aung San Suu Kyi promises that her goal of an open and democratic society might well be achieved in the near future.

"We are Still Prisoners in Our Own Country"

ALAN CLEMENTS: Your father—Aung San—is perhaps the most famous man in Burma's long history. His name today, over fifty years after his death, still evokes awe in the people. He was a spiritual seeker, a heroic freedom fighter and a great statesman. And when you entered your nations struggle for democracy on 26 August 1988, you announced in your speech, delivered at the Shwedagon Pagoda and attended by more than half a million people, that you were "participating in this struggle for freedom . . . in the footsteps and traditions of my father." You have also said, "When I honor my father, I honor all those who stand for political integrity in Burma." Daw Suu, it is here that I would like to begin to explore your story and try to understand what moves you to struggle for your people's freedom. What does political integrity mean to you?

AUNG SAN SUU KYI: Political integrity means just plain honesty in politics. One of the most important things is never to deceive the people. Any politician who deceives the people either for the sake of his party or because he imagines it's for the sake of the people, is lacking in political integrity.

AC: What about SLORC's "political integrity"?

ASSK: Well . . . *(laughs)* sometimes one wonders whether they actually know what political integrity means, because they've deceived the people repeatedly. They've made promises which have not been kept.

AC: Like not honoring the results of their "free and fair" elections in 1990 in which your party, the NLD [National League for Democracy], won a landslide victory? What has been the SLORC's official explanation of why they have not honored the results?

ASSK: There has not been a real explanation. But you can see SLORC has not let the elected representatives play any meaningful role in the drawing up of the new constitution. In the National Convention nobody is allowed to speak freely. The NLD has not even been allowed to protest against undemocratic working procedures. That is why we decided to stay away from the convention until a meaningful dialogue has been successfully initiated.

AC: In examining the crisis in Burma it is so easy to focus on the vast divisions between those struggling for democracy—the NLD—and the ones oppressing democracy—SLORC. Perhaps it's a premature question, but are there actual places of goodwill and trust between both sides—areas where

From *The Voice of Hope: Aung San Suu Kyi Conversations with Alan Clements,* by Aung San Suu Kyi with Alan Clements.

Reprinted by arrangement with Seven Stories Press, c/o Writers House as agent for the proprietor New York, NY. Copyright 1998 by Seven Stories Press.

you find some sense of genuine connection?

ASSK: I would like to think there are but we have not been given an opportunity to find out. This is why we say that dialogue is so important. How can we find out if there are places where we can meet, issues on which we can work together, unless we talk to each other? But I heard a rather shocking report about an interview of one of the SLORC ministers by a foreign journalist. The minister said, "You can do anything with money. If you hold a ten dollar note above a grave, a hand will come out and reach for it. And if you held out a hundred dollar note, the whole body would come out." That seems to indicate that they have no principles whatsoever. If they think that everyone can be purchased with money, that's a shocking revelation.

AC: Sounds like a sociopathic fantasy . . .

ASSK: Well . . . one wonders, why? Why are they like that? I do not think they're interested in the why. There is a phrase the authorities like to use: "We don't want to hear about a leaking water bottle. We only want the water." That means, just do what we tell you, with no excuses. All we want are results. That's a very strange attitude.

AC: How would you define the collective psychology of SLORC?

ASSK: My impression of them as a whole is that they do not know what communication means. They don't communicate, either with the people or with the opposition. And I wonder whether they even communicate with each other. If everybody in SLORC shares this minister's attitude, that money is what decides everything, then I have this rather unhappy image of them simply shoving dollar bills at each other.

AC: Is it fair to say that the regime—SLORC—are Buddhists?

ASSK: I would not like to comment on other people's religious inclinations. It's not for me to say who is Buddhist or who is not. But I must say that some of their actions are not consonant with Buddhist teachings.

AC: For example?

ASSK: There's so little loving-kindness and compassion in what they say, in what they write and what they do. That's totally removed from the Buddhist way.

AC: Removed from people?

ASSK: Yes. This is the problem with a lot of authoritarian regimes, they get further and further away from the people. They create their own isolation because they frighten everybody, including their own subordinates, who feel unable to say anything that would be unacceptable.

AC: Yes, I've noticed that. Back in 1990, when I was in the jungle along the Thai-Burma border, I witnessed SLORC's "ethnic cleansing" campaign against the Karens, and to an extent against the Mons and Shans, as well as their attempt to exterminate the armed democracy forces based in the hills near Mannerplaw. At that time I interviewed a SLORC commander who had been captured after a fire-fight . . .

ASSK: How did they treat him?

AC: Humanely. This, I can testify to. Not only the SLORC officer but also the privates who had been captured. But I asked this commander, "Why are you killing your own people?" He brought out of his pocket a picture of himself as a monk and said, "I don't like killing, but if I don't kill, I will be killed." He then started to cry. His tears looked real . . .

ASSK: Why did he enter the army if he was so against killing? Was there nothing else he could do?

AC: I asked that same question to a group of young SLORC conscripts who were being held in the stockade; "Why do you kill?" And they replied, "If we don't kill we're killed." Then I asked what you asked me: "But why did you enter the army?" They all said the same thing: "If we don't join the army our families are abused. We have no money, there's no other source of income, there's no work, it's the only way we can give money to our parents, otherwise they can't eat."

ASSK: Yes, I have heard that in some parts of the country there is a lot of forced conscription—they do force villages to produce a certain number of conscripts for the army.

AC: Thousands of Burmese students have fled the country as well as hundreds of thousands of refugees from the time of SLORC's coup in 1988. Obviously, you're here in Rangoon struggling with your people for democracy but what about all those other disenfranchised people living in squalor, many of them weakened by starvation, or dying of disease? What are your feelings about those citizens of the nation?

ASSK: It is so they can come back that we're fighting for democracy in this country. Where will they come back to if we can't make this place safe for them? The people need a country where they can feel safe.

AC: What are your feelings specifically towards the young students?

ASSK: We have said from the very beginning that the NLD will never disown students who are fighting for democracy, even though they have chosen to take up arms and we have chosen the way of non-violence. Because we are not in a position to guarantee their security, we do not have the right to demand that they do what we want them to do. We look forward to the day when we can work together again.

AC: Many peace settlements are occurring around the world—in the Middle East, in the former Yugoslavia, possibly in Northern Ireland and of course, the miracle that's occurring in South Africa. SLORC has a precious opportunity to follow suit—a reconciliation could occur. Now, you have repeatedly called for dialogue, but what is it that's preventing SLORC from saying "Daw

Aung San Suu Kyi, let's say hello, have lunch together, and see where it goes from there?"

ASSK: This is exactly what I meant when I said they do not know how to communicate. I think they're afraid of dialogue. I think to this day, they do not and cannot understand what dialogue means. They do not know that it's a process that is honorable, that it can lead to happiness for everybody—including themselves. I think they still see dialogue as either some kind of competition in which they might lose or as a great concession which would disgrace them.

AC: It sounds like fear. What do you think this fear is rooted in?

ASSK: When you really think about it, fear is rooted in insecurity and insecurity is rooted in lack of *metta* [loving-kindness]. If there's a lack of *metta*, it may be a lack in yourself, or in those around you, so you feel insecure. And insecurity leads to fear.

AC: In South Africa, Archbishop Desmond Tutu is leading the Council for Truth and Reconciliation. Already, the former Defense Minister under the apartheid regime has been indicted for his complicity in the murder of thirteen people while in power. Now, if we were to put ourselves in the minds of some of SLORC's main players—I would think that fear would be a legitimate concern. In other words, they have good reason to be insecure. Won't the people seek revenge after democracy is won?

ASSK: I think here they [SLORC] underestimate both the people and us as a movement for democracy. Obviously, there is some hatred among the people, especially among those who have suffered. However, we are confident that we can control this hatred. But there is no hate among the leaders of the NLD. The authorities find this difficult to understand. There are many in SLORC who feel strongly against Uncle U Kyi Maun, Uncle U Tin U, and even U Win Htein [Aung San Suu Kyi's personal assistant who spent six years in Insein Prison and was re-arrested on 21 May 1996], because they are ex-military men who are actively involved in the democratic process.

I think SLORC's reading of the situation is this: if these men, who themselves were in the military, are opposing them, they must be doing so out of vindictiveness. I do not think it occurs to them that these ex-military officers are supporting the democracy movement because they believe in certain principles. It goes back to what I just told you about waving a dollar note above a grave: people who think that anybody can be bought, that human minds and hearts are mere commodities subject to the laws of supply and demand, such people would not be able to understand other human beings who work for a cause and are prepared to sacrifice themselves for that cause.

Mind you, none of these people we are talking about have done well out of joining the movement. They've suffered and their families have suffered, but they're still going on. And it's not as though they are unaware that they could be subjected to even more suffering.

AC: When and if "genuine dialogue" begins between you and SLORC, what would be the first item of discussion?

ASSK: Well, if we got to the dialogue table, the first thing I would like to say is, "You tell us what you have to say." I would like to listen to them first. Why are you so angry with us? What is it that you object to? Of course, they may say, we object to your criticisms. But we've always pointed out that we've been very careful not to attack anybody personally. But criticize we have to, that is part of our duty. Otherwise how can we hold our heads up as a political party that represents the interests of the people? We have to point out whatever is against the interests of the people. If we know that something is detrimental to the good of the people and we don't say anything about it, that would be sheer cowardice.

AC: Many peace settlements have been brokered by middle people, a mediator or intermediary. Have you ever thought about offering that as an option?

ASSK: We don't need an intermediary because we're always prepared to open dialogue at any time.

AC: Is Ne Win [Burma's "retired" dictator] really the person you want to open a dialogue with?

ASSK: I don't know . . . I really don't know. That is what some people say. But I have no hard evidence either for or against the theory that he is still the power behind the throne.

AC: When you call for dialogue, are you calling for a dialogue with Ne Win or with SLORC?

ASSK: We're calling for a dialogue with SLORC. But if we had absolute proof that he's behind everything that SLORC is doing, then perhaps we would decide to seek dialogue with him.

AC: Yesterday, before your public talk began, a Rangoon University student asked me bluntly: "Should Burma's democracy movement engage in an armed struggle rather than continuing in a non-violent way?"

I told him I would ask you the question.

ASSK: I do not believe in an armed struggle because it will perpetrate the tradition that he who is best at wielding arms, wields power. Even if the democracy movement were to succeed through force of arms, it would leave in the minds of the people the idea that whoever has greater armed might wins in the end. That will not help democracy.

AC: Daw Suu, how effective is non-violence in the modern world, and more specifically, with regimes that seem devoid of sensitivity or any sense of moral shame and conscience?

ASSK: Non-violence means positive action. You have to work for whatever you want. You don't just sit there doing nothing and hope to get what you want. It just means that the methods you use are not violent ones. Some people think that non-violence is passiveness. It's not so.

AC: Let me ask the question in another way. In your country there were numerous brave young men and women who literally faced the bullets and bayonets, in their willingness to be non-violently active, yourself included. And the results left at least 3,000 dead. Do you ever have doubts about the effectiveness of non-violent political activism in the face of armed aggression?

ASSK: No, I don't have any doubts about it. I know that it is often the slower way and I understand why our young people feel that non-violence will not work, especially when the authorities in Burma are prepared to talk to insurgent groups but not to an organization like the NLD which carries no arms. That makes a lot of people feel that the only way you can get anywhere is by bearing arms. But I cannot encourage that kind of attitude. Because if we do, we will be perpetuating a cycle of violence that will never come to an end.

AC: It's a matter of debate, but politics and religion are usually segregated issues. In Burma today, the large portion of monks and nuns see spiritual freedom and socio-political freedom as separate areas. But in truth, *dhamma* and politics are rooted in the same issue—freedom.

ASSK: Indeed, but this is not unique to Burma. Everywhere you'll find this drive to separate the secular from the spiritual. In other Buddhist countries you'll find the same thing—in Thailand, Sri Lanka, in Mahayana Buddhist countries, in Christian countries, almost everywhere in the world. I think some people find it embarrassing and impractical to think of the spiritual and political life as one. I do not see them as separate. In democracies there is always a drive to separate the spiritual from the secular, but it is not actually required to separate them. Whereas in many dictatorships, you'll find that there is an official policy to keep politics and religion apart, in case I suppose, it is used to upset the *status quo*.

AC: The Burmese monk U Wisara, who died years ago while in prison, after 143 days of a hunger strike, was an outstanding example of politically motivated non-violent protest. Indeed, Burma has a long history of monks and nuns being actively engaged in political areas when it concerns the welfare of the people. However, I wonder about today. With the crisis at such a critical moment, do you think that the *Sangha*—the order of monks and nuns—can play a greater role in supporting the democracy movement? After all, it's their freedom too.

ASSK: Well, there are a lot of monks and nuns who have played a very courageous role in our movement for democracy. Of course, I would like to see everybody taking a much more significant role in the movement, not just monks and nuns. After all, there is nothing in democracy that any Buddhist could object to. I think that monks and nuns, like everybody else, have a duty to promote what is good and desirable. And I do think they could be more effective. In fact, they should help as far as they can. I do believe in "engaged Buddhism," to use a modern term.

AC: How might they be more effective?

ASSK: Simply by preaching democratic principles, by encouraging everybody to work for democracy and human rights, and by trying to persuade the authorities to begin dialogue. It would be a great help if every monk and nun in the country were to say, "What we want to see is dialogue." After all, that is the way of the Buddha. He encouraged the *Sangha* to talk to each other. He said, "You can't live like dumb animals. And if you have offended each other you expiate your sins and offenses by confessing them and apologizing."

AC: What do you think is preventing the *Sangha* from saying to those SLORC generals who visit their monasteries, "What we want to see is dialogue?"

ASSK: I don't know. I do not think there is anything in the *Vinaya* [monastic discipline] that says that monks should not talk about such things, or is there? I do not know. You're more familiar with the *Vinaya* than I am because you were a monk. Is there anything that says that you cannot say such things?

AC: I don't know of any rule that says you can't tell the truth. But perhaps, there's some blind separation going on . . .

ASSK: I see . . .

AC: I know that you occasionally pay your respects to the Venerable Sayadaw U Pandita at his monastery, here in Rangoon. May I ask you to share some aspect of his teachings that you have found helpful?

ASSK: I remember everything he has taught me. The most important of which was that you can never be too mindful. He said you can have too much *panna*—wisdom—or too much *viriya*—effort; but you cannot overdo mindfulness. I have been very mindful of that *(laughing)* throughout these last seven years.

Also, he advised me to concentrate on saying things that will bring about reconciliation. And that what I should say should be truthful, beneficial, and sweet to the ears of the listener. He said that according to the Buddha's teachings, there were two kinds of speech: one which was truthful, beneficial and acceptable, and the other which was truthful, beneficial but unacceptable, that is to say that does not please the listener.

AC: Throughout my years of lecturing on both Buddhism and Burma's struggle for democracy, I've encountered many people who wish to label you in heroic terms. Even the recent *Vanity Fair* interview with you was entitled on the cover as "Burma's Saint Joan" . . .

ASSK: Good heavens, I hope not.

AC: Which raises my question. In strictly Buddhist terms, I have heard you referred to as a female *Bodhisattva*—a being striving for the attainment of Buddhahood—the perfection of wisdom, compassion and love, with the intention of assisting others to attain freedom.

ASSK: Oh, for goodness' sake, I'm nowhere near such a state. And I'm amazed that people think I could be anything like that. I would love to become a *Bodhisattva* one day, if I thought I was capable of such heights. I have to say that I am one of those people who strive for self-improvement, but I'm not one who has made, or thought of myself as fit to make a *Bodhisattva* vow. I do try to be good *(laughs)*. This is the way my mother brought me up. She emphasized the goodness of good, so to speak. I'm not saying that I succeed all the time but I do try. I have a terrible temper. I will say that I don't get as angry now as I used to. Meditation helped a lot. But when I think somebody has been hypocritical or unjust, I have to confess that I still get very angry. I don't mind ignorance, I don't mind sincere mistakes; but

what makes me really angry is hypocrisy. So, I have to develop awareness. When I get really angry, I have to be aware that I'm angry—I watch myself being angry. And I say to myself, well, I'm angry, I'm angry, I've got to control this anger. And that brings it under control to a certain extent.

AC: Is it ironic that you're dealing with one of the world's most hypocritical regimes?

ASSK: But you know, I have never felt vindictive towards SLORC. Of course, I have been very angry at some of the things they've done. But at the same time I can sense their uneasiness—their lack of confidence in good, as it were. And I think it must be very sad not to believe in good. It must be awkward to be the sort of person who only believes in dollar bills.

AC: How do you perceive their uneasiness? Is it a sense of moral shame or moral conscience in them?

ASSK: I'm not talking about moral shame or moral conscience. I do not know if all of them have it. I have sadly learned that there are people who do not have a moral conscience. All I'm saying is that I think there must be a lot of insecurity in people who can only believe in dollar bills.

AC: When you speak to your people who gather in front of your house on weekends, do you in fact speak to SLORC, trying to appeal to that place in them that might make them pause and reflect on their actions? Or are you just speaking to your people?

ASSK: I'm talking to the people, really. Sometimes, of course, I'm also talking to SLORC, because a lot of the issues that I address are so closely linked to what the authorities are doing throughout the country. But basically I'm addressing people and I do think of SLORC as people. They do not always think of us, who oppose them, as people. They think of us as objects to be crushed, or obstacles to be removed. But I see them very much as people.

AC: During the last month I've spoken with a lot of Burmese people in markets, shops, vendors on the street, and construction workers. I've asked them how they feel about the conditions of their country under SLORC. Almost everyone says that they are afraid of SLORC's wrath; afraid of retribution, afraid that if they speak out they'll pay for it with imprisonment. So in time, I've come to appreciate the importance of your words, "Fear is a habit; I'm not afraid." But is that true, Daw Suu, are you not afraid?

ASSK: I am afraid. I'm afraid of doing the wrong thing that might bring harm to others. But of course, this is something I've had to learn to cope with. I do worry for them though.

AC: Several thousand people attend your weekend talks in front of your house. Three students were recently arrested and sentenced to two-year prison terms . . .

ASSK: Yes. But one must ask why the USDA [Union Solidarity Development Association], which is supposed to be a social welfare organization but is in fact used by SLORC as its political arm, besides its disrupting the activities of the NLD, is having enormous rallies which people are forced to attend.

AC: U Kyi Maung was telling me about this. Are people fined if they don't attend these SLORC-instigated rallies to chant slogans in support of their National Convention?

ASSK: Yes. I had a letter from somebody from Monywa saying that they were made to attend this rally. And every household that could not send a member had to give fifty kyats. For poor people these days, fifty kyats is a lot of money.

AC: How poor is poor in the countryside?

ASSK: You don't have to go to the rural areas . . . just go out to a satellite township like Hlaingthayar [near Rangoon] and take a look. They can't afford to have two meals of rice a day. Some can't even afford to have one. So they are forced to drink rice water instead of eating rice.

On the other hand, some have gotten very rich in Burma—rich as they have never been before. This is an aspect of life today that disturbs me very much—the gap between the rich and the poor has gotten so wide. You must know that there are restaurants and hotels in which people throw away tens of thousands of kyats a night [the official bank rate is 6 kyats to $1]. And at the same time there are people who have to drink rice water to survive.

AC: I know that 80 percent of Burma's population live in the rural areas, and most are farmers. What are their conditions like?

ASSK: The peasants are really suffering. Farmers have told us that they have been forced to eat boiled bananas because they don't have rice to eat. If they can't grow enough rice to provide the quota they [are forced] to sell to the government, then they have to buy rice on the open market and sell it to the government at a loss because the government buys at a fixed price which is lower than the market price. And farmers who refuse to grow the second crop of rice have their land confiscated. The only reason why they refuse to sow a second crop is because they lose so much on it. Not only do they lose what little profits they've made on the first crop but they end up with huge debts. Yet the authorities insist that they must grow a second crop.

AC: Does torture still go on in Burma's prisons? And do you have evidence for this?

ASSK: Yes, torture goes on in all the prisons of Burma. And yes, I do have evidence of this. But it is more important to try to understand the mentality of torturers than just to concentrate on what kind of torture goes on, if you want to improve the situation.

AC: How many political prisoners are still being detained by SLORC?

ASSK: I think it's in the four figures. We can't be certain because we are not even certain how many political prisoners there are in each of the prisons of Burma. The prisoners themselves do not know everybody who is there. They are kept apart.

AC: There is a lot of pent-up anger among some people in this country towards the SLORC. When and if your struggle for democracy succeeds, and perhaps you assume a major leadership role in a democratic Burma, can you guarantee that SLORC will not face criminal charges?

ASSK: I will never make any personal guarantees. I will never speak as an individual about such things. It is only for the NLD to speak as an organization—a group that represents the people. But I do believe that truth and reconciliation go together. Once the truth has been admitted, forgiveness is far more possible. Denying the truth will not bring about forgiveness, neither will it dissipate the anger in those who have suffered.

AC: Could you envision a Truth and Reconciliation Council in Burma after she gains her freedom?

ASSK: I think in every country which has undergone the kind of traumatic experience that we have had in Burma, there will be a need for truth and reconciliation. I don't think that people will really thirst for vengeance once they have been given access to the truth. But the fact that they are denied access to the truth simply stokes the anger and hatred in them. That their sufferings have not been acknowledged makes people angry. That is one of the great differences between SLORC and ourselves. We do not think that there is anything wrong with saying we made a mistake and that we are sorry.

AC: Are there listening devices in your house?

ASSK: Perhaps there are, I don't know.

AC: Does it concern you?

ASSK: No, not particularly. Because I'm not saying anything that is underhand. Whatever I say to you, I dare to say to them, if they would like to come to listen to me.

AC: Is your telephone tapped?

ASSK: Oh yes, probably. If it is not I would have to accuse them of inefficiency *(laughing)*. It should be tapped. If not, I would have to complain to General Khin Nyunt [SLORC's Military Intelligence Chief] and say your people are really not doing their job properly.

AC: What does it feel like to be under such scrutiny all the time?

ASSK: I don't think of it. Most people I speak to on the telephone are just friends and we don't really have anything particularly important to say to each other. You say hello, how are you, I'm so happy to be able to speak to you. Then there are people ringing up for

appointments. And my family rings me every week. But it's just, how's everybody, how are they getting on, what are your plans, can you get this for me, can you send me that *(laughing)*—that sort of thing. Nothing that I mind the Military Intelligence personnel hearing.

AC: So you feel no pressure whatsoever from all the unseen eyes, a tapped telephone, the Military Intelligence men everywhere, and of course, that ever present threat of re-arrest—nothing at all?

ASSK: I'm not aware of this pressure all the time. But sometimes, of course, I am. For example, somebody from America, whom I had not met for years, rang up. His brother had been in Rangoon recently, and he started talking about his brother's meetings with some people in the government. I said, "You do realize that my telephone is tapped. Do you intend that everything you say be heard by the MI?" And he said, "Oh, yes, yes." But he hung up pretty quickly after that, so it was quite obvious that it had not entered his head that my telephone would be tapped. On such occasions, I am aware of my unusual circumstances.

AC: Are measures taken by your colleagues for your security?

ASSK: You see the students who are outside at the gate, on duty as it were. They don't have weapons or anything like that. We screen people who come in to see me. I don't see everybody who says they want to see me. Apart from that, what else are we supposed to do?

AC: Well, you're dealing with a rather violent regime. Has SLORC either directly or indirectly ever verbally threatened your life?

ASSK: You do hear the authorities saying "We'll crush all these elements who oppose whatever we are trying to do," and so on and so forth. One hears that sort of thing all the time.

AC: Soon after Nelson Mandela was released after his imprisonment, international media began labeling you "the world's most famous political prisoner." May I ask your comments about that?

ASSK: I'm not one of those people who think that labels are that important. Recently somebody asked if I felt that I had less moral authority now that I was free. I found it a very strange question. If your only influence depends on you being a prisoner, then you have not much to speak of.

AC: So despite your years of detention, you never felt like a prisoner?

ASSK: No, I have never felt like a prisoner because I was not in prison. I believe that some people who have been in prison also did not feel like prisoners. I remember Uncle U Kyi Maung saying that sometimes he used to think to himself when he was in prison: If my wife knew how free I feel, she'd be furious." *(laughing)* And just yesterday, somebody interviewing me for a television program asked "How does it feel to be free? How different

do you feel? I said "But I don't feel any different." He asked, "How is your life different?" I said, "In practical terms my life is different, of course. I see so many people, I have so much more work to do. But I do not feel at all different." I don't think he believed me.

AC: U Tin U told me that being imprisoned for his love of freedom was one of the most dignified fruits of his life. But he seems to be quite happy to be out and about again. Was it the same for you? Were you happy to reconnect to life and intimate relationships?

ASSK: I never felt cut off from life. I listened to the radio many times a day, I read a lot, I felt in touch with what was going on in the world. But, of course, I was very happy to meet my friends again.

AC: But Daw Suu, you were cut off from life in a fundamental way. You were cut off from your family, your husband, your children, your people. Cut off from your freedom of movement, of expression.

ASSK: I missed my family, particularly my sons. I missed not having the chance to look after them—to be with them. But, I did not feel cut off from life. Basically, I felt that being under house arrest was just part of my job—I was doing my work.

AC: You have been at the physical mercy of the authorities ever since you entered your people's struggle for democracy. But has SLORC ever captured you inside—emotionally or mentally?

ASSK: No, and I think this is because I have never learned to hate them. If I had, I would have really been at their mercy. Have you read a book called *Middlemarch* by George Eliot? There was a character called Dr. Lydgate, whose marriage turned out to be a disappointment. I remember a remark about him, something to the effect that what he was afraid of was that he might no longer be able to love his wife who had been a disappointment to him. When I first read this remark I found it rather puzzling. It shows that I was very immature at that time. My attitude was—shouldn't he have been more afraid that she might have stopped loving him? But now I understand why he felt like that. If he had stopped loving his wife, he would have been entirely defeated. His whole life would have been a disappointment. But what she did and how she felt was something quite different. I've always felt that if I had really started hating my captors, hating the SLORC and the army, I would have defeated myself.

This brings to mind another interviewer who said that he did not believe that I was not frightened all those years under house arrest. He thought that at times I must have been petrified. I found that a very amazing attitude. Why should I have been frightened? If I had really been so frightened I would have packed up and left, because they would always have given me the opportunity to leave. I'm not sure a Buddhist would have asked this question. Buddhists in general would have understood that isolation is not something to be frightened of. People ask me why I was not frightened of them. Was it because I was not aware that they could do whatever they wanted to me? I was fully aware of that. I think it was because I did not hate them and you cannot really be frightened of people you do not hate. Hate and fear go hand-in-hand.

AC: Your country's prisons are filled with prisoners of conscience. Perhaps copies of this book will be smuggled into the prisons. What might you say to those men and women?

ASSK: They're an inspiration to me. I'm proud of them. They should never lose faith in the power of truth. And they should keep in mind what Shcharansky once said, "Nobody can humiliate you but yourself." Keep strong.

AC: One final question. Daw Suu, back in 1989, days before you were placed under house arrest, you made the statement: "Let the world know that we are prisoners in our own country." It has been a few months since the time of your release. Has anything really changed?

ASSK: The world knows better that we are still prisoners in our own country.

Questions

1. What are Aung San Suu Kyi's philosophical principles?

2. What are her political goals and how does she believe they can be reached?

3. What personal character traits of Aung San Suu Kyi emerge from this interview?

Recommended Reading

Aung San Suu Kyi. *Letters from Burma*. New York: Penguin, 1977.

Aung San Suu Kyi. *Freedom from Fear and Other Writings*. New York: Penguin, 1995.

Clements, Alan and Leslie Kean. *Burma's Revolution of the Spirit: The Struggle for Democratic Freedom and Dignity*. New York: Aperture Foundation, 1991.

Film

Beyond Rangoon

Afghan Women

In the 1990s, there has probably been no place on earth where human rights have been violated more thoroughly than in Afghanistan. People from outside of the country have been paying more attention to Afghanistan since the terrorist bombings on September 11, 2001, in the United States because the al Qaeda terrorist network of Osama bin Laden had been given refuge in Afghanistan by the ruling Taliban government. As of May 2002, the war in Afghanistan rages on. Afghanistan is one of those countries like Tibet caught between larger powers and whose strategic importance is due more to its geographical location than any internal resources. As a consequence, it has been repeatedly invaded by great powers over the centuries. In the past 25 years, it has known much conflict. The Soviet government invaded in 1979, overthrew the democratic regime of President Daoud in order to place in power a regime friendly to the Soviets. For the next 10 years, the country was engaged in a ferocious civil war, as opponents of the regime—the *mujahedin*—attempted with American, Arab, and Pakistan military aid to overthrow the Soviet puppet ruler, Babrak Karmal. During the years of Soviet dominance, which was a repressive regime, women were nonetheless allowed to continue to participate in society: to receive an education, to work outside the home, and to hold jobs and positions of importance. Yet there was much opposition to this regime and thousands fled Afghanistan.

By 1989 the Soviet leader, Mikhail Gorbachev, decided to pull all Soviet troops out of Afghanistan due to Soviet failures and high casualties, growing opposition to the war at home and his own plans for reform. With the Soviet pull out, the radical Islamic *Mujahedin*, referred to as the *Jehadi* in the interviews below, soon took over Afghanistan. Opposed to the Western ways which had been established since the 1950s, they began imposing their own rules for society, claiming that they were following the Koran. For the next years Afghanistan experienced continued civil strife as the different ethnic tribes and political groups fought each other for power. By 1994 the Taliban began seizing territories and within two years their control of Afghanistan was complete.

The Taliban continued the process of creating a strictly controlled society in which women, especially, had no rights. Afghan women could not leave their homes without male relatives, were required to paint their windows black, could not get an education or medical care from a male doctor, and were forced to cover themselves in a *burqa,* a veil from head to toe. Many women were stoned to death for violating the Taliban rules. Because of the civil war, thousands of women lost their husbands and yet they were forbidden to work to support their families. Many were forced to beg on the streets. In spite of the overwhelming threat to their lives, they courageously and defiantly formed illegal groups and underground networks so that they could educate their children and give one another support. In her introduction to the interviews below, Rosemarie Skaine, the author of *Women of Afghanistan Under the Taliban,* points out that these women all experienced the break up of their families, violence and death. Nonetheless, they did not submissively accept their fate, but fought against it with remarkable courage. The women in these interviews are not recipients of Nobel Peace Prizes—they are ordinary women whose full names might never be known, but they share with Violeta Morales and the Chilean *Arpilleristas* a desire for freedom and an open democratic society.

Profiles of Afghan Women

. . . [The] perspective on the Afghan conflict that has remained hidden to the West—the perspective of the Afghan women and men whose voices have been silenced . . . should be heard.

—Sima Wali[1]

The Voices Heard

Interviews with Afghan refugee women reveal vividly how they are affected. The women's stories bear a common thread of death, violence, threats of violence, denial of education, denial of work, and the breaking up of families, but also demonstrate their ongoing, unmitigated and unique courage. These women have lived through two bloody regimes, the Soviet occupation and now, that of the Taliban.

The interviews in this chapter were conducted by and translated by the Revolutionary Association of the Women of Afghanistan (RAWA). RAWA provided for this book 30 interviews with Afghan women who either recently had fled, or who had fled after the Soviet occupation.[2] The interviews were received during March, May and July 2000. The interviewees were asked five broad, open-ended questions:

1. What experiences have you had since the Taliban took power?

2. How is your life changed as a result of the Taliban?

3. What was your life like before the Taliban came to power?

4. Do you think your life would be better or worse if the Taliban were no longer in power? Explain.

5. What else would you like to say about your experiences in Afghanistan?

The numbered responses in the interviews correspond to the above numbered questions.

Saleema

1. When the Taliban came, they beat up my husband very seriously and said that he had weapons, but my husband was a farmer and did not have weapons. For some days they detained him and during the investigation they beat him. By paying a small amount as a bribe, we got him released from prison.

2. The change which came to my life was that the Taliban set to fire our home and the wheat we had in our home. They forced us to go to Pakistan with lots of difficulties, and I was injured during the rocketing of the Taliban.

3. Before the Taliban, our life was harsh and bad. During the past 20 years our life went from bad to worse with the

From *The Women of Afghanistan Under the Taliban* by Rosemarie Skaine. McFarland & Company, Inc., publisher. Reprinted by the permission of the author and RAWA (Revolutionary Association of the Women of Afghanistan).

passing of every day, and we had a dog's life.

4. Our life will become stable and good under a government which the people will select and where there is no oppression and brutality.

Asthma

1. The Taliban's first work after capturing power was the closure of girls' schools, and then they started their oppression against women and men.

2. The men cannot trim and shave their beard. Above all, the women have not the right to education and to work in offices. If they go somewhere, they have to cover their body from head to toe with a veil, so that nobody can see them. If the Taliban sees a woman without veil, they beat her very seriously.

   During the Taliban, our life became harsh and unbearable because we could not go to our work. The Taliban closed the only source of our income, i.e., schools and offices. After that, our economic condition became so much worse that we could not buy even a scrap of bread. Then we decided to leave the country and took refuge in Pakistan.

3. Before the Taliban our life also wasn't good. The Jehadis were more brutal than the Taliban. During the Jehadis, every day we were in fear of hunger, rape and other uncountable problems.

Many young girls committed suicide just to save their chastity from the filthy hands of the Jehadis. Hundreds of families sold their children very cheaply because they hadn't anything to feed them.

4. Under whatever organization or government that is in favor of democracy, education and rights of women, our life will become better. If they are against these wishes our life will become worse than the Taliban regime.

Shamsia

1. The Taliban don't allow the women to go outside home. They closed girls' schools and forced the women to wear a veil. They don't allow women to work and even in the beginning, they deprived women of going to the doctor.

2. With the coming of the Taliban, we were forced to stay at home and nothing changed for the better.

3. The Jehadis and the Taliban are chips off the same block. Our life under the Jehadis was also miserable. They both are the arch-enemy of the Afghan people.

4. I don't know that what will happen after the Taliban, and what sort of government will come to the power. If those who are in favor of democracy and women's rights come to power, our lives will become better. But if the

Jehadi parties once again take power that would be another catastrophe.

5. The Jehadis were not better than the Taliban. They raped and looted our people. During the Khaliqi-Parchami regime our villages were under heavy bombardments. Finally, after the killing of a number of our villagers and relatives, we were forced to come to Pakistan.

Palwasha

1. As the Taliban come to power, they curbed freedom of the women and men. During the Khalq-Parcham regime my brother was in Iran. When he came back, the Taliban detained him and beat him pretending that he had weapon. When we gained his freedom by paying a lot of money as a bribe, we fled from the country leaving behind our property and home.

2. The change that came to my life was that I again became a refugee in one of the refugee camps in Pakistan, running my life with uncountable difficulties.

3. In general, since the Khalq-Parcham era, all my life has been in wandering and hopelessness. If that situation continues, we will never enjoy happiness and prosperity.

4. If a good government based on democratic value and respectful of women's rights comes to the power, and prepares the way for our children's education and well-being and opens the door of work for women, our life will change for the better. If it is like the previous regimes, there will be no change in our life. And we will die in hope of that day.

5. All in my life, I have had shocking and heartbreaking experiences. I was 14 when I emigrated to Iran. During the reign of Khalq and Parcham, I got married to one of my brother's friends. I had three children when my husband was killed in an ambush by the Russians as he was on his way from Iran to Afghanistan. I, along with my three children, was living in one of the Afghan refugee camps in Iran with my brother, but the difficulties forced us to go to Afghanistan.

Nooria

1. Destitution, oppression, crime, poverty and the closure of school and putting the women behind the walls of home are things that I have got from the Taliban.

2. Emigration from my home-province to Kabul city and from here to refugee camps in Pakistan is the result of the Taliban takeover. All we know is hunger and wandering from here to there in search of food and shelter in the refugee camps in Pakistan.

3. The Taliban and the Jehadis are both from the same origin. There is no fundamental difference between them.

4. If a government that sincerely works for the people comes to power, our lives will change for the better.

5. Forty days passed from my birth to when my father passed on. Now I am 18 years old and live with hunger and poverty in one of the refugee camps.

Floran

1. The experience I have got since the Taliban came, is that whatever government is based on religion and fundamentalism is the most dangerous one in the world. In the guise of religion, what atrocities are in the world that the Taliban do not commit against our people? I have come to the conclusion that politics should be separated from religion. In our country, the fundamentalists committed uncountable crimes in the name of religion and their first and easy victims are women. I saw hundreds of times how the Taliban whip the women in the streets. Once I went shopping with my sister. The weather was warm and I couldn't take a breath under my veil. I said to my sister that I wanted to raise my veil for a minute. She had forbidden me to do that. So when we reached an alley, we both raised our veils assuming that the Taliban were not there. A few minutes later we heard a terrible voice that echoed to our ear that "aren't you ashamed showing your faces to strangers?" We both stopped and

begin to shiver. In that moment, we thought about those women who are beaten by the Taliban. The Talib who shouted at us wasn't the member of the infamous ministry of "do what are prescribed and don't what are forbidden." Whenever I remember his abuses, I think that we are the most unlucky and ill-fated women of the world. If in some countries the women have been struggling for their rights, we in Afghanistan don't even have the right about what we have to wear on our own body. Our clothing is according to the Taliban.

2. The change which came to my personal life since the Taliban, is that, as I am student, I cannot go to school. We women don't have permission to go to the market. If we do, we must wear a veil. We are always in fear. If the Taliban see us in the street without hejab, they beat us very seriously. It is the whip of the Taliban which mostly makes me prefer to stay at home rather than to go outside and face their cruelty.

3. The television station was closed and the radio programs are full of religious propaganda. There is no music program and the news is a pack of lies. Nobody can hang pictures on the walls of their home or in their shops. Photography is forbidden according to their self-interpretation of the shari'a.

All the women workers and officials have been prevented from working. We are paid a salary after three or four months which is insufficient. With that salary, we cannot even run our life for a week. Although the security is better than the past, unfortunately nowadays the Taliban themselves intentionally create security problems by robbery and thievery. The Taliban failed to uproot the poverty which is deepening every day.

4. In the past, although there was no security, schools and colleges were open for girls and boys.

   From one side the Jehadi groups fought with each other which resulted to the destruction of Kabul city and from the other side, these groups raped women and young girls. A lot of families didn't allow their girls to go outside. In short, the atrocities of the Jehadis know no boundary.

5. About the Jehadis, I expressed my view in the above passage, but about the Khalq and Parcham I don't have any idea in my mind now because during that time I was a little child. But people say they are the real cause of the current situation. I myself know that they forced people to emigrate to neighboring countries.

Marzia

1. When the Taliban emerged in our land, they behaved with us very inhumanely. They beat my husband and brother and told them to hand over their weapons or face lashing and punishment. As they didn't have any weapon and were against Khalq and Parcham and the Jehadis and the Taliban alike, they were forced to flee to Pakistan. Then the Taliban come to our home and compelled us to give them money equivalent to two weapons.

2. We are far from our homeland. Our life is not good. The destiny of our children is not clear. They are not educated and cannot go to school. Our children are working in a carpet-weaving factory. With their insufficient salary we are running our life. I have got six children. My husband works in a brick kiln. But money is the real problem.

3. Before the Taliban, we were in our home-province. We had a small land. But now we are refugees and are wandering in a strange land.

4. I think our life will become worse and the problem will deepen, because every group is just working for its own sake. They are not working for the country's prosperity and bright future.

5. In the past, the Jehadis and the Khalqi and Parchami oppressed our people and uncountable young girls have been raped by the Jehadi forces. The puppet regime of Russia destroyed our villages, detained our people and tortured intellectuals. At the end, I strongly appeal to the U.N. and other democracy-loving personalities and forces to help the people of Afghanistan to put an end to that unfortunate situation.

Shakeba

1. The Afghan people dreamt of a future full of prosperity and happiness. They awaited that, after the withdrawal of the Russians, the situation would get better. But unfortunately, everything's turned upside down. When the Taliban captured power, they did every inhumane thing in the name of Islam and shari'a. Their interpretation of Islam is contrary to the order of the day. They didn't even get a lesson from the past 20 years. The puppet regimes of the Russian commit innumerable crimes and then began the turn of the Jehadis, and now the Taliban white-washed their faces with the passing of every day. Women cannot go to work and are forced to wear a veil.

2. I myself am in Pakistan. Whatever the Taliban put into practice in Afghanistan in the name of shari'a I am fully aware of. In the given situation, I don't hope to go to Afghanistan. Under the Islam which the Taliban forcibly imposed on our people, the women cannot work or have the right of education and studying. In short, this situation really vexes us.

3. I have never seen better days in the past two decades. All the previous regimes oppressed our people and the Jehadis too misused Islam and shari'a. They killed our people in the name of Jehad and Islam. Our economic situation is very bad. We have been living hand to mouth all our life. If our children get sick, we don't have money to go to the doctor and buy medicine. We cannot work because the Taliban don't allow us to work. We cannot solve our day-to-day problems. Our economy goes to the dogs.

4. If our people have got the proper lesson from the past 20 years, I think they will, shoulder-to-shoulder, select their real and just representatives and establish a just and democratic government. We hope that in the near future our land will be liberated and in a free and independent future Afghanistan, the real responsible parties of the current situation will be punished accordingly. Anyway, tomorrow never dies.

5. Since the 27th April coup, I have so many bad and disturbing experiences that it would take sheets of paper to be written down. But in short, every force and government which has come to the power 'til now, did the same thing, i.e., brutality, torture, killing, rape and destruction.

Freba

1. I, with my one son and a daughter, was living in Kabul before the coming of the Jehadis. I lost my husband during the reign of the puppet regime of the Russians. I was working in one of the schools as a handmaid to make ends meet. I, with the salary got, just could save myself and my children from

dying. Though I had never better days, life was good then compared to now under the Taliban. The Jehadis didn't pay us on time so I was obliged to go to my brothers and other relatives to borrow money. The moment the Taliban entered Kabul city, they announced that women cannot work. The school where I was teaching was for girls and so it was closed down. The teachers, students and all the maids were sacked from their jobs. My life went from bad to worse. My son wasn't of age, and couldn't find any job. My economic condition was bad, so I had my 16-year-old daughter married in hope that her husband will help us and could find a "legitimate" relative. But prosperity and happiness left us forever. My bridegroom was poorer than we. He could earn only enough money to feed his own family. Before the Taliban I was also a refugee, now and then I moved from one place to the other. I was in fear that someday or the other, the Jehadis would rape me or my teenage daughter. I was in fear of my children's death because of hunger and cold winters. Every day the martyrdoms of my relatives shocked me. So I was forced to emigrate to Pakistan. Now I live in one of the refugee camps in Pakistan while facing lots of economic problems. There is nobody who can save the Afghan people.

3. If a government which works according to the people's wishes comes to power, our lives will change for the better. But I never have the least hope for my future. I've suffered so much that all my hope has died.

4. During the Khalq and Parcham regime, I lost my husband and 'til now I am in deplorable condition.

5. First the henchmen of the puppet regime didn't tell me that they had killed my husband. I searched for my husband from one prison to the other. I had faced ill treatment and bad handling and got no answer. Finally, I have learned that my husband has been killed. I was the only bread-winner and protector of my two little children.

Hamida

1. The Taliban gave people painful experiences since their eruption. Their first move was against women. They shut down the door of girls' schools and banned women from any public appearance, ordered men to sport beards and women to be clad in burqa and if find anyone deviating from these restrictions, they would give her severe punishment. I myself was the witness of an incident when a teenager Talib was lashing an old man because his beard didn't touch the limit the Taliban had prescribed. Seeing that really shocked me and aroused my aversion to the Taliban. When you visit the Taliban offices in Kabul and other cities, they have hung large banners

written on white cloths and almost all of them are anti-women slogans. It would be interesting to see if most of these anti-women slogans are based on sayings of Prophet Mohammad. A banner I remember was from a saying of the Prophet, that "I have finished all the enemies of the mankind and there are no harmful people but women who are the worst enemies for Muslim people, be careful about them." The Taliban never quote some noble sayings of Prophet in favor of women like "education is necessary for both men and women."

2. With the coming of the Taliban the lives of most people have been changed completely though the previous rulers have left nothing to them. The 20 years of war brought our unfortunate country to the brink of elimination but the Taliban dragged our country more and more in the vortex of economical, political and cultural collaboration. Beggary and prostitution have prevailed in each corner of our country and poverty has reached to the maximum.

   As it was done in other places, I was sacked from my job. I had to feed my family, the little amount that my sons earned from the workshop was too small and therefore I decided to do something at home with my two daughters who are both under 15. I borrowed money from my brother-in-law and bought a carpet weaving means. We work from dawn to sunset and can finish a carpet in a month. From each carpet we can earn about 8 lacks Afghani which is equivalent to 1,000 rupees, but now I can't do work any more because I have a back problem and can't sit for too long. I really see my future as bleak because my children are all illiterate.

3. I was a teacher in a primary school, my husband was killed in the war with the Russians and my salary could hardly feed my five children. My two sons who were six and nine years old at that time were working together in a workshop and earned just enough to buy their schoolbooks and stationery. We lived in a house that had a small garden at its back and could supply us some fruits in the summer. Our life under the Taliban is really disgusting. Sometimes I come to the conclusion that there is no way but to commit suicide, but then I feel what will happen to my children and then I scold myself.

4. Naturally, if the elements that have committed thousands of atrocities and introduced the most backward laws were overthrown and not replaced by a successor worse than them, life would be much better. The Taliban since their emergence has brought up our misery-stricken country to the brink of total economic bankruptcy.

5. The only experience that I have got since the giving of the destination of our people into the hands of the fundamentalists is that fundamentalists of all shades and color will never bring

welfare and justice to the people because they are anti-people and anti-democracy in nature and therefore if I was given a chance to comment on the issue of Afghanistan I would have said that democracy and welfare would come only if these fundamentalists are swept away.

Zakira

1. The three years of Jehadis domination crushed our people both physically and mentally and when they were overthrown by their rival brothers, our mournful people were in the hope that the Taliban will end up their miseries but the Taliban proved them to be worse than the Jehadis. The Taliban claim that they have established peace and stability but what is happening in our country show the opposite. Apart from continuous fighting, the Taliban have imposed restrictions on our people and particularly women. They have kept women locked in the closed walls of their houses and stopped girls from going to school. I haven't seen such miserable life in my lifetime. I know many women who are suffering from depression, a girl in our neighborhood yells a few times a day and asks her parents to hide her because the Taliban are coming to rape her.

2. The Islamic Emirate of Taliban gave people a lot of miseries. Closing girls'

schools and banning women from work brought thousands of women into the home. My three daughters were in school in Pakistan. When the Jehadis snatched the power from the puppet regime, we went back to our homeland with the hope that they would get education there in their own country, and we thought that this will be an end to our long and sad story and the hardships of living in very bad conditions in Pakistan. I admitted them in a school but the studies over there were totally rubbish and the Taliban then struck the last blows to their education.

3. We had a relatively good life. My husband was a shopkeeper and my elder son worked in a mechanic shop.

4. What I have experienced in the last three years under the domination of the Taliban, I can say it certainly that life would be much better no matter who would take their place and I don't think there would exist an element more brutal, backward and anti-women than the Taliban.

5. The 20 years of war and especially the last eight years of Jehadis and Taliban rule gave me a lot of experiences and I reached to some solid conclusions that unless there is foreign meddling in internal affairs and unless there is fundamentalist peace, freedom, democracy and social justice would remain at the level of dreams and imaginations.

Parvin

1. I have a lot of experiences of the tyrannic rule of the Taliban. The Taliban are against our people and especially the helpless women. They are not Muslim. What they are doing with our poor people is totally against the Islamic law. Where else and who else has seen the way people are beaten in the street for not obeying the ridiculous restrictions the Taliban have imposed? Where else are women given punishment because their shoes make noise while walking? The Taliban are committing thousands of atrocities in the name of Islam. They have shut the doors of girls' schools and at the same time don't allow women to be treated by male doctors. It has stuck in my mind and I still remember the whole story of a girl who was beaten by a Talib near our house. Brutal!

2. My husband had a cosmetic shop at the Shahri Now market in Herat city. The backward Taliban, without giving any warning, smashed all the items because, according to them, cosmetics are un-Islamic. My husband requested from the Taliban to give him a few days so that he could take his properties to Iran but the Taliban didn't listen and crushed everything to pieces. This was our only source of income but after that blow our condition started shrinking. My husband is handicapped and the only work he could do with was as a shopkeeper. We had neither saved money nor any property to start another business. My two sons who are 14 and 16 left school and began to work in a workshop which give them each 250,000 Afghanis (U.S. $7), and with that salary we can only buy the flour we need, therefore we had no other option but to leave our house and rent it out and move to the village where we had an old house. It took three months to make some repairs to that old house with the help of my two sons and their two other cousins. I had a sewing machine and began to do some business with it at home, which can bring me around 300,000 Afghan ($8) per month. My husband is now searching for a light job in the village but no one is ready to give him a job.

3. We had a very comfortable life before the emergence of the Taliban. My two sons were attending their school regularly. My husband had a cosmetic shop which could provide us with a handsome income.

4. Life would certainly be better if these enemies of our people are kicked out. These elements have brought nothing to our people but misery, destruction, homelessness, increasing poverty, prevailing prostitution and beggary and collapsing the economy of our war-torn country. I do believe, and this is because of my experiences of seven years of domination by the Jehadis and Taliban, that these creatures would not

get in power if they are being openly controlled and backed by the foreign countries, and it is quite right that a foreign country see only its own interest and has no concern for what is coming out of its interference. United States of America and Saudi Arabia through Pakistan from the east, Iran from the west and Russia through central Asian countries from the north squeezed our countries in their claws and each of them snatched a part of it for their benefit. The 20 years of war was nothing but just a war between these aggressive neighboring countries. Through history, it has been proved and this was confirmed that why our country has remained undeveloped and backward lies in this fact, that through the ages these aggressive countries have destroyed our homeland and drained our resources and I must say that we are very proud of ourselves that we always stood firm against these invaders.

5. I got that experience from the tyrannical rule of the Taliban and Jihadis that one should not trust what the rulers says. Taliban and Jihadi have always misused Islam for their personal whims and political interests. They killed thousands of people and made thousands of others homeless in the name of Islam. All of them had Koran in one hand and gun in other. I realized that the real Muslims are those who don't just induce people to pray or obey the Islamic law but they themselves act in accordance to the tradition of Islam.

Gulalai

1. Before the entrance of the Taliban into Herat city, I had heard about them that they were very pious and good people and they carry the banner of Islam and would sweep away all the Jehadi gangs who had committed lots of crimes. When they entered in Herat I prayed to Allah and thanked him for his blessing that finally peace had come and our sorrow has flown away, but this joy was very short lived. The Taliban, at the very first day, took off their mask and showed their real selves. They proved themselves to be worse than the brutal Jehadis, especially their attitude toward women is very cruel. I realized that when we had a wedding ceremony in our village. According to our traditions, we had brought a music band to the occasion, the ceremony was still going on when a group of Taliban came in and disturbed the ceremony. Like wild animals they rushed to the band and kicked the musical instruments, among these instruments was an expensive electronic keyboard, which was crushed to pieces as an angry Talib hit it with the gun. The owner was weeping and crying for his keyboard. The wedding ceremony turned to grieving ceremony and ended in the middle.

Seeing that ominous act, we all at the ceremony got angry. After that I changed my mind and realized that the Taliban are not the ones who carry the banner of the Islam but are the most corrupted and the most backward minded elements. The Islamic regime of Iran which is famed for being the most fanatic Islamic regime in the world, is much more progressive than these medieval-minded people. In the three years of their domination in Herat, they exposed themselves as the agent of misery, poverty, homelessness and thousands of other sufferings.

2. One of the "reforms" that the Islamic government of Taliban has introduced was banning music and watching television, this resulted in the collapse of the electronic workshop of my husband. My husband stayed in the middle, he didn't know what to do. He had invested a big amount on this shop, now he couldn't sell the devices and he could not open another shop. After three months waiting, thanks to Allah, he was employed as a guardsman in the custom which give him 600,000 Afghanis ($12) per month, but this amount could not meet our basic necessities therefore my husband decided to send my elder son who was about to finish his secondary school to Iran to work there. Crossing Iran's border was very difficult, it needed a permission slip (Nama) from the Iranian government. It was a lengthy process as well as expensive and to

some extents impossible. My husband met many people and one of our relatives made a fabricated Nama. Thank God that my son reached Iran without any major difficulty. It has been exactly two years that I haven't seen my son, during that time he has sent once 500,000 Tomans ($60) and 400,000 Tomans ($50) eight months later. But I am always afraid if the Iranian regime capture my son they will send him to a special prison designed for Afghan refugees in Zahedan called "Tal-e-Sea" where they treat the prisoners worse than what the Taliban do with people.

3. Our life was much better than what we have now. My husband had a large electronic workshop. The money we earned was more than enough to meet all our needs plus some extra money, which my husband gave to his widow sister. My three sons and my younger daughter were going regularly to school.

4. I think not only our lives but also the lives of all people would be much better. If you ask any person, he would have certainly some problem with restrictions and some laws that the Taliban have imposed on many things. The Taliban has closed the girls' schools, which had two bad effects, it deprived thousands of girls of education and cost the jobs of hundreds of women teachers. The Taliban have cost the jobs of thousands of women. The Taliban banned music, television and

many other entertainments. The Taliban don't allow people to hold Nowruz (Persian New Year) which is a special tradition of our people rooted deep in the history. What I do believe is that if a force came and opposed these restrictions, life naturally will be better, but if the Taliban are replaced by the element similar to them then the wounds of people will never be healed.

5. Russian invasion and then the civil war between the Jehadi rival and now the tyranny rule of the Taliban destroyed our country and made the life of our people miserable. Though thousands of our innocent people have been killed in the resistance war against the Russians, but it was a war against a foreign aggressor and our people unanimously participated and devoted their whole property. But the seven years of civil war really crushed our people mentally and physically. With my little knowledge of Afghanistan history, I can say that Afghanistan has not seen in its 5,000 years, cruel, uncivilized and anti-women elements like Jehadis and Taliban. Abdur Rahman Khan and Allauddin Ghuri were famous for their cruelty, but the Taliban in many ways have white-washed them. Some of our people now say the communist regime was better than these dirty criminals. Dr. Najibullah was called "cow" by people, but when the seven so-called fundamentalist leaders, Hekmatyar, Rabbani, Massoud, Sayyaf, Khalili, Mazari, Mojadadi, took power and committed many crimes now there is a joke among our people which goes like "Oh God, please smash these donkeys and return our cow!" This shows the depth of hatred our people have against them.

Nooren

1. After the coming of the Taliban and fleeing of Jehadis, Kabul's picture has been completely changed. The presence of men with beards and women with burqa is a scene that attracts the attention of everyone. Some people say that the shine our city had before has disappeared and the city looks like a cartoon, men with long beards and a cap in head and women in burqas. Poverty has struck so much that by a glancing through the faces of people one can easily predict their miserable conditions.

Every day, thousands of men, women and children make rows in front of bakeries waiting for long hours and get breads by the cards that have been distributed to them by the U.N.'s committees. Economic problems are great blows which have struck our devastated people, and for the survival of their children, they have gone to Iran and Pakistan. The majority of the residents of Kabul have sold their property so that they could buy at least a sack of flour. Prices are so much high that most of the people spend their day with only bread. Most of the people say that they have survived the Jehadis's rocket shelling but these bad economic conditions are another way of making our people miserable.

2. I am a student of the 11th class. I was very fond of my studies and my only hope was to become a doctor. Though there was not any proper school neither in Dr. Najibullah era nor during the Jehadi domination, but uncivilized Taliban even took this from our people and in this way doomed our hopes.

3. When I was born my country was burning in the flame of wars but I remember that those time people had a relatively better life. We had a comfortable life, my mother was a teacher and my father was a government officer. I could go to school without feeling any fear and worry.

4. In my opinion if a government is established by an election and grant people democracy and freedom then the lives of most people will get better, but this government must be saved from any foreign meddling and clean from the reactionary and anti-democracy elements. I think women also must have the rights to vote for the future government of Afghanistan.

5. The 20 years have given me a bitter experience that if people are given their own right to decide their fate and no external power meddle in it, certainly peace, security and democracy will come in our country.

Zohra Samad

1. Khalq and Parcham, the puppets of Russia, have destroyed our country and killed thousands of our innocent people but the religious militia, the Taliban, tortured our people in another way. The Taliban in their very first days disclosed their hostility with women, science and culture. They deprived women of their basic rights. Thousands of women are being lashed savagely in the streets because they don't have a burqa or wear white socks.

They have allowed only doctors to do a job but in my opinion it is not enough, the next generation would be scarce of doctors if they don't get education. The Taliban must keep the schools open for both sexes otherwise there would be no doctor. I also see it as really ridiculous that the Taliban have banned women to be treated by a male doctor.

Most of the patients that I have treated had different psychological problems because they were mostly widows and it is quite natural. There are many instances that these widows have sold their darlings or left them in the streets because they had nothing to feed them.

Most of the intellectuals living in Afghanistan have a tough life. Intellectuals are very sensitive to the political events and this resulted in their departure from Afghanistan.

2. I am doctor. I have four children. My husband is also doctor. Though no peace and stability was there when Jehadis had the power, the people had a relatively good life than that they have now. There was not any prevention when I was going to my job and the conditions were fine for both my husband and me. When the Taliban came they introduced a lot of restriction on female doctors in hospitals. Once I was in my office treating a patient, when a wild teenager Talib came in and with cursing ordered me to wear burqa. It was really hard for me to bear that rudeness but I convinced myself that the Taliban are not the people who should know how to deal with people. I have decided to help my people any time and in any condition but the conditions over here compelled me to leave the country.

3. Our life was in a relative good condition but it was not as good as it is expected. The Jihadi gangs were not far behind in crimes and atrocities compared to the Taliban. In their four years rule the Taliban have left nothing for our misery-stricken people who have been already crushed and tortured by the Russians and their puppets, the Khalq and Parcham. The different Jehadi parties in Kabul put our innocent mass in their claws and each of them tortured them in different ways. These religious murderers sow the seed of differences between different communities. Pushtun fell in hostility with Hazara and Uzbek with Tajik. The first targets of the Jihadis were women. Apart from depriving women of major jobs and giving no attention to women's education, they have committed lots of crime. They have kidnapped girls and forced them into marriage. Raping was happening every day in Kabul and prostitution has been prevalent over most part of the country. When the Taliban snatched the power from their rival brother, our country was in complete destruction, but the religious militia even didn't have any mercy on the war-stricken country.

4. Naturally, life will be better if these religious militia whose crimes and atrocities have no example neither in the 5,000 years old history of Afghanistan nor in any other history. But one thing is more obvious, that the roots of all miseries lie in the foreign intervention and therefore I do believe that attention should be paid to this part otherwise talking about the Taliban would be useless. When the Jihadis were in power, everyone was of that opinion that peace and justice would come if the Jihadis were removed from power, but the opposite happened and the reason is clear, the instruments of the machine were changed but its engine remained untouched. And it is also noteworthy to say the world communities, and especially the U.S., are really just spectators.

5. Of what I have read in history during my school time and what I have experienced in 46 years of my life, one thing has been confirmed to be right, that if there is foreign handling of our affairs, our people will never see a progressing Afghanistan. And I must say that our people throughout history have proved their opposition to the foreigner and never have accepted any kind of slavery. I have a piece of advice for U.S., Pakistan, Iran and Saudi Arabia that before taking any decision on Afghanistan, spend a few minutes and flick through the pages of Afghanistan's history, I am sure they would find some useful materials. The 20 years of wars have struck our innocent nation severe blows that they are incapable to speak out against the external and internal aggressors, but a time will come when our people will stand on their feet and sweep out the enemies of Afghanistan.

Footnotes

1. Ansima Wali (same as Sima Wali) (President, Refugee Women in Development {RefWID} Inc. Washington, D.C.), "Ansima Wali: America's Debt to the People of Afghanistan," *The Boston Globe,* Dec. 4, 1999, 3rd ed., A19.

2. Revolutionary Association of the Women of Afghanistan, Interviews with Afghan Women provided to and translated for the author, Mar. 14, 2000, May 15, 2000, and Jul. 2, 2000.

Questions

1. What happened to the husbands and male relatives of these women?

2. How did the Mujahedin *(jehadi)* and Taliban treat girls and women? Why were they treated differently?

3. How was the Koran and Islam distorted by the Mujahedin and Taliban?

4. What hope do these women express in their future?

Recommended Reading

Benard, Cheryl. *Veiled Courage: Inside the Afghan Women's Resistance*. New York: Broadway Books, 2002.

Brooks, Geraldine. *Nine Parts of Desire: The Hidden World of Islamic Women*. New York: Anchor, 1995.

Zoya with John Follain. *Zoya's Story: An Afghan Woman's Struggle for Freedom*. New York: Morrow, William & Co., 2002.

Film

Beneath the Veil